Netbooks

FOR

DUMMIES®

Netbooks
FOR
DUMMIES®

by Joel McNamara

WILEY

Wiley Publishing, Inc.

Netbooks For Dummies®

Published by
Wiley Publishing, Inc.
111 River Street
Hoboken, NJ 07030-5774

www.wiley.com

For general information on our other products and services, please contact our Customer Care Department within the U.S. at 877-762-2974, outside the U.S. at 317-572-3993, or fax 317-572-4002.

For technical support, please visit www.wiley.com/techsupport.

Wiley also publishes its books in a variety of electronic formats. Some content that appears in print may not be available in electronic books.

Library of Congress Control Number: 2009935829

ISBN: 978-0-470-52123-6

Manufactured in the United States of America

10 9 8 7 6 5 4 3 2 1

WILEY

About the Author

Joel McNamara started using computers in the early Cenozoic era of personal computing (1980 to be exact). If NorthStar Horizon, ARPANET, PDP-11, Kaypro, and Apple Lisa ring a bell (when dinosaurs roamed the earth), like in the movie *Zelig,* he was there. Over the years, Joel has worked as a programmer, technical writer, and manager for a number of companies in the high-tech sector.

Joel currently consults and writes on things he finds interesting. Living in an undisclosed location somewhere in the Pacific Northwest, he likes boats of all kinds and is fond of old-school technologies such as celestial navigation and Morse Code.

Joel is also the author of *ASUS Eee PC For Dummies, GPS For Dummies* (1st and 2nd Editions), *Geocaching For Dummies,* and *Secrets of Computer Espionage: Tactics & Countermeasures* — all brought to you by Wiley Publishing, Inc.

Author's Acknowledgments

Thanks to ASUS and Dell for loaning me a few of their latest netbook models. And much gratitude to the talented folks at Wiley for transforming a collection of ideas and words into a real, live book — specifically acquisitions editors Katie Mohr and Tiffany Ma, project editor Chris Morris, technical editor Jim Kelly, copy editor Virginia Sanders, and anyone else who was involved with this title that I didn't have a chance to virtually meet. It's always a pleasure working with pros.

Publisher's Acknowledgments

We're proud of this book; please send us your comments at http://dummies.custhelp.com. For other comments, please contact our Customer Care Department within the U.S. at 877-762-2974, outside the U.S. at 317-572-3993, or fax 317-572-4002.

Some of the people who helped bring this book to market include the following:

Acquisitions, Editorial

Sr. Project Editor: Christopher Morris

Acquisitions Editor: Katie Mohr, Tiffany Ma

Copy Editor: Virginia Sanders

Technical Editor: Jim Kelly

Editorial Manager: Kevin Kirschner

Editorial Assistant: Amanda Graham

Sr. Editorial Assistant: Cherie Case

Cartoons: Rich Tennant
(www.the5thwave.com)

Composition Services

Project Coordinator: Katherine Crocker

Layout and Graphics: Carl Byers, Joyce Haughey, Melissa K. Jester, Melissa K. Smith

Proofreaders: Melissa Cossell, Penny Stuart

Indexer: Infodex Indexing Services, Inc.

Publishing and Editorial for Technology Dummies

Richard Swadley, Vice President and Executive Group Publisher

Andy Cummings, Vice President and Publisher

Mary Bednarek, Executive Acquisitions Director

Mary C. Corder, Editorial Director

Publishing for Consumer Dummies

Diane Graves Steele, Vice President and Publisher

Composition Services

Gerry Fahey, Vice President of Production Services

Debbie Stailey, Director of Composition Services

Contents at a Glance

Table of Contents

Part III: Netbook Add-On Accessories and Hardware... 185

Introduction

*1*t's always pretty boring to start a book with a bit of history. But hey, this is important, so I'll make it quick and painless. You have my word. (I plead guilty to falling asleep in history classes myself, so I can relate.)

In October 2007, a Taiwanese company named ASUS, which was primarily known for making computer motherboards and other components, started selling a diminutive laptop called the Eee PC. The laptop had an itsy bitsy, 7-inch screen, an underpowered processor (compared with the latest and greatest dual core chips), a dinky keyboard, and a user interface that looked like it was designed by Toys"R"Us.

Pundits immediately dismissed the little laptop. Some of the quotes I remember hearing include the following: "Who in their right mind would buy something like that when for a bit over a hundred dollars more they could get a full-size, low-end laptop with a usable screen, decent processor, and built-in DVD drive?" "The keyboard keys are too small for typing unless you have toothpick-size fingers." "A 900 MHz processor? You have to be kidding! I didn't know they even made anything that slow anymore." And finally, "Well it might be okay for little kids, but adults will never go for it."

Ah, you've gotta love those pundits. They make the world go round. They had no clue — and I suspect ASUS didn't either — that the Eee PC would be an industry game changer. It was one of those right-place-at-the-right-time products that opened up a huge new market niche. By the end of 2007, around 400,000 little laptops were sold — mostly to adults, by the way. In 2008, an estimated 11.4 million units were purchased. ABI Research predicts 35 million units will ship in 2009 and a whopping 139 million of the little laptops will be sold in 2013.

It turns out there was (and is) a huge demand for a portable computer that's somewhere between the size of a cell phone and a conventional laptop. And because there was money to be made, more than a dozen companies jumped on the bandwagon and began selling their own versions of Lilliputian laptops.

These small wonders, now pretty much universally known as *netbooks,* are lightweight and compact laptops (right around two pounds and a little bit bigger than this book), durable enough not to mind getting knocked about a bit, cheaper (for the most part) than a conventional laptop, and are loaded with all sorts of hardware and software that you need for accessing the Net (thus the name). They're perfect for doing a variety of personal, work, and entertainment-related tasks from home or on the road.

So with that bit of history out of the way, I can get right down to business and start telling you about this book. As you probably guessed from the title, it's all about netbooks. In the coming pages, I tell you everything you need to know about these nifty little laptops, including their capabilities, limitations, and how to get the most from them.

Who This Book Is For

If you're browsing through this book at your favorite bookseller right now (either online or in a good old fashioned bookstore) and you're trying to decide whether you should shell out some hard-earned cash for this book, ask yourself these three simple questions:

- ✔ Are you thinking about purchasing a netbook?
- ✔ Have you recently bought a netbook (or maybe scored one as a gift)?
- ✔ Have you owned a netbook for a while, but want to get more out of it?

If you answered yes to any of these questions, you can immediately proceed to the cash register or online shopping cart because this book is for you. (If you're still not convinced, feel free to continue flipping through the pages to make your decision.)

Although your netbook user manual covers the basics, there's a good chance it doesn't go into a whole lot of depth (which is perfectly understandable from the manufacturer's perspective; you don't want a big user manual when your goal is to offer an affordable computer).

With this book, I take you beyond the user guide and the online help, expanding on topics and programs, presenting a variety of subjects that aren't covered, and pointing out places where you can get more information on the Internet — all in the easy-to-read-and-understand style of the *For Dummies* series.

Setting Some Expectations

Before getting started, I'd like to set a few expectations about what you'll be reading, just so you and I are on the same page (literally and figuratively):

- ✔ I'm not one of those netbook fanboys who say netbooks are the be-all, end-all perfect computer. (I personally don't think such a thing will ever exist.) Netbooks have some distinct limitations, which I honestly share with you.

✔ When the first netbooks debuted, most of them ran one version or another of the Linux operating system. You can still get Linux netbooks, but the Windows models have proven much more popular, and because of that I primarily focus on Windows netbooks. (Take heart Linux users: I still discuss Linux netbooks here and there, as well as provide a few resources.)

✔ I expect you've used Windows before and are familiar with the operating system, so I don't spend time walking you through how to use a mouse, copying and pasting, and other basics. However, I focus on things that make a netbook a little different to use compared to running Windows on a desktop or conventional laptop.

✔ Don't expect Consumer Reports–style, specific product recommendations. New models are released much too quickly, and any netbook I recommend today could easily be yesterday's news in a matter of months. (Although you won't find any product endorsements, I do arm you with plenty of information to make a good choice if you're in the market for a netbook.)

How This Book Is Organized

This book is conveniently divided into several parts. The content in each part is related (more or less), but, by all means, feel free to skip around and read about what interests you the most.

Part 1: Getting Started with Netbooks

This part of the book introduces you to netbooks. I start with a chapter that provides a quick roadmap to everything I cover in this book. Then I launch into telling you all about netbooks, especially how they differ from conventional laptops. I help you make sense of the myriad of features and select a netbook that will work for you. Because netbooks come with a number of different operating systems, I provide a chapter that compares and contrasts the various options. And I conclude with a chapter that tells you what to expect and what you should do when you pull a shiny new netbook out of the box for the first time.

Part 11: Using Your Netbook

In this part of the book, I get down to business (and fun), stepping you through what you need to know about using your netbook. I begin with a chapter on networking. (Hey, it's called a *net*book, and you're going to be using it a lot to connect to the Net, so this is a good place to start.) I devote a chapter to productivity suites (both traditional software such as Microsoft Office and the newer generation of online applications like Zoho). All work and no play makes for a dull netbook, so I devote a chapter to entertainment (including video, music, and games). I also cover security issues and provide a survey of Net communication programs and social networking sites that lend themselves to the netbook form factor. I wrap up this part with a chapter that introduces you to the wonders of GPS and tells you how to turn your netbook into a mobile navigator.

Part III: Netbook Add-On Accessories and Hardware

With a cutting-edge solid state drive, 802.11 wireless, an Ethernet jack, and webcam, you might think your netbook is all ready to go. Well, yes and no. Many users expand the storage with Secure Digital (SD) memory cards, maybe add a DVD player/writer, perhaps charge the laptop in a car or plane, or connect any number of peripheral devices to the USB (Universal Serial Bus) ports. This part is about add-on netbook hardware and accessories, and I discuss everything from hooking up external devices to appropriate carrying cases.

Part IV: Checking Underneath the Hood

In this part, I pop the hood (or *bonnet* if you're from the U.K.) on your netbook and see what makes it tick. I cover a collection of slightly more advanced — but not too geeky — topics compared with elsewhere in the book. I start with a chapter on troubleshooting your netbook — hopefully, you'll never need to refer to it. I also cover backing up and restoring your netbook, upgrading memory and internal drives, and changing Windows settings. I tell you what you need to know about drivers (I'm talking about system software here, not golf) and considerations for dealing with BIOS. (BIOS is an abbreviation for basic input/output system, which is code a computer runs when it is powered on before the operating system loads.)

Part V: The Part of Tens

All *For Dummies* books have a part called The Part of Tens, and this one is no exception. In this part, you can find a chapter devoted to the best netbook Web sites, blogs, and forums on the Internet. I also give you a list of ten real cool netbook hardware hacks.

Icons Used in This Book

If you've ever pawed through the pages of a *For Dummies* book before, undoubtedly you've seen all sorts of little icons scattered throughout the book. In keeping with that fine *For Dummies* tradition, this one is no different. So as a reminder (or first time explanation), here's the scoop on the various icons you'll encounter in the coming pages:

This is just a friendly little reminder about something of importance. Because I can't be there in person to tap you on the shoulder or clear my throat, this icon will have to do.

Every now and then, I may need to get a little geeky on you. Maybe it's to provide a bit more detail on a topic or clue you in to something cool that's a little techy. In such cases, rest assured I either give you a plain-English explanation or point you off to a Web site where you can find out more.

This is a tip or trick designed to make your life easier; usually gained from practical experience and often not found in the user guide or online help; or if it is there, it's buried deep in some obscure paragraph or maybe perhaps requires a suitable translation.

The little bomb icon means "Danger, Will Robinson!" (Not a "Lost in Space" fan? Look it up on Google.) While I'm digressing here, between you and me I've always thought they needed to update this icon with something a little more contemporary. The icon first appeared in conjunction with computers back in 1984 when the Apple Macintosh first came out. And honestly, when was the last time people even used bombs that looked like that? Anyway, whenever you see the bomb, be sure to pay close attention. It means something you do (or don't do) may cause the kind of trouble most rational people like to avoid.

Some Things to Keep in Mind

Before you get going with the rest of the book — and I know you can't wait — I'd like to mention a couple of things:

- As I mention earlier, this book is not meant to replace your netbook's user manual — especially considering the large number of different netbooks that are available on the market. This is *Netbooks For Dummies*, not a leather-bound, multivolume set of the Encyclopedia of Netbooks.

- I'm a self-admitted cheapskate who likes good values. That means I'm going to tell you about a variety of free and low-cost programs as well as offer tips on how to get the best deal on a netbook. In these hard economic times, every dollar counts, and hey, it's hip to be frugal!

✔ You can find lots of references to Web sites in this book. I'm sure you've noticed that Web sites change (and appear and disappear) about as fast and randomly as the stock market rises and falls. If you try entering a Web address in your browser and it doesn't work, don't get frustrated and walk away. I provide you with enough information to find what you're looking for with some follow-up Google searching.

✔ You're not going to find every netbook or netbook-compatible program in existence mentioned in the book. I've tried my best to list many of the more popular netbook manufacturers and programs, but as with any author, I'm faced with the harsh realities of page count constraints. So please don't get upset if I didn't mention your netbook or a program you use.

✔ Some days I wish the pace of technology and the consumer electronics marketplace would take a short vacation and stand still for a moment or two. It's a foregone conclusion that between the time I write these words and this book is published, new netbooks will appear sporting spiffy new features and technology. Because I can't see into the future, keep in mind this is a snapshot of the general state of the netbook world circa late 2009/early 2010.

Okay, that finishes up the introduction, so on with the show!

Part I
Getting Started with Netbooks

By Rich Tennant

"I tell him many times—get lighter laptop. But him think he know better. Him have big ego. Him say 'Me Tarzan, you not!' That when vine break."

In this part . . .

In the fall of 2007, a small laptop called the Eee PC appeared on the market and took the world by storm. Dubbed a netbook, this Lilliputian laptop ushered in a new era of affordable and ultra-mobile personal computing. These go-anywhere, Internet-enabled laptops proved to be a perfect combination of size, price, and performance, and consumers quickly opened up their wallets and purses.

This part introduces you to netbooks. I start with some general information about the little laptops — as well as provide you with a roadmap of what you can find in the book. I then tell you exactly what netbooks are and how they differ from laptops. If you're in the market for a netbook, you're faced with a confusing array of models and features. Considering this, I bring you up to speed on all the options and provide guidance on selecting and purchasing a netbook that best meets your needs. I conclude this part with a chapter that gets you familiar with your new netbook and shows you how to easily exchange data with another computer.

Chapter 1

Everything You Need to Know about Netbooks

So you want to know about netbooks? Well you've come to the right place. Obviously, this entire book is about the Lilliputian laptops, but in this chapter, I distill essential information to give you an overview of everything you need to know about netbooks.

After you read this chapter, you should be able to talk knowledgably about netbooks at cocktail parties, and you may even gain a reputation for being techno-savvy — be careful though, as such status often results in a never-ending stream of phone calls from family and friends asking for help with their computer problems.

In addition to the big picture view, this chapter also serves as a roadmap to the rest of the book. In the coming pages, I refer you to specific chapters where you can get more info about a certain topic or find out how to get your netbook to perform a specific task.

Netbook Nuts and Bolts

More than likely, you've wondered just exactly what a netbook is and how it's different than a laptop. Here's the lowdown. A netbook (also called a mini-laptop, sub-notebook, or mobile Internet device) has these key features:

- ✔ **Compact size and light weight:** Netbooks are lighter, usually below or right around 3 pounds, and come in a smaller case than a conventional laptop. The smaller size is achieved with a smaller screen (typically 10 inches or less) and a smaller keyboard that doesn't have full-size keys. See Figure 1-1 for a size comparison between a laptop and a netbook.

Figure 1-1:
A full-size laptop with a netbook resting on top.

- ✔ **Internet ready:** As the name suggests, a netbook is ready to connect to the Internet. Netbooks have 802.11 wireless cards and an Ethernet jack for wired connections.

- ✔ **Minimal hardware features:** Unlike a full-size laptop, you won't find a DVD drive, internal modem, FireWire port, PC card slot, or more than two or three USB ports on a netbook. Netbooks also have slower processors compared to full-size laptops. All of this helps keep the costs down, which is a nice segue into the next bullet.

✔ **Affordable:** Netbooks are currently priced between $250 and $600. Many are under $400, with the average price falling on a regular basis.

When you see a netbook for the first time, you may be surprised by its size. However, don't let the toy-like appearance of the mini-laptop fool you. This is a real computer, and for the most part, it can do just about anything a normal PC can — with a few exceptions that I discuss coming up.

A netbook isn't just a cheap laptop. Its diminutive size allows you to carry it around more often and take it places where carrying a full-size laptop would be a hassle.

I want to emphasize that a netbook isn't really designed to be your primary computer. Its purpose is to be a highly mobile, convenient laptop you can take just about anywhere. It's great for browsing the Web, sending e-mail, using Skype (a service for making phone calls over the Net), and other Internet-centric activities. It's also suitable for basic word processing and spreadsheet work. However, the under-powered processor (and small screen and reduced-size keyboard on some models) limits its usefulness for certain tasks, such as playing graphics-intensive games, desktop publishing, or running computationally intensive programs.

That's a brief description of what a netbook is. For more information, read Chapter 2, where I provide a lot more detail.

Picking the Perfect Netbook

When you've decided you need (or want) a netbook, now comes the challenge of selecting one that earns the Goldilocks rating of "just right."

When ASUS released the first netbooks in the fall of 2007, making a selection was simple because there were only a few models to choose from. Now, thanks to the popularity of the little laptops, there are dozens of models available from a wide variety of manufacturers.

In Chapter 3, I provide a list of netbook manufacturer Web sites so you can check what's currently available on the market. And in Chapter 22, I list a number of netbook news and review sites.

When selecting the perfect netbook, start with your wallet or your purse. How much money do you want to spend? At the time I'm writing this, netbooks are priced between $250 and $600 — with many models in the $350 range. (I expect the entry-point models to drop to around $200 or perhaps even lower, so make sure to look around at prices.)

Just like most other computers, the more money you spend, the more whistles and bells you get. Don't dismiss low-priced netbooks, though. In most cases, they provide more than enough function to get basic tasks done.

Next, sift through the features. Netbooks come with a laundry list of sometimes confusing features. (I go into lots of detail on features in Chapter 3.) When it comes to specifications, here are the primary features you should key in on:

- **Processor:** Netbooks sport a number of different processors. Don't expect the performance you get from a conventional laptop with a fast CPU. Netbooks aren't designed to be high-performance computers; however, this isn't to say they're as slow as molasses. Instead of horsepower, focus on the processor that provides decent performance coupled with low power consumption. (I discuss available processors in depth in Chapter 3.)

- **Battery life:** The processor and the battery used (batteries typically are 3-cell or 6-cells; the more cells, the more power stored) dictate how long you can use the netbook without plugging it into a power source. Whether you have wireless turned on or off and what programs you're running also impact battery life. The first generation of netbooks got only a few hours of battery life. Current models can easily achieve upwards of five or more hours.

Longer battery life means a bigger battery. Netbooks that claim eight-to-ten-hour battery lives are noticeably heavier and thicker than models with smaller batteries.

- **Storage:** Netbooks models come with a variety of internal storage options. Solid state drives (SSDs) are the wave of the future and use memory chips to store data. They're lighter and have no moving parts to malfunction, but they're currently more expensive and hold a limited amount of data compared with traditional hard drives. Hard drives add a bit more weight to a netbook, but offer more storage space at a lesser price than an SSD.

- **Keyboard size:** To fit a netbook in such a small package, manufacturers need to make some compromises, and one of them is the size of the keyboard. Different models have different reduced-size keyboards. Some users with larger hands and fingers may find it difficult to type on smaller keyboards. The size of the keys can vary between manufacturers and models. Most 10-inch-screen netbooks have very usable keyboards although they are reduced in size.

✔ **Screen size:** Netbooks generally come with screens ranging from 7 to 10 inches, with different levels of resolution. Ten-inch screens are the standard these days. Smaller-screen models are more compact (see Figure 1-2) but have smaller keyboards and don't have as much screen real estate — which means more scrolling when browsing the Web.

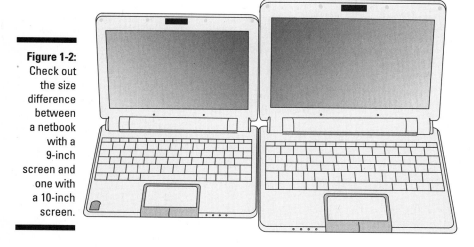

Figure 1-2: Check out the size difference between a netbook with a 9-inch screen and one with a 10-inch screen.

Another one of the decisions you'll need to make when selecting a netbook is what operating system you'll use. Netbooks come installed with different versions of Windows and Linux (and there's currently talk of other operating systems being available in the future, including Apple's OS X and Google's Chrome OS). Based on sales figures, most people opt for Windows (which I primarily focus on in this book). I list all the operating systems currently used on netbooks and discuss their pros and cons in Chapter 4.

After you've narrowed down which netbook model you want to purchase, the last step is pulling out your credit card and buying the little laptop. I provide you with advice on this in Chapter 3, but in the meantime, here are some essential points:

✔ **Stick with one of the larger netbook manufacturers**. Although a lesser-known brand laptop may work great, it's usually safer to go with a well-known brand. The more units that have sold, the greater the chance an online user community has formed. In many cases, online user communities offer faster and better support than the manufacturer.

✔ **Read buyer reviews and feedback (especially from online retailer Web sites such as Amazon and Newegg).** Get as many opinions as you can. If you remember your statistics class, the larger the sample size, the more meaningful the data.

✔ **If you get a chance, find a local retailer who stocks netbooks and check them out in person.** In the early days of netbooks, this was tough because only online stores carried the little laptops. Now, more brick-and-mortar retailers are stocking the wee computers, as my Irish cousins call them.

✔ **Shop around because prices can vary — especially online.** Every dollar saved counts, and you can easily save 20 bucks on up, depending on where you purchase your netbook.

Getting Started with a New Netbook

Pulling a new computer out of its box for the first time reminds me of opening up presents at Christmas when I was a kid. The year's "big" present almost always came in a large box. But in the case of netbooks, the big gift from Santa comes in a small package.

First things first. Read the manual! It may be only a quick-start guide, with the full user manual tucked away on a DVD or installed on the netbook's hard drive, but in any case, read it. It will make your life much easier — trust me.

I always like to plug in the power and fully charge the battery before I start using a new laptop. If you're impatient, go ahead and fire up the netbook but keep it plugged in to a power source, and after you shut it down, let it fully charge.

While the netbook is charging, read the user manual (yes, I sound like a broken record) and get familiar with all the buttons, keys, jacks and connectors.

If your netbook didn't come with a paper user manual for you to read while you're patiently waiting for the laptop to charge, visit the manufacturer Web site with another computer and download a PDF version of the manual to peruse.

When the netbook first starts up, more than likely you'll need to go through some initial setup screens that customize the laptop for your location and time zone. This process is painless, so just follow the instructions and fill in the requested information.

In Chapter 5, I provide more information on what to do after you get your new netbook out of its box. I also discuss the very important topic of moving data between your netbook and another computer.

I'm guessing you'll want to connect to the Internet — more sooner than later — so I talk about that next.

Netbooks and Networks

The word *net* in netbook doesn't apply to a hair net, fishing net, or Annette Funicello. Nope, *net* refers to *Internet* (or *network*), because when connected to the Net, the little laptop really shines.

All netbooks have an 802.11 wireless card for connecting to the Internet. If you've used Windows to connect to the Internet, a netbook works the same way. That means you need to do the following:

1. **Make sure the wireless card is turned on.**
2. **Select an access point you want to connect to; use a correct password if the connection is encrypted.**
3. **Start using the Internet.**

In addition to a wireless network card, netbooks also come with an Ethernet port for making a wired connection to the Internet or a local area network (LAN). You'll need an RJ45 cable to do this. Just plug one end of the cable into the netbook and the other into a network jack, and Windows should automatically do the rest and connect.

If you need more details on connecting to the Internet, be sure to read Chapter 6. In addition to the basics, I also cover 3G modems, sharing files on Windows networks, and using your netbook to remotely connect to another computer.

Aside from doing e-mail and browsing the Web, an Internet connection provides you and your netbook with a wealth of opportunities for taking advantage of second-generation Internet communications programs and social networking sites. The bring-it-anywhere nature of a netbook and a wireless Net connection allows you to use instant messages (IMs); Internet telephony (such as Skype); and social networking sites like Facebook, MySpace, and Twitter to your heart's content. If you haven't used these programs or sites before, be sure to read Chapter 10 to come up to speed.

Business or Pleasure

Because of their small size and portable nature, netbooks get a lot of use while on the road or around the house — either for business or pleasure. I find a netbook especially useful for the following:

- Checking and sending e-mail
- Browsing the Web
- Watching videos

- Listening to music

- Instant messaging and using Skype

- Working on word processing and spreadsheet documents when away from a primary computer

- Viewing digital photos

- Traveling (especially on airplanes, trains, and buses)

If your netbook uses Microsoft Windows as its operating system, it's compatible with all Windows programs — with the exception of some games. Just keep in mind that processor-intensive programs (such as graphics applications) run slower due to the netbook's under-powered CPU. Also, a netbook's small screen can make life a little challenging for programs that expect more screen real estate.

Business sense

When it comes to business, productivity suites like Microsoft Office or the free, open-source OpenOffice are a must — many netbooks come bundled with Microsoft Works, which is adequate for very basic word processing and spreadsheet work, but may not offer all of the features users come to expect for real business.

Aside from traditional productivity suites, it's worthwhile considering Web-based collections of programs such as Google Apps and Zoho (see Figure 1-3). If there's a Net connection nearby, these Web programs have a number of benefits. I fill you in on everything you need to know about both traditional and online productivity programs in Chapter 7.

Fun and games

Of course, netbooks are great for work, but they're also great for play. All netbooks have sound cards that allow you to record (there's a microphone jack) and listen to music and words (through the speaker/headphone jack). In addition to the jacks, netbooks also have a built-in microphone and speaker. With some basic software, you can turn your netbook into an over-sized MP3 player or a handy digital tape recorder for recording classroom lectures and meetings.

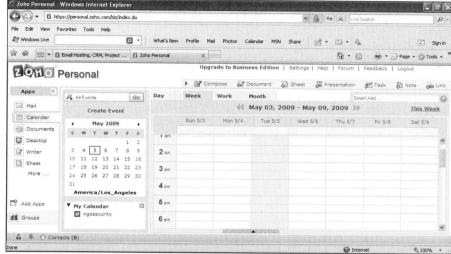

Figure 1-3:
Zoho:
Web-based
productivity
software on
a netbook.

Most netbooks are about the size of a portable DVD player. In addition to size, they also share the ability to play movies. Because netbooks don't have built-in DVD drives, you'll need to purchase an external drive that plugs into the netbook's USB port if you want to watch a movie on a disc. Another alternative is to use *ripping* software to convert the DVD movie into a file that can be played on a computer — this is usually an AVI format file. If your netbook doesn't have an external DVD/CD-ROM drive, you can rip the movie on another computer and then transfer a copy to your netbook.

Many netbooks also have built-in webcams for recording video or streaming with video-conferencing programs.

If you're a computer gamer, you're probably wondering whether you can use your netbook to play some of your favorite games. The answer is yes, with a few caveats.

Many Windows games load and run seamlessly on a Windows netbook — for example, Figure 1-4 shows the ever-popular time-waster Solitaire. The exceptions are games that require lots of memory or a high-end graphics card. Most netbooks have pretty basic graphics chips that get bogged down or don't work well (or at all) when playing graphics-intensive, 3-D games. In addition, the relatively under-powered processor and limited amount of memory found in netbooks can also slow things down to a crawl.

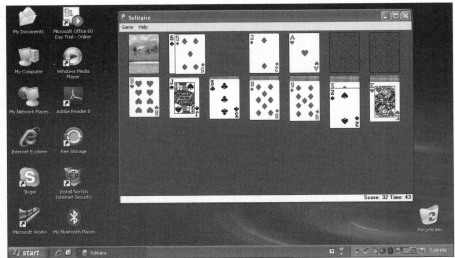

Figure 1-4:
Playing
Solitaire on
a netbook.

If your favorite game requires a lot of graphics and CPU (also known as the *processor chip* or the *central processing unit*) power, don't hold your breath that it will work to your satisfaction on a netbook. Also, just because a game runs on a netbook doesn't necessarily mean you'll have fun playing it — keep in mind the small screen and touchpad. That said, some new netbooks with faster graphics processors and more memory make better game machines than others. And there are active gaming communities on the Internet that provide a wealth of information on which games work on various models of netbooks and which don't.

In Chapter 8, I go into much more detail on the fun and games aspects of netbooks. I show you how to use your netbook to watch videos, listen to music, and turn it into a game machine.

Better safe than sorry

Lots of early Internet users had high hopes that the Net would usher in a utopian era of greater community through worldwide inter-connectedness. Unfortunately, the architects of the Net never expected all the spam, viruses, worms, and other malware that lurk in the digital shadows waiting to pounce on an unsuspecting victim. Because a netbook is at its best when connected to the Net, it's critical that you have your shields up when you're zooming around in Internet-space. Chapter 9 is devoted to security, and in it I bring you up to speed on the latest programs and techniques for keeping the bad guys out of your netbook.

In addition to electronic threats, a netbook's small size makes it a tempting target for theft. (The small size also makes it more prone to accidental loss.) There are a number of ways to reduce the chances of this happening and to protect your data just in case it does. In the chapter on security, I also discuss physical security approaches to keep your netbook out of harm's way.

Going places

Although many cell phones have built-in GPS (Global Positioning System) functionality that tells you where you are and how to get places, if you have a netbook you might consider turning it into a netbook navigator. It's easy to connect a GPS receiver to a netbook, and a number of available mapping programs can tell you where you are and how to get from Point A to Point B. Chapter 11 is all about netbooks and GPS.

Accessorizing and Expanding

After you purchase a netbook, if you're like most users you'll also eventually buy some additional hardware or accessories to go with it.

The first purchase is usually something to carry the netbook around with. I really encourage you to have some type of padding to protect your netbook from the inevitable bumps and bruises when toting it around town.

Because of its compact size, you have all sorts of carrying options available, including cases and sleeves (padding with no carrying straps) designed specifically for a specific model, cases originally designed for something (portable DVD players work great), and cheap do-it-yourself carriers. If you need some ideas, check out Chapter 12.

If you're going to be using your netbook for trans-Pacific or Atlantic flights (or anytime you're away from a power source for an extended period), you'll probably want to consider carrying a spare battery. Battery life can vary dramatically between netbook models, ranging from a few hours to five hours plus — I just tested a netbook that achieved an amazing eight hours of run time. This has to do with the size of the battery (the more cells, the longer the life); the type of processor (some are more energy efficient than others); the screen brightness; whether the wireless card is turned on; and what you're doing (for example, watching a movie drains the battery faster than working on a spreadsheet).

In Chapter 13, I charge up your brain cells with everything you need to know about batteries — including third-party and universal batteries. I also discuss different ways to maximize battery life.

Netbooks typically don't have as much hardware as comes with a full-size laptop (no DVD drive, dialup modem, mouse, and so on). However, most netbooks have at least two USB ports that you can use with all sorts of external USB devices. That includes flash memory drives, external hard drives, and DVD/CD-ROM drives (such as the one shown in Figure 1-5). You can find much more on expanding storage for your netbook in Chapter 14.

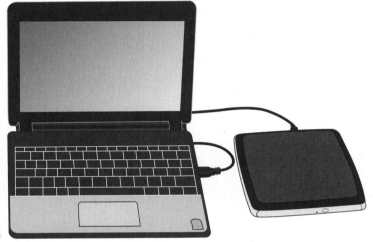

Figure 1-5:
An external
DVD drive
connected
to a
netbook.

Unlike laptops, most netbooks don't have PC card slots — a few models are coming with newer and smaller ExpressCard slots though. For adding hardware, always think USB or SD memory card. (Most netbooks feature an SD card reader slot.)

In addition to storage devices, you can also connect mice, keyboards, modems, Bluetooth cards, and so on, to your netbook. And don't forget that most netbooks feature a VGA port that allows you to connect an external monitor or multimedia projector — a netbook, PowerPoint, and a projector makes a killer presentation system. I go into a lot more detail on netbook peripherals in Chapter 15.

Technically Speaking

Technically speaking, a netbook is no different than a conventional laptop or desktop PC. Although some of the hardware components may be a little different, what works with Windows should work with your Windows netbook. You should be aware of a few technical details, though.

Underneath the hood

First off, if your netbook came with Windows, you can make various tweaks to the operating system to improve performance and free up drive space. In Chapter 19, I tell you about various tune-up hints and tricks.

Related to the operating system are drivers — and I'm not talking about motor vehicle operators or what Tiger Woods uses. *Drivers* are programs that allow the operating system to interact with a computer's hardware. And your netbook has a number of drivers you should know about — especially as manufacturers often release new versions of drivers to fix bugs or add features. Chapter 20 is the place to go for information on netbook drivers, including how to download and install new versions.

With a standard laptop or desktop computer, most users never deal with the BIOS (basic input/output system). If you pay attention when your computer starts up, you may see a very brief message about pressing a certain key to change BIOS settings. BIOS settings include options for which device to use for startup (such as hard drive, CD drive, or perhaps a memory card) and whether hardware components such as wireless cards and webcams are turned on. At times you may need to change BIOS settings for your netbook, and Chapter 21 tells you what you need to know — including how to upgrade the BIOS.

You can swap out the hard drive (or solid state drive) on a number of different netbook models, replacing it with a larger drive for more storage. Many netbooks also allow you to upgrade the internal memory (RAM) to speed up performance. I discuss both of these types of upgrades in Chapter 18.

If you're technically inclined and like to mess around with hardware, you'll have hours of fun with your netbook. There is an active hardware hacking community on the Internet that's doing all sorts of modifications to different netbooks, such as backlit keyboards, internal GPS receivers, homebrew touch screens, and even modified cases. Chapter 23 tells you more and points you to a number of Web sites that have do-it-yourself hardware hacking projects.

When bad things happen to good netbooks

Always remember that a netbook is just a computer. And like any computer (or mechanical or electronic device) it may break. Because you can take netbooks just about anywhere, the more you use it and carry it around, the greater chance you could accidentally drop it, spill something on it, soak it during a downpour — you get the picture.

Although it's a good idea to periodically back up any computer, with a netbook backing up is a must. Consider that a computer is cheap to replace compared to the Great American Novel you've been working on for the past couple of years, a final paper for a class, or a sales presentation for work. Enough said. In Chapter 17, I fill you in on various backup strategies and discuss restoring your netbook back to its original state if something bad happens.

Most netbooks are dependable performers, but every now and then a gremlin may decide to pay a visit and cause you an inordinate amount of frustration and hair pulling. In Chapter 16, I present a list of troubleshooting tips for common netbook problems. Also be sure to read the next section, "Netbook Information on the Net."

Netbook Information on the Net

If you purchase a netbook, you'll unquestionably use the Internet to get the most out of your little laptop. When you have a question about your netbook, you can turn to the manufacturer's Web site. Most companies have support sections where you can read frequently asked question (FAQ) lists, download updated versions of important files and utilities, replace a lost copy of a user manual, and submit technical support questions.

In addition to manufacturer sites, many popular netbook brands and models have independently operated Web sites and user forums. In my opinion, these are often better than "official" technical support, in that you hear the voices of many netbook users — some of them incredibly knowledgeable and helpful.

Finally, if you really catch the netbook bug, you may want to stay up-to-date on the latest news and industry gossip. Because of a relatively low price point and releases of new models with new features, some users often purchase new netbooks to replace old models — similar to upgrading cellular/ mobile phones. There are a number of Web destinations devoted to the latest netbook news to keep you well informed.

Make sure your old netbook goes to a new home instead of gathering dust in a closet or sent on a one-way trip to the landfill. Give it to your children, favorite niece or nephew, or perhaps an older relative who doesn't own a computer.

You can find netbook Web resources by doing a bit of Googling, or better yet, go to Chapter 22, where I provide you with a list of what I consider are some of the best netbook sites on the Net.

Chapter 2

Introducing Netbooks

*Y*ou hear about them on the news. You read about them in magazine articles. You may have even played with a friend's or perhaps tried out a demo model in a store. They're netbooks. They're hot, and they're taking the world by storm.

These tiny laptops are inexpensive, versatile, and trendy. But what exactly are they? How are they different from full-size laptops? And what makes them so popular?

I'm glad you asked, because in this chapter I answer all these questions and more.

Honey, 1 Shrunk the Laptop!

That's what a netbook looks like, doesn't it? If you've never seen one, check out Figure 2-1. It's as if you absentmindedly put a laptop into the washing machine, left the setting on hot water, and when you pulled it out, to your dismay you discovered it shrank. (By the way, don't try this at home.)

Figure 2-1:
Netbooks come in different sizes and designs. Shown here are two 10-inch-screen models with a 7-inch-screen netbook.

But a netbook is more than just a laptop that was left in the washer or was zapped by a mad scientist's shrink ray. It's important to understand some of the differences between the netbook and its full-size laptop cousins — especially a netbook's capabilities and limitations. The following sections get the ball rolling.

Just what exactly is a netbook?

For starters, a netbook is a small laptop. But you already knew that, right?

Netbooks are also known as mini-laptops, sub-notebooks, and mobile Internet devices (MIDs). For the purpose of this book, I refer to them by their most commonly used name, netbook.

Here are some of the things that make netbooks different from conventional laptops:

✔ **Compact size:** Netbooks are smaller than conventional laptops. This is achieved through a smaller screen (typically 10 inches or smaller) and a reduced-size keyboard.

To get a better idea of the size of a netbook compared with a laptop (and other things), visit a cool Web site called sizeasy (`http://sizeasy.com`). It compares physical dimensions of various products. Search for your favorite netbook and see how it stacks up measurement-wise.

✔ **Light weight:** Netbooks are lighter than most laptops and usually weigh in around 3 pounds or less. The compact size and feather weight make carrying around a netbook a breeze — especially compared with a typical 6-pound-plus laptop.

✔ **Internet ready:** Netbooks could be more appropriately called *internetbooks.* The reason why is these little laptops are all ready to connect to the Internet — take your pick of built-in 802.11 wireless or cabled Ethernet connections. The growing abundance of Wi-Fi hotspots makes the easy-to-carry netbook perfect for quick sessions of Web browsing or e-mail checking.

✔ **No-frills hardware:** You won't find a DVD drive, internal modem, FireWire, PC card slots, or half a dozen USB ports on a netbook. Additionally, netbooks have relatively low-powered processors compared with full-size laptops. All of this helps keep the cost down, which is a nice segue into the next bullet.

✔ **Affordable:** You don't have to pay an arm and leg for a netbook — list prices currently range between $250 and $600, with many models priced under $400. If you shop around, you can pick up a basic netbook for around $250 or even less.

Some manufacturers are pushing models they call netbooks that come with screens larger than 10 inches. Don't fall for the hype — these are more like lightweight laptops than netbooks. If you buy something someone calls a netbook with an 11- or 12-inch screen, you're getting a bigger case to accommodate the screen and a heavier computer. In my opinion, only computers with 10-inch screens (plus or minus a tenth of an inch or two) or smaller are representative of true netbooks.

In Chapter 3, I go into depth about all the features you find in various netbook models so you can make an informed buying decision.

Prehistoric netbooks

The road to modern netbooks is littered with the fossilized remains of small laptops that, for one reason or another, never quite achieved popularity. Put on your Indiana Jones fedora for a moment or two so you can unearth a few evolutionary ancestors of the contemporary netbook.

Going through a closet filled with dusty, obsolete junk (er, I mean my historical computing device collection), I come across a mid-1990s HP 100LX, shown in Figure 2-2.

Figure 2-2:
Oldies but goodies: an HP 100LX from 1993 (front center); a Toshiba Libretto from 1999 (right); and, for comparison, a first-gen Eee PC 701 from 2007 (left).

The 100LX came out in the days before Windows 3.0 — that was the first version of Windows that enjoyed widespread popularity. It fit in your palm, had a bunch of productivity applications built in, sported a full, yet tiny keyboard, ran DOS, and was powered by ubiquitous AA batteries.

The popularity of Windows squeezed the HP family of palmtops out of the market. And because of the success of Windows, Microsoft rolled out an operating system specifically designed for mobile devices — mostly to compete with the popular Palm PDA. Called Windows CE, the OS had a Windows look and feel.

Computer manufacturers started building small laptops, similar in form to today's netbooks, which ran Windows CE. Unfortunately, the operating system never caught on with consumers, who complained it was buggy and didn't run "real" Windows programs that ran on a PC. Coupled with that, the Windows CE mini-laptops were priced between $700 and $1,000 — viewed as too costly for the limited features they provided. (Microsoft finally got the bugs out with the rebranded Pocket PC operating system, but by then the mini-laptop market was viewed as a lost cause.)

However, the little laptop idea just wouldn't die. Companies like Toshiba still pressed forward. In the late 1990s, its Libretto line (refer to Figure 2-2) used the standard version of Windows — which meant you could run any Windows program on it. Aside from being about twice as thick as contemporary netbooks and lacking built-in networking capabilities, it matched the form factor of today's mini-laptops.

Meanwhile, on the other side of the Atlantic, a British company called Psion (see the "Netbook name calling" sidebar) was making a nifty organizer similar to the HP 100LX. It evolved into a product called the Psion 5, which had a speedy processor and ran a custom graphical user interface operating system called EPOC. The subsequent Psion 7, which was marketed as the *netBook,* was pretty close to today's netbooks, featuring a 7-inch color touch screen and network connectivity. Unfortunately, by the early 2000s, Psion stopped producing its mini-computers, instead opting to focus on developing and licensing operating systems for cellular phones.

Netbook name calling

You may have thought the term *netbook* is a generic way of describing a small laptop. But guess what, the term *netbook* is trademarked. And a nasty little legal fight broke out because of it.

Computer manufacturer Psion applied for the trademark in Europe and the U.S. in 1996 — it was registered by the U.S. Patent and Trademark Office in 2000. Psion used the trademark on two of its products, the netBook and NetBook Pro, which were discontinued long before ASUS debuted its Eee PC. (The Eee PC is generally considered the first netbook.)

In March 2008, Intel started using *netbook* to describe "small laptops that are designed for wireless communication and access to the Internet." Intel's legal-beagles felt they were on solid ground because they weren't offering a branded line of computers under the name. (The U.S. Patent and Trademark Office had already rejected some product names, such as MSI's proposed "Wind Netbook" citing a "likelihood of confusion" with Psion's trademark.)

In December 2008, Psion began sending cease-and-desist notices to OEMs (Original Equipment Manufacturers) and Web netbook news sites telling them to stop using the term *netbook.* Most people blew the letters off until February 2009, when Google declared it was banning the use of *netbook* from AdSense advertisements. This got people riled up. An organization called Save the Netbooks was formed and stated it was going to sue Psion. Dell beat them to the punch and sued to legally quash the trademark. Intel joined in and accused Psion of fraud and demanded the trademark's immediate dismissal. Psion fired the next shot, counter-suing Intel for $1.2 billion. Sheesh. Can't we all just get along?

Time will tell how this will all play out, but even if Psion does have legal ownership of the term, the genie is out of the bottle, and the company will be hard pressed to stop a whole lot of people from generically referring to mini-laptops as netbooks. As I write this, rumors are swirling that Psion has relinquished claim to the netbook name. Hopefully this little tempest in a teapot is over and everyone can get back to business.

Microsoft decided to give the mini-laptop market one last shot, and in 2006, it began marketing a concept called Origami, which later became known as UMPC (Ultra Mobile PC). Manufacturers that released the small tablet computers, which ran a custom version of Windows, never really found much commercial success.

So what happened? Why didn't these prehistoric netbooks ever gain the crazy success that netbooks have enjoyed over the past few years? There are a number of reasons why, including

- ✔ **Price:** These netbook ancestors weren't cheap. And most consumers didn't see enough bang for the buck to buy them. In many cases, cheaper components and more efficient Asian manufacturing processes that are present today weren't available.

- ✔ **Performance:** Oh dear, performance of these computers compared to the full-size laptops and PCs of the time was pretty dismal. Today's netbooks still aren't as fast as a low-end dual core PC, but performance is more than adequate for browsing the Web, watching videos, and using productivity software.

- ✔ **Wireless Internet availability:** Today, many coffee shops, airports, libraries, restaurants, airplanes, ferry boats, truck stops, marinas, parks, and so on have free (or paid) Wi-Fi. Wireless Internet availability, and consumer dependence on e-mail and Web sites, were virtually nonexistent when these prototype netbooks emerged from the primordial muck.

First-generation netbooks

First-generation netbooks can be traced back to the fall of 2007, when ASUS released the Eee PC, which is generally hailed as the first true netbook. The stars and planets were in perfect alignment for a smash hit. Wireless Net availability had taken off, and people wanted an inexpensive, portable (yet usable) computer they could tote around that was somewhere between the size of a cellular phone/PDA and a full-size laptop.

The surprise popularity of the Eee PC brought a succession of competitors (and follow-up models from ASUS), all sharing the same basic features. First generation netbooks can be identified by:

- ✔ **Internet connectivity:** Models featured a built-in wireless card and an Ethernet port.

- ✔ **Solid state drive (SSD):** To keep the weight down and provide super-fast startup times, first generation netbooks featured SSDs. Instead of relying on a spinning platter like conventional hard drives, SSDs use memory chips. The downside to SSDs is they are considerably more expensive than conventional drives, so to keep the cost affordable, small SSDs providing 4 to 8GB of storage were offered.

The OLPC XO-1

Although it's not really a consumer product, I consider the One Laptop Per Child (OLPC) XO-1 to be the mini-laptop that started the whole netbook revolution.

Nicholas Negroponte, who ran the Media Lab at MIT among other things, had a wonderful vision of producing a laptop priced at $100. It would be primarily designed as an educational device for children all over the world. This evolved into the One Laptop Per Child program, which created and produced the XO-1.

The XO has some pretty slick features like a screen you can read in direct sunlight, a spill-proof keyboard, a solid-state design that doesn't generate heat, and a built-in wireless card with a pair of antennas you can rotate for the best signal reception. (Part of the original design spec called for a hand crank for charging the laptop's battery, but unfortunately this never made it into production.) The XO also sports a very simple user interface called Sugar that was built from the ground up for use in education. Don't go looking for windows, folders, and other elements of the common desktop metaphor — you won't find them.

The whole concept got other manufacturers thinking about producing competitive small, cheap laptops for the educational market. Out of that, ASUS released the Eee PC. (The XO-1 never quite lived up to its $100-laptop reputation, instead costing a bit under $200. And there's a recent move to use Windows XP instead of the Linux-based Sugar for its operating system.)

Negroponte's original market for the XO-1 was education ministries of developing countries, who would order thousands of units at a time. There was a limited Give One Get One program, where individuals could buy two laptops for $399, keeping one and having the other donated to a child in a developing country.

This means XO-1s show up for sale on eBay, Craigslist, and other places from time to time. However, unless you want one for your child or are a geek who likes to play with technology, I wouldn't recommend purchasing one. In my opinion, the speed and performance are considerably lacking compared to first-generation netbooks like the Eee PC 701 (although a faster chip in the upcoming XO-1.5 version may address this), and the keys lack the tactile touch and feel of a normal keyboard. Also, even though it's improved greatly from the initial release, the custom Linux operating system isn't rock solid reliable. (It's possible to load other operating systems on the XO-1, though.)

Despite the shortcomings, I'm still hanging onto my XO-1 just in case I need a rugged little laptop I can use outdoors — one that sips small amounts of electricity and can be powered by a small solar panel. If you're interested in the OLPC and the XO computers, check out www. olpcnews.com.

- **Celeron processor:** A low-voltage version of Intel's Celeron chip was used. Running at around 900 MHz, the processor was no speed demon, but performance was acceptable for basic computing tasks.

- **7-inch screen:** First-generation netbooks sported fairly small screens, which made browsing Web sites a little painful. Resolution was limited to a meager 800 x 480.

- **Small keyboard:** The first-generation netbooks were about the size of this book. To accommodate the small case size, reduced keyboards were used — between 80 and 85 percent of normal size. The cramped keyboards were functional, especially after some practice, but certainly not as usable as a full-size keyboard.

✔ **No-frills hardware:** Early netbooks sported a touchpad, several USB ports, a VGA output for connecting an external monitor or projector, audio input and output jacks, built-in speakers and microphone, an SD memory card reader, and all but the most basic models came with a webcam.

✔ **Not-so-great battery life:** You may think a small laptop would have a great battery life. However, the catch is that with a small case, you have to use a smaller battery — which means less power storage capacity. Depending on how you used them, first-generation netbooks provided around 2.5 hours or less of battery life.

✔ **Linux operating system:** As another cost-saving measure, versions of the free, open-source Linux operating system were used instead of Windows. (Microsoft charges a licensing fee for each copy of Windows a manufacturer distributes on a computer.) Customized, easy-to-use user interfaces were deployed to conceal some of the complexities of Linux. (If you owned a licensed copy of Windows, it was possible to replace Linux with Windows on your own, but the process was both time consuming and a bit technical.)

Second-generation netbooks

The first-generation netbooks caught on like wildfire, and based on customer feedback, a second generation of products appeared by mid-2008. These mini-laptops still shared many of the same characteristics of their predecessors but included some important changes:

✔ **Intel Atom processor:** When the first-generation netbooks arrived, Intel was just finishing work on a new low-voltage processor specifically designed for mobile devices. Codenamed *Atom,* the chip was perfect for netbooks. In fact, when the chip started shipping in 2008, there was such a large demand Intel couldn't fill all the orders, and many manufacturers were forced to continue using the older and cheaper Celeron chip in their netbooks.

From a performance standpoint, the first Atom chips offered no measurable improvements compared with the older Celeron chips. The Atom wasn't faster, but it consumed much less power, thus increasing battery life. Subsequent Atom processors feature better performance.

✔ **Conventional hard drives:** Although users liked the speed and fast startup of solid state drives, they didn't appreciate the measly amount of storage space — when a single movie takes up just under 1GB of storage,

Order #77232080

(Amazon order #104-0435060-4691437)

Date ordered: 2010-12-27 13:43:58

We hope you enjoy your order!

From: whypaymorebooks@gmail.com

Ship via: Standard

Payment: Prepaid

Ship To:

Bernard L. Gorda
9477 BATTLER CT

COLUMBIA MD 21045-3904 United
States

Bill To:

ncbm59d8hmgmm50@marketplace.amazon.com
Jennifer A. Mannix

QTY	SKU/ISBN/UPC	Condition	Loc	Description	Media	Price
1	X15-WILEY-14690 0470521236	New NEVER USED! MAY CONTAIN MINOR SHELFWARE IF ANY. SHIPS IMMEDIATELY!!	[X15]	Netbooks For Dummies [Paperback] ... Joel McNamara	Paperback	$0.74

an 8GB drive just doesn't cut it. Although you could boost storage space by using inexpensive SD memory cards and USB flash drives, manufacturers decided to start offering cheaper, conventional hard drives alongside the SSD models. Hard drives of 100GB and up made much more sense for adequate storage.

✔ **Larger screens:** The 7-inch screens didn't offer enough screen real estate for most people, and manufacturers soon began to shoehorn 9-inch screens into roughly the same size case as the smaller-screen models. Some 10-inch-screen models were also offered, and even though they had larger cases, they were much smaller than full-size laptops.

✔ **Larger keyboards:** Many people had difficulty using the small keyboards found in first-generation netbooks. Eager to please, manufacturers started to introduce models with larger keyboards — up to a very usable 90 to 95 percent of normal key size. A 10-inch-screen netbook has a larger keyboard than smaller models thanks to the larger case needed for the screen.

Keyboard layout, key size, and key feel vary from manufacturer to manufacturer — and sometimes even between models.

✔ **Windows XP:** Although Linux netbooks work great, most people use Windows and are more familiar with it. Because of this, consumers sent a strong message to netbook manufacturers that they wanted the Microsoft operating system. The companies obliged and started offering models with Windows XP installed. (In fact, Windows netbooks currently outsell Linux netbooks by about 9 to 1.) Check out Chapter 4, where I go into more detail about all of the different netbook operating systems.

✔ **More memory:** First-generation laptops had 512K of RAM. That was fine for a lean version of Linux, and although Windows XP can get by with that meager measure of memory, it ran better with a little more oomph. That led manufacturers to start boosting the RAM on most models to at least 1GB.

Microsoft nixed netbooks from having as much memory as conventional laptops. The Redmond giant stipulated that manufacturers who licensed Windows XP could use it only on netbooks with 2GB or less of RAM.

✔ **Better battery life:** The Atom processor combined with larger batteries boosted netbook battery life by an hour and upwards. Users could look forward to 4.5 to 5 hours (or even more) of battery life, depending on use.

Battery life depends on how you're using your netbook. Far less power is required working on a word processor document compared to surfing the Net with wireless on and watching a movie at the same time.

✔ **More hardware:** Manufacturers started offering models with new hardware options including Bluetooth.

Third-generation netbooks

For only being on the market a few years, netbooks have undergone a fairly rapid evolution. The third generation of netbooks is just about ready to emerge from its cocoon — or likely already will have by the time you read this. Some of the newer-is-better features you'll find include

- **Touch screens:** Since the first-generation netbooks, hardware hackers have been retrofitting touch screens into their mini-laptops. Manufacturers have now clued into this as a good idea, and touch screen models are available. Some designs have a rotating screen that turns the netbook into a tablet computer.

Nostradamus on netbooks

Instead of doing the popular pundit party pleaser of proffering predictions (for the future of netbooks that is), I decided to channel the legendary seer Nostradamus to get his take on what lies ahead — that way, if he blows it, hey, you can't blame me.

Here's what old Nostradamus had to say about the future of netbooks (sorry, he didn't have time for French quatrains):

- **Lower prices:** The $100 laptop may actually be realized in the near future. Cheaper processors and decreased manufacturing costs will continue to lower netbook prices, with basic models falling below the $200 and eventually $150 price points.

- **Longer battery life:** Technology advances in fuel cells and batteries will power your netbook all day without a charge. Nine-cell batteries are already coming on the market that offer eight hours plus of unplugged computing — just remember that bigger batteries weigh more and mean bigger or thicker cases.

- **New chips:** Although they won't run Windows, expect netbooks powered by ARM chips to appear — especially on inexpensive, basic models. ARM processors consume a tiny amount of power and likely will run some type of Linux operating system, such as Google Chrome OS.

- **Thin is in:** Look for netbooks to go on diets and get thinner cases.

- **Better screens:** Mary Lou Jepsen was the brains behind the high-resolution, easy-to-read-in-the-sun screen that comes with the OLPC XO-1. She started her own company, called Pixel Qi (http://pixelqi.com), to provide innovative screens to computer manufacturers. They should start showing up in netbooks soon.

- **Ruggedized cases:** Look for drop-proof, water-resistant netbooks to hit the streets — and not get broken in the process.

- **GPS:** Global Positioning System chips are getting smaller and cheaper, and it's just a matter of time before they become standard inside netbooks.

- **TV tuners:** You can watch movies on your netbook, so why not watch digital TV with a tuner card that comes standard?

- **Instant-on:** Instant-on startup code like Splashtop (www.splashtop.com) will find its way onto netbooks. An instant-on computer allows you to access Internet applications like a Web browser, e-mail, and Skype without waiting for the primary operating system to boot.

✔ **Windows 7:** The popularity of netbooks took Microsoft by surprise, and the company would like to see something other than the dated Windows XP running on small laptops — and I'm talking about a Microsoft brand product, not Linux or any other operating system. Microsoft has been getting a lot of press on its upcoming Windows 7 operating system, including how it will run better on netbooks than the venerable XP.

✔ **Increased connectivity:** In addition to Wi-Fi and Ethernet connections, manufacturers are offering netbooks with 3G (Third Generation) tele-communications hardware that allows you to have mobile broadband access through a cellular phone network.

✔ **Increased performance:** Faster versions of the Intel Atom chip are becoming available, and netbooks are appearing with other processors. In addition, some netbooks now come with high-performance graphics cards that support graphics-intensive games and other programs.

Nuts About the Net

As I mention in Chapter 1, the *net* in *netbook* doesn't apply to a hair net, a fishing net, or Annette Funicello. Instead, it refers to the Internet. A netbook is defined by its affordable, small form factor coupled with widely available wireless Net access. Because the little laptop is so easy to tote around, just about anywhere you find a wireless connection you can

✔ Check and send e-mail.

✔ Browse the Web.

✔ Watch streaming videos.

✔ Use instant messaging, Twitter, and Skype.

✔ Stay in touch through social networking sites such as Facebook and MySpace.

All netbooks offer two ways of jacking into the Internet (or a Local Area Network):

✔ **Wireless:** Netbooks have a built-in, wireless 802.11 card (typically 802.11 b/g) for quick and easy connections to Wi-Fi access points.

✔ **Wired:** If a faster, wired Net connection is available, just plug a cable into your netbook's Ethernet port.

With Windows netbooks, accessing the Net is no different than making a connection with a Windows laptop or desktop PC.

Head in the clouds

You can't talk about netbooks without mentioning *cloud computing*. Here's a brief description of what this buzzword means in case you ever hear it in a conversation.

Think of the Internet as one big cloud. Lots of complex things are going on inside the cloud, but the puffy, white billows prevent you from seeing the inner workings — that would be Web services and software, from companies such as Google, Microsoft, Amazon, Zoho, and Yahoo! (to name a few).

You don't need to know what's happening inside the cloud to benefit from it. An example of cloud computing is Google Docs, where you access documents with a Web browser while the actual applications and data are being stored on a server. (I discuss Google Docs in Chapter 7.)

Netbooks make cloud computing more viable, because they are easy to pack around and can access the Internet from any wireless hotspot.

That's what cloud computing is in a nutshell. If you want to learn more details, check out this great YouTube video with various industry "names" explaining cloud computing in their own words: www.youtube.com/watch?v=6PNuQHUiV3Q.

Although not as popular in the United States as other places in the world (at least as of yet), 3G, as in Third Generation, cellular phone services provide high-speed Internet access for mobile devices. Newer netbook models have built-in 3G modem cards. With a cellular data plan, they allow you to access the Net from just about anywhere you can use a cell phone.

Netbooks versus Laptops: Bigger Isn't Necessarily Better

A common criticism leveled against netbooks is that they're too similar to a full-size laptop. That is, for just a bit more money why wouldn't you buy a cheap, full-size laptop instead?

Yes, it's true that over the past few years traditional laptop prices have plummeted. You can easily find a decent, low-end laptop loaded up with an internal DVD drive, memory card reader, wireless card, 15-inch screen, Bluetooth, a fistful of USB ports, a fast processor, a couple GB of RAM, and a big hard drive for $500 or less.

However . . .

Looking at full-size laptop downsides

First, take a look at some of the downsides to a standard laptop compared to a netbook.

- ✔ **Cost:** If you're on a tight budget, a laptop, even a cheap one, is going to cost you more than a netbook. (However, some manufacturers are producing models they call netbooks, which are actually more like a laptop in terms of price and size.)

  In Chapter 3, I give you tips on how to get the best buy when purchasing a netbook.

- ✔ **Weight:** A good guideline is the heavier a laptop, the less it will get carried outside the home or office — unless it's a work-issued model that you're forced to lug around. Yes, you can get ultra-light laptops like the MacBook Air or Dell Adamo, but they still have a large, albeit thin, case compared to a netbook. And for the price, you could pick up about a half a dozen basic netbooks.

- ✔ **Size:** Laptops have larger cases than netbooks. Take a gander at Figure 2-3, which shows a 10.1-inch-screen netbook next to a standard 15.4-inch-screen Dell laptop. (And just so I don't offend any Mac users out there, Figure 2-4 shows a 13.3-inch-screen MacBook with the same netbook.) Netbook or laptop? You tell me which is going to be easier to carry around.

Figure 2-3:
A 15.4-inch-screen Dell laptop next to a 10.1-inch-screen netbook.

Figure 2-4:
A 13.3-inch-
screen
Apple
MacBook
next to a
10.1-inch-
screen
netbook.

✔ **Hardware:** Be honest with me: When was the last time you actually used the built-in DVD player in your laptop? Or that dialup modem? For most users, a full-size laptop has a fair number of hardware components that are seldom if ever used. These components make the laptop heavier and add to its cost.

Missing in action: Features you don't find on a netbook

The truth is, when comparing netbooks to laptops, some of the features you normally expect to find on a laptop are going to be missing in action on a netbook. Just so you know, that includes

✔ Larger screen

✔ Larger hard drive

✔ Full-size keyboard

✔ Faster processor

✔ Performance graphics card

✔ DVD/CD-ROM player/burner

✔ PC Card slots

✔ Serial port

✔ Dialup modem

✔ FireWire

Life is all about compromises. Millions of netbook users are willing to trade off these standard laptops features for the portability and convenience of a netbook.

Deciding between horsepower or more miles per gallon

When I grew up, 1960s and 70s muscle cars were the big thing. A monster engine with lots of horsepower and a blistering fast quarter mile speed was all that counted. Ah, misspent youth.

Now that I'm older, wiser, and greener, a more practical and functional car that gets good gas mileage, is reliable, and is easy to maintain is much more important to me (although I still like old-school sports cars).

You can apply the same analogy to laptops and netbooks. Do you really need the 160 mph top speed and tire-melting torque of a zoomy laptop running the fastest possible processor? Or does it make more sense to have a zippy and nimble little netbook that didn't cost you an arm and a leg for going into town and taking on long trips?

I've been using netbooks since they first came out, and in all honesty, for everyday tasks such as e-mail, Web browsing, word processing, and so on, low-horsepower chips such as Celerons and Atoms actually work quite well.

Don't let what appears to be a slow processor speed fool you. You don't need a high-horsepower, fast processor for the kind of things you'll likely be using your netbook for. Instead of muscle car, think a peppy and fun little economy car.

A Laptop and a Netbook?

Heck, I say if you can afford it, you should have a laptop *and* a netbook — or a desktop PC and a netbook. Use a standard laptop (or desktop) for doing serious work and running computationally intensive programs. Use a netbook as an ultra-portable travel companion for doing small bits of work and accessing the Internet while away from home (or even at home in unconventional places such as the kitchen, garage, or patio).

Intel recently launched a marketing campaign (`www.intel.com/consumer/learn/netbook.htm`) around the theme of "laptops are for creating" (as are desktop PCs) while "netbooks are for viewing and sharing." Although the company obviously stands to benefit from increased sales of any device that uses its chips, conceptually, the marketing team isn't wrong. There are some things (creating and editing photos, encoding music, playing graphics intensive games, and using desktop publishing and graphics software) that a traditional laptop is going to be much better at compared with a netbook. Save these heavy-lifting tasks for a full-size laptop or desktop PC and avoid the frustration of trying to get your poor little netbook to perform them.

Chapter 3

Selecting a Netbook

*Y*ou've decided you want a netbook. I really can't blame you; they're versatile, fun, and useful little computers. But now comes the hard part: sorting through a sea of models with all sorts of different (and similar) features. Who would have thought buying such a small, simple computer could be a large, complicated task?

It's certainly possible to buy a netbook based on looks or an online review or two, but most people like to do a little more research before purchasing a computer. In this chapter, I take some of the mystery out of selecting a netbook. I tell you about various netbook features and hardware components and provide guidance on which netbooks are best suited for your needs. With that information in hand, I tell you where and how to purchase a netbook.

Time's a-wasting, and you'd better get started. The quicker you get through this chapter, the sooner you'll have a netbook of your own.

Meet the Manufacturers

When netbooks first hit the marketplace, only a handful of computer manufacturers were offering the little laptops. Now it seems everyone and his brother is making a version of a netbook.

When selecting a netbook, it's best to start by seeing what's available on the market and who makes what. As a handy reference, here's a list of the major companies currently offering netbooks along with the addresses for their Web sites:

- ✔ **Acer,** www.acer.com
- ✔ **ASUS,** www.asus.com
- ✔ **Dell,** www.dell.com
- ✔ **Everex,** www.everexstore.com/everex
- ✔ **Fujitsu,** www.fujitsu.com/global/services/computing
- ✔ **HP,** www.hp.com
- ✔ **LG,** www.lg.com
- ✔ **Lenovo,** www.lenovo.com
- ✔ **MSI,** www.msi.com
- ✔ **Samsung,** www.samsung.com
- ✔ **Sony,** www.sony.com
- ✔ **Toshiba,** www.toshiba.com

ASUS model madness

For when you start shopping for netbooks, I need to give you a little heads-up about ASUS — the firm that got the ball rolling with netbooks. If you look at the company's little laptop offerings, there are enough models to make your head spin. When I was writing *ASUS Eee PCs For Dummies* (Wiley Publishing, Inc.), it seemed like a week didn't go by that ASUS wasn't announcing a new netbook with a different model number. It was crazy trying to keep up with them all, and netbook pundits were constantly chiding the manufacturer about having too many models to choose from and confusing the buying public. The company's release pace has slowed down, but their model numbers can be cryptic.

At first it looks simple. For example, a 701 model has a 7-inch screen, a 900 model has a 9-inch screen, and so on. Then it starts to get confusing. Here's why: Another netbook manufacturer may have a model ABC and offer it in several different configurations; perhaps with Windows or Linux, solid state drive or hard drive, and so on. ASUS, on the other hand, tends to use a unique model number for each configuration. So instead of having just a model ABC available with different options, you'd probably find an ABC-W, ABC-L, ABC-HD, and so on. Heck, the company might even release a CBA model, making you think it's something entirely different than an ABC, when in reality it isn't.

My point is, when you're looking at ASUS netbooks, don't get all hung up on all the model names and numbers — this holds true for any manufacturer. In fact, forget them. Look at the features and figure out what you want. I guarantee if you try to make sense of the extensive and frequently confusing model numbers, you'll probably go a little crazy in the process.

This isn't a complete list of all netbook manufacturers — there are more. I don't include some companies because they currently have limited distribution channels. Some great netbooks are made in Taiwan and Korea by lesser-known manufacturers that aren't as readily available to international consumers outside of Asia.

To stay up-to-date with the latest netbook manufacturers and models (including many lesser-known brands), one of my favorite places to visit is the Liliputing.com product database. Point your Web browser to `http://products.liliputing.com`.

The netbook market is in its infancy. Expect more companies to start selling their own versions of little laptops in the near future. As I write this, Nokia is working on a netbook, and there are persistent rumors Apple will release a netbook soon.

Picking a Price Point

When selecting the perfect netbook, start with your wallet (or purse). How much money do you want to spend? Currently, netbooks are priced between $250 and $600. (I expect the price of new entry point models to drop to around $200 and lower in the near future.) The sweet spot is presently in the $350 to $400 range.

If you shop around, it's possible to find refurbished and discontinued netbooks for $200 or less. These models may not have all the whistles and bells of newer netbooks but are easier on the budget and definitely usable.

As with any consumer electronics product, the higher the price, the more features (otherwise known as whistles and bells) you can expect. The guideline is . . .

- ✔ The larger the screen
- ✔ The faster the chip
- ✔ The better the graphics chipset
- ✔ The more memory
- ✔ The bigger the drive
- ✔ The more features (Bluetooth, 3G modem for broadband Internet connection through a cellular phone service provider, and so on)

. . . the higher the price.

A higher price netbook doesn't necessarily mean better. Basic, no-frills models are perfectly acceptable for many tasks. In my opinion, part of what defines a netbook is its affordable price.

All in common

When you purchase a netbook, no matter which brand or model, a number of features seem to universally come standard — of course, always get the model specs just to be sure. Common features include

✔ 10/100 Ethernet port

✔ 802.11 b/g wireless card (some models support 802.11 n)

✔ Audio-in jack (microphone)

✔ Audio-out jack (headphones or speakers)

✔ Built-in speakers (many models feature a built-in microphone)

✔ SD card reader

✔ Touchpad

✔ USB ports (2 or 3)

✔ VGA out (for external monitor or projector)

Choosing Chips

When you look at netbook specifications, you'll notice several types of CPU (central processing unit) chips are used to power different models. The following sections describe what you need to know about these chips.

The general rule is the faster a processor's clock speed (that's the MHz or GHz number associated with a CPU), the more performance it will offer.

Intel Celeron-M

The first generation of netbooks, and even some current models, sport Intel Celeron-M (*M* as in mobile) processors. The Celeron is in the x86 family of processors and is based on the Pentium chip. Manufacturers use this chip in value and bargain laptops. It offers adequate performance but is getting a bit long in tooth and is being replaced by more efficient chips such as the Intel Atom, described next.

Intel Atom

Because of the growing popularity of mobile devices, Intel decided to develop a new low-voltage chip. Dubbed Atom (see Figure 3-1), the chip debuted in 2008 and was quickly adopted by netbook manufacturers. Netbooks powered by Atom processors have longer battery lives compared with similar configured models that use Celeron chips. At present, the Atom processor dominates the netbook market.

Figure 3-1: The Intel Atom processor sits next to a penny to give you an idea of size.

Graphics chipsets

When netbooks were first introduced, they used fairly rudimentary graphics chipsets. There is currently a move by netbook manufacturers to start including higher-end graphics chips that will support 3-D graphics for games and high-definition (HD) video. Here's some brief information about common graphics chips and chipsets found in netbooks:

- **Intel GMA:** GMA stands for Graphics Media Accelerator, and this is Intel's line of graphics processing units (GPUs) built into motherboard chipsets. The 500, 900, and 950 GPUs are commonly used in netbooks.

- **Intel 945 GSE:** A graphics chipset (based on the GMA 950 architecture) included with netbooks that use the N270 Atom processor. It's power efficient but lacking in performance when it comes to working with graphics intensive programs and data.

- **Intel GN 40:** Intel's latest graphics chipset for netbooks that supports high-definition (720p) video and 3-D. This chipset is included with netbooks powered by N280 Atom processors. Initial reports say the chipset offers more performance but slightly less power efficiency.

- **Nvidia Ion:** Graphics giant Nvidia is getting into the netbook game with a chipset called Ion. This is an Atom processor paired with GeForce 9400M graphic chip. Nvidia is promising 5x faster graphics and 10x faster video transcoding compared with an Atom-powered netbook with a 945GSE chipset. (Nvidia's Tegra platform includes a graphics chip paired with an ARM processor.)

If you're a heavy-duty gamer or want to watch Blu-ray videos, get a netbook with a fast graphics chipset. If you just plan on using your netbook for general computing and accessing the Net, you don't really need a higher-power (and more costly) graphics chipset.

Silverthorne was the original codename for the Atom chip. It was designed for ultra-mobile PCs. *Diamondville* is the version of Atom designed for netbooks. There's also a dual-core Atom on the drawing board, and it's supposed to offer higher performance.

Atom N270 processors run at 1.6 GHz. Intel's new Atom N280 runs at a slightly faster 1.66 GHz. Both processors draw about the same amount of power.

Both of these chips are expected to be phased out by mid-2010 and replaced by the next generation Atom N450 — codenamed *Pine Trail.* This single core processor will use less power and run at a faster speed.

Atom chips are more expensive than Celeron chips. That's why Celeron model netbooks had a lower price than their Atom cousins. As Intel expands its Atom line of chips, look for netbooks using lower-speed Atoms to be cheaper than models with faster processors.

VIA

VIA Technologies is a Taiwanese manufacturer of computer components. The company produces a processor called the C7-M, which is used in a handful of netbooks. The C7-M is more or less equivalent to the Celeron in terms of processing power. VIA recently released a new processor called Nano, which is designed to compete against the Atom in the notebook market.

AMD

Advanced Micro Devices (AMD) is Intel's perennial competitor in the processor market. AMD was initially skeptical about the netbook market and decided it wasn't a development priority. The company has since announced that it's working on a chip dubbed *Neo* that will compete with the Atom. (Whether *Neo* means "new" or is a reference to the movie *The Matrix,* I don't know.) After AMD releases a suitable netbook processor, expect some manufacturers to jump on the bandwagon.

ARM

ARM stands for *Advanced RISC Machine.* This is a 32-bit, Reduced Instruction Set Chip (RISC) architecture developed by ARM Limited. If you have a cell phone, there's a very good chance it's powered by one or more ARM chips. ARM chips are also widely used in PDAs (personal digital assistants), MP3 players, and handheld game machines.

ARM processors aren't the only alternative chips to perhaps find their way into netbooks. Companies like Freescale Semiconductor, Qualcomm (see the "Smartbooks" sidebar) and Samsung Electronics all make inexpensive, power-saving chips used in cell phones and are eyeing the netbook market.

As I write this, a few ARM-powered netbooks have been announced, and some of the larger netbook manufacturers are hinting about future production. ARM chips are cheap compared with the Intel Atom. And while they don't offer the performance of an Atom processor, manufacturers are considering the chips for use in the next generation of netbooks.

The Windows operating system was developed to run on Intel x86 processors. ARM chips don't use the same instruction set as Intel chips, which means Windows and Windows programs won't run on ARM netbooks.

An industry goal is to eventually create a $100-or-less netbook. ARM chips would likely power such an inexpensive netbook, running a custom operating system based on Linux. Such a device would have enough horsepower for basic Net activities such as e-mail, Web browsing, instant messaging, and watching streamed videos.

Smartbooks

What do you get when you cross a netbook with a smartphone? According to chipmaker Qualcomm, you get a *smartbook*. In May 2009, the company started promoting the idea of a device that looks like a typical netbook but uses Qualcomm's Snapdragon chipset, which is based on an ARM-based processor that comes with 3G mobile broadband, Bluetooth, GPS, and Wi-Fi. In addition to the connectivity features, a smartbook also has enhanced graphics capabilities that allow you to play 3-D games and watch HD video.

The catch is a smartbook won't run Windows or any familiar Windows programs. The little laptop will need to run some variety of Linux or perhaps an updated variation of a Microsoft PDA operating system.

Qualcomm has been showing off prototypes of various devices using its chipsets for awhile now, but Atom netbooks still rule the market. The success of any ARM-processor little laptop is going to depend on aggressive (meaning *cheap*) pricing coupled with an outstanding user interface and operating system — Google Android and Chrome as well as Moblin show promise. At this point, I'm not ready to make any bets on the smartbook concept taking off.

Mesmerized by Memory

Like any computer, netbooks have internal random access memory (RAM). Over the years, as memory prices have declined and programs and operating systems have gotten more bloated (er, I mean have greater memory requirements to support new and exciting features, yeah, that's it), traditional laptops and desktop PCs have come with more and more RAM. It's not uncommon to see low-end PCs stuffed with 3–4GB of RAM.

When you start looking at netbooks, you may be shocked that some models come with only 512K of RAM. "How can that be?" you say. "Won't the computer run as slow as frozen molasses in the middle of December?"

Actually, no. Both Windows XP and Linux can easily run on 512K RAM and still have acceptable performance — as long as you don't have a lot of programs or files open at once or try to run memory-intensive programs.

That said, 1GB of RAM will give you snappier performance, and you don't need to worry so much about curbing your multitasking.

Manufacturers may offer 512K of RAM in a basic netbook with 1 to 2GB in higher priced models — 1GB seems to currently be the standard.

The maximum for any netbook running Windows is 2GB. This has nothing to do with technology but everything to do with Microsoft's licensing agreement, which stipulates manufacturers cannot sell netbooks with more than 2GB of memory that run Windows XP.

Opt for at least a 1GB netbook, or if you're stuck with less, make sure it's possible to upgrade the RAM at some future time. (I discuss adding more RAM in Chapter 18.)

A few manufacturers are offering Microsoft Vista on their netbooks. If you're thinking about running Vista, you need at least 2GB of RAM. I talk more about Vista in Chapter 4.

Stumped by Storage

Why should you be stumped by storage? That shouldn't be a hard decision. You just get a netbook that has a big enough hard drive to hold all of your stuff. Well, it's actually a little more complicated than that because many netbooks offer two options for storage, solid state drives and traditional hard disk drives. Here's the lowdown on both.

Solid state drives (SSDs)

Instead of relying on spinning platters (found in standard laptop and desktop PC hard drives), some netbook models feature a solid state drive (SSD) — one is shown in Figure 3-2. An SSD uses a memory chip to store data and doesn't have any moving mechanical parts — this makes them lighter and less prone to failure. They start up and power down very quickly, are quiet, and have fast read and write times.

Figure 3-2:
A solid state
drive case
and
internals.

SSDs have two downsides:

- ✔ **Cost:** Because they're a rather new storage technology, they're quite expensive. At the present, the retail price of a 256GB SSD is around $500. Compare that with a conventional hard drive you can get for about $50.

- ✔ **Capacity:** Due to the cost, netbook manufacturers use low-capacity SSDs — storage capacity is usually under 20GB. On very small SSDs, Linux is typically installed.

SSDs are the wave of the future for laptops. Prices are starting to fall, but it will be several years at the least before SSDs are comparably priced to traditional hard drives that have large amounts of storage space.

Hard disk drives (HDDs)

Over the years, hard disk drives have become the storage medium of choice for laptops and desktop PCs. They work by reading and writing data on rapidly spinning platters that have magnetic surfaces. A relatively inexpensive HDD can store a large amount of data. Compared with a solid state drive, hard drives are considerably cheaper, a little heavier, consume a bit more power, and because they have moving mechanical parts, aren't quite as robust.

Early netbooks didn't have HDDs, but customer demand for more storage prompted manufacturers to start offering conventional hard drives. HDD-equipped netbooks are now more popular than SSD models and commonly come in 80, 120, and 160GB sizes, with Windows typically installed.

It's also possible to have a hybrid storage system. As I write this, a netbook that uses a small SSD for the operating system and a HDD for data and installed programs was just announced. This design would be the best of both worlds.

Deciding between SSD and HDD

Which would you choose? A netbook with a 16GB solid state drive or one with a conventional 160GB hard disk? Oh, I forgot to mention, both retail for the same price.

"No way," you exclaim. "That must be a typo. You'd have to be crazy to limit yourself to only 16GB of storage when you could have ten times more for the same price."

This is a dilemma netbook buyers sometimes often face. As I mention earlier, because solid state drives are much more expensive than traditional hard drives, manufacturers use low-capacity SSDs to keep prices down. Here's a bit of guidance if you're having trouble making a decision.

Choose a netbook with an SSD drive if you

- Want the lightest weight configuration possible
- Like very fast startup times
- Don't plan on adding many other programs beyond those that were preinstalled
- Are primarily using the netbook for accessing the Internet

Choose a netbook with a conventional hard drive if you plan on

- ✔ Installing lots of programs
- ✔ Storing movies and MP3 files on the drive
- ✔ Running programs that use large data files (such as mapping or professional graphics applications)

Personally, I'd opt for a netbook with a hard drive versus a solid state drive. SSDs are cool, but the low capacity due to the price doesn't make them as versatile. When 80 or 120GB SSDs come down in price, I'll change my tune. In the meantime, laptop hard drives are an affordable, reliable, and known commodity — and are usually easy to swap or replace.

Just because a netbook with a hard drive comes preinstalled with Windows doesn't mean you can't install Linux on it. And conversely, if you have a Linux netbook with an SSD, you can always install Windows on it. I discuss more about this in Chapter 4.

Keyboard Conundrums

When you purchase a desktop PC or a conventional laptop, you get a standardized keyboard. Although some of the keys might be in different places, you at least know they'll all generally be the same size and shape.

This isn't the case with netbooks. The size of the keys, how they feel when you press them, their shape, and even their layout differ from manufacturer to manufacturer — and sometimes even among models. See Figure 3-3 to get an idea of how key size can vary.

Because of this, I strongly recommend — if you have a chance — trying out several netbooks before you buy. More retail stores are carrying netbooks with the undersized keys, and it's important to select a model you and your fingers will be happy with. If you can't demo a model or two, make sure the online retailer has a reasonable return policy just in case you find out your fingers and the netbook can't be friends.

Generally, you'll find the keys on most 10-inch-screen netbooks quite usable. On smaller netbooks, the keyboards can definitely be challenging to get used to.

Figure 3-3:
From top
to bottom,
in scale,
a full-size
laptop key,
a 10-inch
netbook
key, a 7-inch
netbook
key, and a
key from an
OLPC XO-1.

 Full-size laptop (Dell Vostro 1500)

 10-inch netbook (ASUS 1000HE Eee PC)

 7-inch netbook (ASUS 701 Eee PC)

 OLPC XO-1

Baffled by Batteries

When you read netbook specifications, you'll undoubtedly see information about the battery. All netbooks currently use rechargeable lithium ion batteries. Pay attention to these two things:

✔ **mAh:** This stands for milliamp hour, a technical term that states how much power a battery holds. Batteries with higher mAh values last longer without recharging.

As a battery ages, its storage capacity decreases. For example, a new 2,200 mAh battery may last longer between recharges than an old 4,000 mAh battery.

✔ **Cells:** A netbook's plastic battery case contains a series of battery cells. The more cells a battery has, the more power it stores, and the longer it will last away from a power outlet. Netbook batteries typically have three, four, or six cells — extended batteries may even have more.

The more cells in a battery, the heavier the battery. Also, you can stuff only so many cells into a netbook-sized battery case. Beyond a certain number of cells, the manufacturer needs to either extend the battery case (which means it won't fit flush inside the netbook) or expand the netbook's case so it will fit larger batteries.

Take a netbook manufacturer's bragging about battery life with a grain of salt. The numbers they sling around are for absolutely best case scenarios — wireless off, dimmed screen, limited processor activity, and so on. Under real world conditions, always expect to get somewhat less than advertised time.

Settling on a Screen

Netbooks come with a variety of nice and compact screen sizes. Figure 3-4 gives you a relative idea of how screens compare size-wise. Generally, the larger the screen and the higher the resolution, the more the netbook costs. Here's what to expect in the way of netbook screens.

- ✔ **7-inch:** First-generation netbooks featured a dinky 7-inch display. It's kind of a pain to surf Web sites with these size screens because the whole page isn't displayed horizontally — forcing you to scroll quite a bit. Additionally, the resolution of the 7-inch screens was a meager 800 x 480. Netbooks with these screens have mostly gone the way of the dinosaur and are available only on the used and discounted markets.

- ✔ **9-inch:** Manufacturers quickly wised up that 7-inch screens just didn't cut the mustard. From an engineering standpoint, it's possible to shoehorn a 9-inch-screen into a 7-inch netbook case and make the case only slightly larger.

In fact, many 7-inch-screen netbooks had a plastic bezel around the screen which, when you tallied up the screen and bezel size, was roughly equivalent to a 9-inch-screen model.

Most screens this size have a 1024 x 600 resolution. If you're looking for ultimate portability, go with a 9-inch-screen model. The downside is you still may be faced with a small keyboard.

Want to get a feel for what browsing the Web at 1024 x 600 is like? If you use the Firefox browser, enter this command in the address bar:

```
javascript:resizeTo(1024,600);
```

Be forewarned that many manufacturers seem to be doing away with their 9-inch models in favor of the more popular and usable 10-inch-screen netbooks, which I talk about next.

- ✔ **10-inch and beyond:** When you put a 10-inch screen in a netbook, its case needs to be enlarged. With the bigger case, you can add a larger keyboard and a bigger battery. Netbooks with 10-inch screens are pretty much standard these days, although different models have different maximum screen resolutions — generally, the higher the resolution, the better.

Despite what a manufacturer may advertise, I personally don't consider any netbook that has a screen larger than 10 inches (a few tenths of an inch over is okay), a true netbook. Models touting 11- and 12-inch screens are really more like laptops than netbooks because you're giving up the compact size, light weight, and inexpensive price tag.

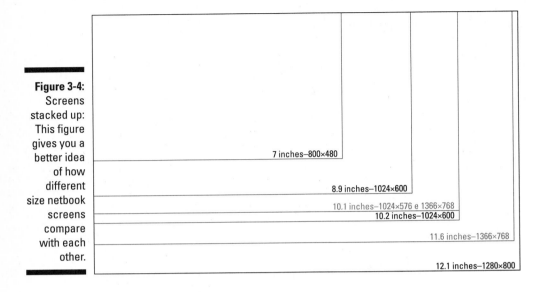

Figure 3-4:
Screens
stacked up:
This figure
gives you a
better idea
of how
different
size netbook
screens
compare
with each
other.

7 inches–800×480

8.9 inches–1024×600

10.1 inches–1024×576 e 1366×768
10.2 inches–1024×600

11.6 inches–1366×768

12.1 inches–1280×800

I'm guilty of rounding screen size numbers just to make it easier to understand. Most netbook screens described as 9 inches are actually 8.9 inches. A 10-inch screen can be 10, 10.1 or 10.2 inches based on manufacturer specs. But what's a few tenths of an inch between friends?

Many netbooks have glossy screens — the surface is reflective. Some models have matte screens, which don't reflect. Research by the Queensland University of Technology in Australia suggests high-gloss screens may cause back problems because users adopt awkward positions to avoid glare and reflections typically not present with matte screens. For more information, see www.hrd.qut.edu.au/healthsafety/worksafely/highGloss.jsp.

Operating System Opinions

With some netbook models, you have a choice between Linux and Windows operating systems — and in the future, you likely will have even have more options.

Although netbooks running Windows are currently the most popular, that doesn't necessarily mean you have to follow the crowd. There's a lot to say on this subject, so I devote all of Chapter 4 to discussing operating systems. Be sure to check it out.

Case in Point

At a quick glance, most netbooks look fairly similar. However, you can find a lot of variation among the cases that house the internal parts and pieces. When you're shopping for a netbook, don't get so focused on hardware specifications that you forget about the case. Here are a few case laws:

- ✔ **Check out photos.** Just about every netbook that comes on the market gets reviewed, and many of the reviews have detailed photos from different angles — much more useful than the official product pictures on the manufacturer Web sites. Check out the photos! You'll find that some netbooks are definitely more aesthetically pleasing than others — just remember that beauty is in the eye of the beholder.

- ✔ **Read the dimension specifications.** When you're comparison shopping netbooks, pay attention to the case dimension specifications. All netbooks are not created equal when it comes to length, width, thickness, and weight. These dimensions are important if you're looking for an ultra-portable travel companion.

- ✔ **Decide on a style and color.** Some manufacturers offer cases with stylish metal trim and in colors other than basic white or black — there are also a few netbooks on the market with metal cases. You might have to pay a little extra for a different case color, material, or a snazzy design on the case, but if fire engine red is more you, don't be afraid to go for it.

Plastic netbook cases come with either matte or glossy finishes, depending on the model. Glossy cases in dark colors are notorious for showing fingerprints — in case that bothers you.

You may narrow down your choices to several different netbooks that all have the same features and the same general price. In such cases flip a coin or make your decision on case aesthetics.

If you want to make a personal statement with your netbook, be sure to read Chapter 12, where I tell you about laptop *skins* (decals for adorning your netbook).

Ferreting out Other Features

In the previous sections of this chapter, I cover most of the primary features you should consider when selecting a netbook. However, there are still a few more miscellaneous features that come with different models that I want to tell you about.

3G modems

The term 3G stands for Third Generation. This term refers to cell phone companies providing high-speed wireless Internet access from your phone through their systems — after you sign up for a data plan, of course.

Mobile phones aren't the only beneficiaries of 3G networks. Newer netbook models are coming equipped with built-in 3G modems — that means you don't need to be near a Wi-Fi hotspot to access the Net. In fact, some cellular providers are beginning to offer discounted netbooks with their data plans. (See the "Netbooks for nothing" sidebar in this chapter.)

If your netbook doesn't have a built-in 3G modem, you can purchase add-on products. I discuss these in Chapter 6.

Bluetooth

Some netbooks have built-in hardware for interacting with Bluetooth devices such as cell phones, speakers, and GPS receivers. If your netbook didn't include Bluetooth, you can purchase an add-on card. I talk more about Bluetooth in Chapter 6.

Touchpads

Like most laptops, netbooks primarily use a touchpad instead of a mouse for interfacing with the operating system and programs — you can still use a USB mouse at the same time if you like. (If you're a new laptop or netbook user and have never used a touchpad before, be sure to read the section on touchpads in Chapter 5.)

Some netbook touchpads support a feature called *multitouch*. Multitouch lets you use two fingers at the same time to navigate the screen. It's the same technology found in Apple's iPhone, iPod touch, MacBook Air, and MacBook Pro products.

Multitouch is pretty cool, state-of-the-art technology. In programs that support it, you can zoom out by placing two fingers on the touchpad and moving them apart — pinch them together to zoom in. You can also scroll windows by placing both fingers together on the touchpad and then together dragging them up or down.

Webcams

A number of netbooks have Web cameras (webcams) built into the case above the screen. This is a handy feature if you plan to use your netbook for video conferencing (or chatting) or shooting quick photos or videos.

Don't expect image quality and resolution to be as high as a standalone digital still or video camera though. If your netbook is equipped for video, it will have a lowly 0.3 or 1.3 megapixel camera built in — compare that with digital still cameras that commonly feature 7 to 10 megapixel resolution.

ExpressCards

No, I'm not referring to that credit card you should never leave home without. I'm talking about the ExpressCard hardware standard which replaces PC Cards (also known as PCMCIA cards). An ExpressCard is smaller and faster than older expansion cards — laptop manufacturers have started adopting the standard within the past few years, and it proves to be the wave of the future. Currently, only a few netbooks sport ExpressCard slots, but I expect this to change as manufacturers try to outdo each other with features in the increasingly competitive market.

ExpressCards can also be referred to as *Peripheral Component Interconnect Express, PCIe,* or *PCI-E* cards. ExpressCards are derived from the PCIe standard.

Selection Suggestions

I'm not going to recommend a specific brand or model of netbook — sorry, that would take away all the fun of deciding exactly what's right for you. Once you know about the features, and start looking at the specs and prices, I have no doubt you'll quickly come up with a short list of models to choose from.

If you're stuck, here are a few general recommendations on what type of netbook to consider, depending on who will be using it:

✔ **Children:** Go for a basic, no-frills model. They're relatively inexpensive and are fairly immune to minor bumps and drops — especially SSD models. A smaller keyboard is perfect for littler hands. Consider models designed for the education market.

✔ **Students:** Having been a starving student once, look for the most features with the best price. Battery life should be a big consideration. Bluetooth is a plus if you have a compatible cell phone. The lighter and smaller the better — with a usable screen and keyboard, of course.

✔ **Businesspeople:** Go for a model with a larger, more usable-size keyboard and screen. Because the business world seems to revolve around Windows, select it as your operating system for easy networking inter-operability and data synchronization. Again, look for long battery life.

✔ **Home computer users:** Netbooks are a great second computer. If you have a wireless access point at home, a netbook's light weight and size make it perfect for accessing the Internet anywhere you want — kitchen, patio, bedroom, wherever. It's also convenient to toss in a bag or purse when you head to the coffee shop. Find a balance between size and usability that works for you.

✔ **Senior citizens:** For seniors, I recommend a netbook with at least a 10-inch screen — get something you don't have trouble seeing. A larger keyboard is also important. If you're going to be using the mini-laptop mostly around home, don't worry about battery life, because a power outlet will always be nearby.

✔ **Techies:** Take your pick — depending on how much you've got to spend. Some netbooks lend themselves more to tinkering and customization than others, so do a quick Google search for a model you're interested in and for *hacking*. And check out Chapter 23 for a collection of projects to get you started.

Buying Basics

Great! You've persevered through this chapter, did all of your homework, and now have one or more netbooks on your short list. You're almost there, and I want to close with some final buying advice:

✔ **Go with a larger netbook manufacturer.** Unless you're technically savvy, it makes sense to go with a netbook made by one of the manufacturers I mention at the beginning of this chapter. Although a lesser-known brand may work great, it's usually safer to go with a well-known name brand. That's because you'll likely get better technical support from the manufacturer, plus, the more units that are sold, the greater the chance an online user community will develop. In many cases, I've found online forums offer faster and better support than what you get from the factory.

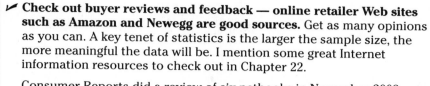

✔ **Check out buyer reviews and feedback — online retailer Web sites such as Amazon and Newegg are good sources.** Get as many opinions as you can. A key tenet of statistics is the larger the sample size, the more meaningful the data will be. I mention some great Internet information resources to check out in Chapter 22.

Consumer Reports did a review of six netbooks in November 2008, and although that seems like forever considering the way technology changes, it's worthwhile reading the free review at `http://blogs.consumerreports.org/electronics/2008/11/six-windows-net.html`. Check the site to see whether any updated reviews have been written with newer products. Consumer Reports reviewed and rated netbooks and other laptops in its June 2009 magazine issue, but as I write this it hasn't appeared online, so visit your friendly local library.

✔ **Price shop.** Prices vary, especially online. Every dollar saved these days counts, and you can easily bank an extra 20 bucks on up, depending on where you purchase your netbook. Amazon (`www.amazon.com`), Newegg (`www.newegg.com`), and Buy.com (`www.buy.com`) all stock netbooks, as do many smaller online retailers — Google is your friend in finding them.

If you're on a really low budget but still want a netbook, consider a first- or second-generation model. With manufacturers getting rid of older, discontinued models, I've seen some limited quantity, great bargains on various deal Web sites — and don't forget about eBay. As I write this, it's possible to pick up new first- and second-generation netbooks for around $150 or less.

✔ **Shop local.** If you get a chance, find a local retailer who carries netbooks and check it out in person. (In the United States, Target, Best Buy, Costco and even Toys"R"Us stock some models of netbooks, and a number of smaller retailers are beginning to carry different lines.)

Some manufacturers offer discounted prices on *refurbished* netbooks. These are netbooks that have been returned to the manufacturer for one reason or another and then are tested and repaired if necessary. Most come with full warranties. Check the manufacturer's Web site (there's a list at the beginning of the chapter) to see whether you can score any deals. I've also found that sites like Buy.com often carry refurbished netbooks.

Netbooks for nothing

"Pssst. How'd you like a netbook for free? I've got this brand-new little gem right here that could be yours."

You might be getting this pitch soon, and it won't be coming from a shady character lurking in the shadows of a darkened alley on the wrong side of town.

No, this offer may be coming from your friendly neighborhood cellular provider. As I write this, some of the large providers are starting to offer brand-new netbooks for $50 to $100 when you sign up with them for a 3G data plan. If the past predicts the future, there's always a possibility they may eventually start giving away netbooks for free just like cell phones.

However, don't be penny wise and pound foolish when it comes to cheap netbooks bundled with cellular data plans. As an example, one retailer (who shall remain nameless) is offering a popular netbook for $99 when you sign up for a data plan that costs $70 a month. However, if you look around, you can get plans that include both voice and data for the same price or less. Do some window shopping and brush off any rusty math skills before being lured in by a discounted netbook deal.

Also, beware of suicidal netbooks. Unlike a mobile phone, which is pretty useless without a service provider, with a netbook, you still have a functional computer when you cancel your data plan (or don't pay the bill). LM Ericsson AB, the Swedish company that makes many of the modems that go into laptops, has a plan to prevent this. The company recently announced a new modem dubbed a "kill pill" that allows a carrier to send a signal to the netbook and completely disable it. Ouch!

Chapter 4

Netbook Operating Systems

*A*ll computers need an operating system (OS) to manage files, run programs, print documents, and perform other basic tasks. A netbook is no exception.

When you buy a computer, you usually don't need to worry about the operating system. If you buy a PC, you get Windows. If you buy a Mac, you get OS X. But as you start looking at different netbooks, you'll soon find that manufacturers offer a number of different operating systems on their little laptops. In fact, you may even have a choice between two operating systems on the same model.

This chapter is all about netbook operating systems. I tell you about what operating systems are available now (and what's in the pipeline), list key differences between different operating systems, and even weigh in on the sometimes heated Linux-versus-Windows question.

Working with Windows

When you think about operating systems, Microsoft Windows naturally comes to mind. Since the 1990s, Windows has been the dominant operating system across all PCs — and it continues its reign among netbooks. Follow along as I describe past and present versions of Windows that are used on netbooks.

XPerience counts

Because netbooks first came out at the end of 2007, you would think the little laptops would be running the latest, greatest, cutting-edge operating system. But guess what? The most popular netbook OS is the venerable Windows XP (shown in Figure 4-1), which was first released in October 2001.

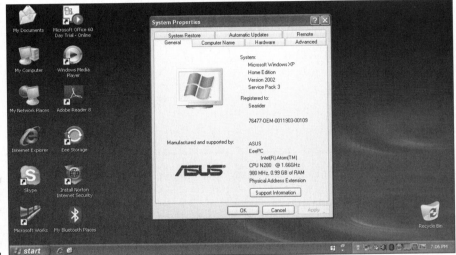

Figure 4-1:
Microsoft XP running on a netbook.

Microsoft has tried its best to replace the dated operating system, but hasn't had much success. (Although the company has ended mainstream support for XP, it will continue offering free security fixes until 2014.) Microsoft's problem is that plain and simple, XP just works. It's reliable, predictable, easy to use, supports all manner of hardware devices and programs, and is as comfortable as an old sweater. According to March statistics from research company Hitslink, 63 percent of computers connected to the Internet are running XP — compare that to a meager 24 percent for Vista, with the remainder split up between Linux and Mac.

Aside from general consumer popularity, XP is well suited for netbooks. Even a first generation netbook with 512K of RAM and a 900 MHz processor can run XP and most Windows programs reasonably well. More memory and a faster processor are even better. Aside from a smaller screen, you can expect XP to run on your netbook just like it does on a full-size laptop or desktop PC — and that means nearly all the Windows programs work the same.

Conspiracy nation

The popularity of Linux netbooks took many by surprise — including Microsoft. When netbooks first came out, they exclusively ran Linux operating systems. Manufacturers provided instructions for installing Windows XP if you happened to have a spare copy, but you couldn't buy an off-the-shelf netbook with the Microsoft OS.

Then suddenly, Windows XP models became available — for the same price as Linux models. This was curious because Linux was free and didn't require any manufacturer licensing fees, but Windows did. Some industry analysts (and conspiracy theorists) believed Microsoft recognized a threat to its hegemony. The rumors go that the Redmond giant started offering netbook manufacturers some really good licensing deals and incentives if they offered Windows XP Home edition netbooks. And in a very short amount of time, Windows netbooks were outselling their Linux cousins by a margin of 9 to 1. The Wall Street Journal recently ran an article that suggested Microsoft was making around $15 from a netbook that comes with XP — compare that to around $50 to $60 each time a computer with Vista is sold. We'll probably never know the real story, but hey, that's business.

Viewing Vista

The Microsoft Vista OS hasn't been the smash success the company expected it to be. Since Vista was released in 2007, a lot of PC users expressed their content with Windows XP by deciding not to upgrade. And with sales of new traditional laptops and desktop PCs (which come preinstalled with Vista) down, Microsoft hasn't made as big of a dent in the user base as it thought it would.

Vista requires more memory and computing horsepower than previous versions of Windows, and this is where Microsoft made a faulty assumption. Up until now, computers have evolved very predictably — new computers have faster processors, more memory, and bigger hard drives than previous generations. Microsoft assumed this Darwinian process would continue, and that computers would naturally and eventually beef up to meet Vista's demands. However the emergence of netbooks in 2007 flipped that assumption on its head — no-frills, underpowered computers are selling like hot cakes. The Internet has taken priority over the traditional desktop computer.

Because most netbooks have a gigabyte or less of RAM and relatively low-performance processors, Vista isn't the best operating system to use. Some netbook users have tried installing Vista on their tiny laptops and were disappointed at the speed and performance. That's why the majority of netbook manufacturers have stuck with Windows XP as their operating system of choice. (A cost factor is also involved because copies of XP have a cheaper licensing fee compared with Vista.)

Although a few manufacturers do offer Vista Home, with various system settings tweaked to accommodate underpowered netbooks, at the present, I'd stick with a model that runs Windows XP or Windows 7, which I discuss next.

Seeking 7

Next up at bat from Microsoft's operating system team is Windows 7. (Figure 4-2 shows you an example of the updated desktop and user interface.) The new OS is a more advanced and improved version of Windows Vista. It runs faster, requires less memory, and has a number of user interface enhancements that make it more intuitive and friendly to use — perfect for a netbook. In my opinion, Microsoft has learned from the less-than-entirely-successful Vista and has put much more thought (and user feedback) into this operating system.

Voting for Vista

If you're bound and determined to run Vista on your netbook, you're a hardy soul, and the least I can do is give you a few tips to make the installation easier:

✔ Upgrade your system memory to at least 2GB. A 512K memory is painful, and 1GB is usable, but slow.

✔ Make sure you have enough storage space. Vista is big, and I wouldn't recommend installing it on a low-capacity solid state drive.

✔ Use vLite (www.vlite.net), a free utility that creates a stripped-down version of Vista. You need to own a copy of Vista; vLite creates the lite version of Vista from the installation disc.

✔ You need an external DVD player to use the installation disc (either a vLite version or the original). It may be possible to install Vista from an SD memory card or a USB flash drive, but the DVD route is the easiest.

✔ You need Vista-compatible drivers for your netbook hardware. The netbook's manufacturer Web support should have the drivers available for download.

✔ Search Google for your netbook model and Vista (for instance, type **Eee PC Vista** as your search term) to get information from other users who may have successfully installed Vista. Also check some of the forums I mention in Chapter 22.

Or, better yet, skip all the preceding steps, sell your old netbook, and buy a new one that has Vista preinstalled.

Figure 4-2:
Windows 7
operating
system.

The OS comes in a variety of editions, with Windows 7 Home Premium
targeted at home computers, laptops, and netbooks — there are also
Professional and Ultimate versions for business and enterprise users. A
Windows 7 Starter Edition is also available on some netbooks. Microsoft has
traditionally released starter editions in developing countries. This software
is an inexpensive version of the operating system with some features pared
down. The goal is to get more Windows users in non-industrialized countries,
where most people or computer manufacturers couldn't afford a fully priced
retail or licensed version. Using a special Starter Edition for netbooks ensures
a Microsoft operating system ends up on $200-or-less netbooks without
cutting into the manufacturers' margins too much.

Don't expect the Starter Edition to have all of the functionality of the full
editions. It has a number of limitations including no support for multitouch
on touchpads, no DVD playback, and limited customization options such as
not being able to change your desktop wallpaper. If your netbook comes with
this basic version of the operating system, you can always upgrade to the
Home version to get more features.

If you're trying to decide whether you should upgrade your Windows XP netbook to Windows 7, check out this great article from Maximum PC that compares real-world performance between the two operating systems (and even contrasts a few Linux distributions): www.maximumpc.com/article/features/windows_7_vs_linux_whats_best_os_your_netbook.

For more on Windows 7, visit Microsoft's official Web page at www.microsoft.com/windows/windows-7.

Don't think the venerable Windows XP will disappear as soon as Windows 7 hits the shelves. Microsoft announced that netbook manufacturers will be able to sell little laptops with XP for one year after Windows 7 is generally available.

Loving Linux

When the first netbooks hit the market, they all ran Linux. Some netbook manufacturers continue to offer Linux models, and if you don't know much about the operating system, this is the place to find out about it — or at least get a good, general overview.

Penguin pointers

If you're not a Linux aficionado, you're probably wondering what's up with the title of this section. When you start using Linux, you'll notice there's an overabundance of references to penguins, especially a cute, cuddly one named Tux — the official mascot of Linux as shown in Figure 4-3. Here's the story: In 1996, developers were trying to think up a mascot for Linux. Sharks and eagles were considered, but Linus Torvalds (the father of Linux, as in LInus uNIX) mentioned he was fond of penguins. So a contest was proposed to come up with a suitable-looking bird. Larry Ewing's design won best of show, and because penguins appear to be wearing tuxedos, someone suggested the name Tux. The rest is history.

Figure 4-3:
Tux, the
Linux
mascot.

If you want the full, illustrated history of Tux, head over to

```
www.sjbaker.org/wiki/index.php?title=The_History_of_Tux_
            the_Linux_Penguin
```

Okay, with that fowl explanation out of the way, I need to get back on track.

Linux is a free, open-source operating system. Lots of programmers all over the world volunteer their time, contributing to its development — some of the reasons they do this include altruism, ego, and beefing up their reputations and resumes.

Just because something is free doesn't mean it doesn't have value. Linux is a very mature and solid operating system — easily in the same league as the latest offerings from Microsoft and Apple.

Linux, which is based on Unix, started out as a command-line operating system. In an effort to modernize Linux with a desktop, windows, and menus, two graphical user interface projects were started: KDE (www.kde.org) and Gnome (www.gnome.org). Both generally work the same but have a slightly different look and feel and associated programs. KDE is Windows-like, and Gnome is more Mac-like. Versions of Linux that run on netbooks typically use either KDE or Gnome as their user interface. Now let me tell you about those different versions of Linux.

Discussing distros

A number of different versions of Linux are available — these are called *distributions* or *distros* if you want to sound clued in. You may have heard of Ubuntu, Fedora (formerly Red Hat), PCLinuxOS, or Slackware; to name a few. A company, organization, or group of people creates a distribution based on a version of a common Linux kernel. It then includes various packages and software. This distribution is then packaged up and released on a disc or over the Internet for download. (Head over to www.linux.org to find out more about all the different distributions.)

No single Linux distribution has been standardized for netbooks, and you can find manufacturers offering different distros with their products. Here's a list of the distributions some of the main netbook players currently offer:

Netbook Manufacturer	Linux Distribution
Acer	Linpus
ASUS	Xandros
Dell	Ubuntu
HP	SUSE
Lenovo	SUSE
MSI	SUSE

Manufacturers further customize their distros, optimizing them for their own netbooks. For example, ASUS uses a Linux distribution called Xandros, customizing the user interface and code for the Eee PC (as shown in Figure 4-4).

Figure 4-4: ASUS Eee PC customized version of Xandros Linux.

If you don't like the version of Linux that shipped with your netbook, it's relatively simple to install a different distro that has features you like. Take ASUS as an example again: Many techie users don't like the simplified user interface on Linux Eee PCs and end up replacing the Xandros distro with a version of Ubuntu (shown in Figure 4-5) or another distribution.

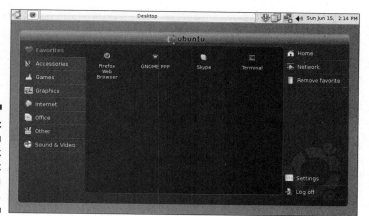

Figure 4-5:
Ubuntu
Netbook
Remix
running on a
netbook.

The main differences between Linux distributions are the user interface and included programs. Linux is Linux, and no matter which distro you use, the operating system functions and the commands you use all remain the same.

Going mobile

Most Linux distros were designed to run on PCs — whether they're desktops or laptops. But a few ongoing projects are working on creating versions of Linux operating systems specifically for netbooks and mobile Internet devices (MIDs) — think netbook functionality, but smaller with a touch screen and no keyboard.

These projects could make a big impact in the netbook world, perhaps moving manufacturers to begin supporting a standardized Linux operating system — including a common user interface designed specifically for small screens. Here are some of the projects worth keeping an eye on:

✔ **Moblin:** Intel is a big backer of this open-source project, and the Moblin 2 operating system is designed to run on Atom processors. Check out `www.moblin.org` for more.

✔ **Ubuntu Netbook Remix:** Canonical, which develops and distributes the very popular Ubuntu Linux, has been working on a version of its operating system expressly designed for netbooks. See `www.canonical.com/netbooks`.

✔ **Ubuntu MID:** This is another Ubuntu project, but this one targeted at MIDs. To find out more, visit `www.ubuntu.com/products/mobile`.

Asking for Apple

As of the summer of 2009, Apple doesn't include a netbook in its product lineup. But that's not to say the secretive company is not working on a tiny laptop, perhaps a cross between an iPod and MacBook. It seems a week doesn't go by without rumors about such a device.

At the end of April 2009, Tim Cook, Apple's Chief Operating Officer said, "When I look at netbooks, I see cracked keyboards, terrible software, junky hardware, very small screens. It's just not a good consumer experience and not something we would put the Mac brand on. It's a segment we would not choose to play in."

I personally wouldn't take those words at face value. First, Apple often says one thing then does something else. Second, from a marketing standpoint, it would make sense for Apple to release a netbook product but call it something else to differentiate it from other netbooks. We shall see.

If you're a frustrated Apple fan and can't wait for a Cupertino netbook, you do have an alternative. Be forewarned, though, you're treading in a legally gray area. Here's the scoop.

It's technically possible to hack a netbook and install a copy of OS X on it. I'm certainly not endorsing the practice, but you heard that right. The hardware internals of some netbooks, such as the MSI Wind and Dell Mini, make some netbooks more suitable than others for this operation. But it's generally not that difficult to play mad scientist and create a *Hackintosh* netbook — you don't even need Igor for an assistant.

Just remember that even if you own a Mac and the OS X installation DVD that came with it, it's a violation of the licensing agreement to install OS X on a PC. And Apple doesn't have much of a sense of humor when it comes to things it deems proprietary.

In February 2009, Apple's lawyers compelled Wired.com to remove a video tutorial on how to load OS X on a netbook. Here's a URL for the censored Web page if you're interested; the page still contains some unedited instructions which gives you an idea about the process:

```
http://blog.wired.com/gadgets/2008/12/gadget-lab-vide.html
```

Despite the Wired video's demise, if you're handy with Google, there are still other sources on the Net where you can find out more information. Before you do so though, check out this MacWorld article that talks about a reviewer's experience running OS X on a non-Apple netbook:

```
www.macworld.com/article/138900/2009/02/apple_netbook.html
```

Just because a netbook runs OS X, that doesn't make it a Mac. Performance is going to be less than a vintage G4 PowerBook, and you'll be missing many of the design and engineering features that define Apple products.

Me, I'll patiently wait for a real Mac netbook. Hopefully it'll be on the market by the time you read this.

Getting Google Android

I fondly remember the days when Google was just a Web search engine, and it was the new kid on the block, gunning for market leader AltaVista. Now Google seems to be everywhere and has its fingers in everything — including operating systems.

Google Android is an operating system for mobile phones. It's optimized for using a number of Google's Internet services (Google Maps, Google Apps, and so on). The OS is open source (based on the Linux kernel) and allows developers to easily write programs that run in it.

Android is a new operating system, and phone manufacturers such as Motorola, Samsung, and Sony Ericson are currently working on products that will use it.

What's interesting about Android is that it could be scaled up to work on a netbook. In fact, some netbook companies have publicly stated they're examining the OS for potential use in future products. (Telecom giant Nokia is also talking about using its phone operating system in netbooks.)

The next generation of netbooks will likely diverge into two lineages: netbooks with Atom processors running Windows (much like what currently is on the market); and cheap, $100-to-$200, no-frills netbooks with ARM processors running some type of open-source operating system such as Android. Considering Google's bankroll and the importance of taking a leading role in this space, I wouldn't be surprised if the company becomes a major player in the netbook game.

For more information on Android, visit www.android.com. You can also download a free, prerelease version of the operating system that will run on a netbook from: http://code.google.com/p/live-android.

Contending with Chrome

But wait, I'm not done talking about Google just quite yet. During the summer of 2009, the company dropped a bombshell and officially announced it would be releasing a brand new operating system for netbooks — which will later appear on desktop PCs and laptops.

Dubbed *Chrome OS,* the free operating system is designed to run on ARM and x86 processors, boot almost instantly, work with Google Web apps (Google is calling it "a browser-based operating system"), and offer a security system that eliminates users worrying about viruses and security updates. Wow!

Google has stated it will make the Chrome OS source code open source toward the end of 2009, and netbooks running the operating system should be available by the second half of 2010. (When the operating system is released, you'll also be able to download it and install it on older netbooks.)

This operating system has the potential to make serious waves in the computer world, especially as a number of industry heavy hitters are working with Google on the project — including Acer, Adobe, ASUS, Freescale, Hewlett-Packard, Lenovo, Qualcomm, Texas Instruments, and Toshiba.

The best place to get the latest on Chrome OS is to visit the official Web site at http://chromestory.com.

Windows versus Linux

Now that you have a general idea of what operating systems are available for netbooks, I need to lead you through a small minefield and talk about Windows versus Linux — just in case you may need to make a choice between the two operating systems.

Pros and cons

I'm not going to advocate for one system or the other (there are already enough flame wars on the Internet). Like most things, each operating system has its pros and cons. To give you some perspective, here are a few key advantages of each:

Windows advantages

  ✔ The user interface is more familiar.

  ✔ More programs are available (including specialized applications).

  ✔ Commercial applications tend to have a more polished user interface.

  ✔ It offers better hardware compatibility (especially with printers and scanners).

Linux advantages

- ✔ Microsoft doesn't make it, and it's free. (More than a few people don't have warm fuzzies about the software giant.)

- ✔ Many free, open-source programs are available (with similar functionality to popular Windows applications).

- ✔ It's more secure (fewer viruses, worms, and Trojans).

- ✔ It provides better performance on computers with slower processors and less memory.

This whole discussion is probably moot as the Microsoft juggernaut continues to steamroller Linux in the netbook market. Windows netbooks outsell models running Linux by a wide margin now, and there's a good chance manufacturers will start dropping Linux models because of poor sales. If you're a Linux lover, take heart. You can always format the drive and install your favorite distro. And in the future, things may be different when Linux-based operating systems such as Chrome OS and Moblin debut.

Which to choose?

If you're having trouble making up your mind, here are a few suggestions to steer you in the right direction:

Pick Windows if you . . .

- ✔ Have experience with Windows and don't want to learn the nuances of a different operating system's user interface.

- ✔ Plan on using Windows programs that aren't available for Linux.

- ✔ Have hardware (printer, scanner, and so on) that isn't compatible with Linux.

Pick Linux if you . . .

- ✔ Like the idea of free, open-source software.

- ✔ Already use Linux.

- ✔ Are willing to trade off a few quirks for a very secure operating system.

- ✔ Are ready to invest some time in learning a new operating system. (You should be up to speed in a week or two.)

- ✔ Are technically inclined — you don't need to be a techie to use a Linux netbook, but being a little more technical makes it easier to do advanced procedures at times.

As much as I like Linux, at this point I have to say I'd steer most new netbook users to a Windows model. Linux is getting close to being a worthy competitor to Windows on the desktop, but it still has some quirks that can frustrate many people who have been using Windows for a while. I reserve the right to change my mind when $100-to-$150 netbooks running Android, Moblin, Chrome OS or whatever become available.

If you visit retail outlets to shop for netbooks, there's a good chance you won't find a Linux netbook to try out. Increasingly, retailers are stocking only Windows netbooks — several reports have shown Linux netbooks have a higher return rate than Windows models; this is likely because the user interfaces are different enough to initially frustrate an impatient Windows user. If you want a Linux netbook, you need to go online. And if you do, make sure the retailer has a decent return policy just in case the operating system isn't for you.

The old switcheroo

If your netbook has an Intel x86 family processor (Celeron or Atom chip), keep in mind you're not tied to using the preinstalled operating system. That means you can dump Windows for a Linux distro or give Linux the boot and replace it with Windows (a licensed copy of course). If you don't like the new OS, just install the old one.

For Linux, first find a suitable distribution. Check out some of the online forums I mention in Chapter 22 — you can usually find a lot of discussion about distros and how to install them.

Download the distro and burn it to a CD. (You can also put the distribution image on an SD memory card or a USB flash drive, but having an external DVD/CD-ROM is usually the easiest.)

Back up any files you want to save.

Boot from the distribution disc — this typically involves changing a BIOS setting or pressing a certain key sequence at startup to get a menu

of choices. (I discuss this more in Chapter 21.) After the operating system has started, follow the installation instructions.

Many distributions come in "live" versions, which means you can boot and run the operating system in virtual memory, without reformatting the hard drive and replacing the original OS. It's a great way to test drive an operating system.

Restart your netbook, and the new OS will run.

One very important warning when switching operating systems: Instead of supplying an install disc, some netbook manufacturers place a copy of the installation program and files on a separate partition of the hard drive. If for some reason you need to reinstall the operating system, these files are used. If you format the hard drive and install a new operating system, you're going to be out of luck if you want to restore the original operating system. If an operating system install disc didn't come with your netbook, contact the manufacturer to see whether you can get one.

Chapter 5

First Things First

. . . .

. . . .

You took the plunge (or are preparing to) and went out and bought yourself a shiny new netbook. Good for you. You're going to find it's a lot of fun and incredibly useful. But before you getting rolling with the fun and usefulness, you should know a few things.

Before a pilot can captain an aircraft he or she hasn't flown before, another pilot with experience in the plane gives a *check ride.* The seasoned pilot goes over all the controls and gauges and explains important details. Then the inexperienced pilot starts the engine, taxis down the runway, and takes off for a short ride — all under the watchful eye of the check pilot.

Because I can't be with you when you pull your new netbook out of the box, consider this chapter an official check ride. Now if you'll step out onto the runway, you can get started.

Read the Manual

Would you please, pretty please with sugar on top, before doing anything else with your brand-new netbook, take a moment of your time, and ever-so-thoughtfully peruse the pages of the user manual, paying careful attention to what it says?

More succinctly, read the first part of the user manual before you do anything else. Yes, I know you want to play with your new toy, but the manufacturer has some important things to say before you do — and the manual is where you find them.

This book is about all netbooks, and not one specific brand or model. Although many netbooks have common features and functionality, always check your user manual for specifics.

There's a trend for manufacturers to skimp on user manuals and include only printed quick-start guides or posters with their products. They're trying to keep the costs down so they can pass the savings on to you; margins on consumer electronics products are notoriously slim.

If that's the case, read the quick-start information first. If there's no printed user manual, it's probably already installed on the netbook's drive, and you'll have to start up the little laptop first to view it. (The manual may also be on an included CD-ROM or DVD, in which case, use another computer with a DVD drive to read it.)

If you lost the user manual in the excitement of opening up the box, pay a visit to the support section of the manufacturer's Web site and download a PDF version of the manual. I like to keep a copy of the manual stored on my primary PC so it's easy to reference.

Power to the People

After you've read the manual (at least the "Getting Started" section — hint, hint), it's time to feed your netbook a little juice. Your netbook's battery should be charged to some extent, but if not, it's a good idea to top it off.

If you just got a new netbook, I'm sure you're eager to use it. But before powering on your netbook for the first time, I recommend you fully charge the battery. That means

1. **Make sure the battery is properly inserted into the netbook.**

2. **Plug the power supply adapter cord into a wall socket.**

3. **Plug the power supply adapter into the netbook.**

Most netbooks are rated to handle 100 to 120 volts and 220 to 240 volts of AC (alternating current) — check your user manual to verify this. That means you can use the computer almost anywhere in the world you can get electricity from a wall socket. Depending on where you travel, you may need to purchase an inexpensive adapter so the plug correctly fits the socket type.

4. **Wait until the charging status light says the battery is fully charged.**

   Depending on the netbook, this could be an orange light turning off or a green light turning on or something else. Check your user manual for details.

   Charge time depends on how much charge the battery has and its capacity. For example, a fully discharged 3-cell battery will charge faster than a fully discharged 6-cell battery. As a ballpark estimate, figure around 2 to 3 hours for a full charge. I discuss batteries at length in Chapter 13.

If you're impatient and can't wait to use your new netbook, you won't hurt it if you don't initially top off the battery — just keep the netbook plugged in to an electrical socket and let it fully charge when you're done. It's just good practice to do this with any battery powered device and it helps prolong overall battery life.

When some netbooks are plugged into a wall socket, the USB ports are powered even if the computer is turned off. This means you can use the netbook to charge your USB devices (such as MP3 players), even when the laptop isn't turned on.

When you're done using your netbook, turn it off like you would any Windows PC. In Windows XP, choose Start⇨Turn Off Computer⇨Turn Off.

Signing on the Dotted Line

Locate your netbook's power switch — it can be inside or on one of the case's sides — and turn it on for the first time. Your netbook happily comes to life, and you are greeted with a series of screens that prompt you to enter information such as the nationality of keyboard you'll be using, a user account name and password, your time zone, and other bits of data that will configure the operating system.

To keep the lawyers happy, you're also asked to agree to licensing terms. Most people blow this off and never read them, but feel free to if you have the time and inclination — especially around bedtime if you're having trouble getting to sleep.

You only have to go through this initialization process once — when you first get your netbook. (However, if you ever have to reinstall the operating system, you'll need to go through the sequence again.) When setup is complete, your netbook is now officially ready to use.

You Light Up My Life

With your netbook powered up, you'll see various lights twinkling on the case — as an example, Figure 5-1 points out the status lights on an ASUS Eee PC model. These LED lights let you know at a glance whether your netbook is running and what it's up to. Some netbooks may have only a single status light, whereas others have several. Typical lights include

- **Power:** Tells you whether the netbook is powered on or off. The light may be incorporated into the power switch or located elsewhere.

- **Drive:** Whenever the operating system or a program accesses the hard drive (or solid state drive) this light flashes.

- **Battery:** The battery status light provides information about the battery charge. Status lights vary from netbook to netbook; for example, the light may change from green to orange as the battery discharges and start flashing when there are only minutes of power left. When you're charging your battery, this light also tells you when it's fully charged. (In some models, the power and battery lights are combined.)

- **Wireless:** When the Wi-Fi card is on, a status light is illuminated.

  If you can't get a wireless connection, always check the wireless status light. If it's off, you need to turn on the wireless card. I tell you all about networking in Chapter 6.

- **Bluetooth:** If your netbook supports built-in Bluetooth, a light lets you know whether it is on or off.

- **Webcam:** If your netbook has a built-in Web camera (or *webcam*), it should have a status light that comes on when the webcam is on. This prevents potentially embarrassing moments.

- **Keyboard status:** Some netbooks have LED lights that indicate whether the Caps Lock or Num Lock keys have been depressed. Press the respective key to enable or disable.

If a program or Web site repeatedly refuses to accept a password, check the Caps Lock. On small netbook keyboards, it's easy to accidentally press this key.

Check your user manual for more information on what status lights mean and where they're located on your particular netbook.

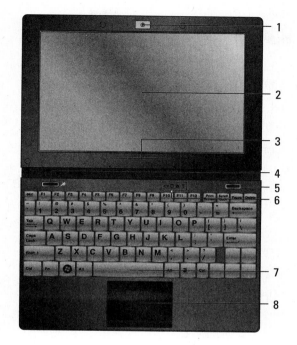

Figure 5-1:
Inside an
ASUS Eee
PC netbook.
(Components,
features, and
locations
vary by
brand and
model.)

1. ⦿ Built-in Camera

2.   Display Panel

3. 🎤 Microphone (Built-in)

4. 🏃 Super Hybrid Engine Key

5. ▭ Power Switch

6. 💡 Status Indicators

        ▱ Battery Charge Indicator

        ◰ Drive Indicator

        🔒 Capital Lock Indicator

        📶 Wireless/Bluetooth Indicator

7.   Keyboard

8.   Touchpad and Buttons

Handling Parts and Pieces

Pick up your netbook. Wow, it's really light. Now take a look at it, paying attention to the sides and bottom of the case. Here's what you find:

- ✔ **USB ports:** Your netbook should have two or three USB 2.0 ports. This is where you can plug in a mouse, keyboard, DVD drive, light, fan, coffee cup heater, or any other useful or useless USB device. (Figures 5-2 and 5-3 show the location of USB ports on an ASUS Eee PC model.)

Right Side

Figure 5-2: The right side of an ASUS Eee PC netbook. (Components, features, and locations vary by brand and model.)

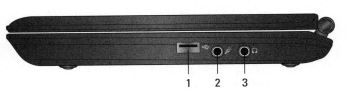

1 2 3

1. ⟜ USB Port

2. ⌖ Microphone Jack

3. ⌒ Headphone Output Jack

Figure 5-3: The left side of an ASUS Eee PC netbook. (Components, features, and locations vary by brand and model.)

Left Side

1

1. ⟜ USB Ports

- ✔ **Ethernet port:** This port looks like a slightly oversize phone jack, but don't try to plug your phone or a modem cable into it. Instead, this port is for connecting to the Internet (or a local area network, LAN) with a cable that has an RJ45 connector — I talk more about this and networking in Chapter 6. Figure 5-4 shows the location of the Ethernet port (called the LAN port) on an ASUS Eee PC model.

Rear Side

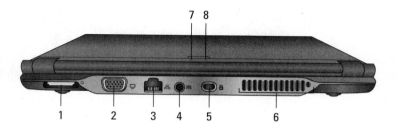

1. L꜀ꞏM Memory Card Slot

Figure 5-4:
The back
of an ASUS
Eee PC
netbook.
(Components,
features, and
locations
vary by
brand and
model.)

1. L꜀ꞏM Memory Card Slot

2. ▭ Display (Monitor) Output

3. ⿳ LAN Port

4. DCIN Power Input

5. K Kensington® Lock Port

6. Air Vents

7. ▱ Battery Charge Indicator

8. ♀ Power Indicator

✔ **Audio-in port:** This port is for attaching a microphone.

✔ **Audio-out port:** The audio-out port is for plugging in headphones or speakers. When a jack is plugged in to this port, sound doesn't play through the built-in speakers. Refer to Figure 5-2 for the location of audio-in and -out ports on an ASUS netbook.

The audio-in port usually has a small icon of a microphone next to it. The audio-out port has an icon of a pair of headphones. On a netbook, both icons are pretty tiny and difficult to see. To make distinguishing the ports easier, some netbooks use color coding: Pink is audio in, and green is audio out.

The audio-in/out ports of most netbooks support a standardized ⅛-inch (3.5mm) mini-jack.

✔ **Built-in speakers:** Your netbook has a pair of built-in speakers. Their location varies from model to model — look to the sides of the screen or somewhere on the case. (Figure 5-5 shows their location on an ASUS Eee PC.) Don't expect high-quality, stereophonic sound. If you want to listen to decent sounding music, use headphones.

Bottom Side

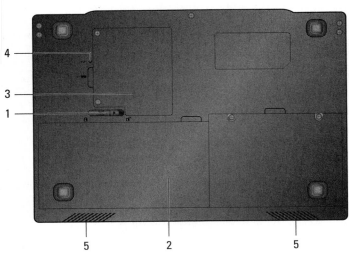

Figure 5-5:
The bottom of an ASUS Eee PC netbook. (Components, features, and locations vary by brand and model.)

1. Battery Lock

2. ▭ Battery Pack

3. ▥▥ Memory Compartment

4. ▸○◂ Reset Button

5. ◁)) Audio Speaker

✔ **Built-in microphone:** Many netbooks have a built-in microphone handy for recording lecture notes and meeting presentations or for video conferencing. (Refer to Figure 5-1 for the location on an ASUS netbook.) Like the built-in speakers, don't expect a high-level of audio quality — use an external microphone instead.

✔ **Card reader:** Most netbooks have a built-in SD (Secure Digital) memory card reader — typically the reader also supports MMC (MultiMedia Card) and SDHC (Secure Digital High Capacity) cards; some netbooks have readers that support additional types of memory cards. Press the memory card in the slot until it clicks into place. Press the card again to release and remove it. Refer to Figure 5-4 for the location of the card reader port on an ASUS netbook model.

I discuss SD cards at length in Chapter 14.

✔ **VGA port:** This port is for plugging in an external monitor or projector — it's easy to identify with its three rows of five holes, which take a 15-pin connector. Your netbook sends a video signal of whatever appears on the screen to a device that's connected to the VGA port. Refer to Figure 5-4 for the location of the VGA port (display output) on an ASUS Eee PC.

Instead of a VGA port, some netbooks have an HDMI port. This is a high-definition multimedia interface port for sending an uncompressed, all digital, high-definition audio and video signal to an HD television, monitor, or other device.

✔ **Kensington lock:** This is a slot (refer to Figure 5-4) for attaching an optional security cable. I discuss netbook security, including Kensington locks, in Chapter 9.

✔ **Webcam:** Many netbooks have a built-in webcam. Look at the case above the screen and smile. (Figure 5-1 shows the location of the webcam on an ASUS Eee PC.) Don't expect high-definition quality out of these low-resolution (0.3 to 1.3 megapixels) cameras. They do, however, perform fine for video conferencing, using Skype (a program that allows you to make phone calls over the Internet), and instant messaging.

✔ **Battery compartment:** A netbook wouldn't be a netbook if it had to be plugged into an electrical outlet all the time. Your battery needs a place to live and depending on your netbook, the battery compartment may be at the back of the case or on the bottom (refer to Figure 5-5). Check your user manual for information on removing and inserting batteries. (I provide more details on netbook batteries in Chapter 13.)

✔ **Memory compartment:** On netbooks supporting memory that can be upgraded, you can typically find a compartment on the underside of the case. (Refer to Figure 5-5.) There may also be a compartment for accessing the drive to replace it. In Chapter 18, I discuss upgrading memory and drives.

If you can't figure out where any of the preceding parts and pieces are located or your netbook has a connector, compartment, port, slot, or thingamajig that you have no idea what it is, consult your friendly user manual.

Touching on Touchpads

The *touchpad* is the recessed rectangular area below the keyboard (refer to Figure 5-1). Directly below the touchpad, you find the mouse buttons. (A few netbooks incorporate the buttons to the right and left of the touchpad or directly on the touchpad surface so there are no visible buttons.) Some netbook models have two distinct buttons, whereas others feature what looks like a single, long button — clicking the left side of the bar is equivalent to a left mouse click, and clicking the right side is the same as a right mouse click.

If the mouse buttons feel a little stiff and clunky, most netbook touchpads support *tapping* — a single tap on the touchpad is treated as a mouse click, and two quick taps are a double-click. You can change touchpad settings in the Windows Control Panel — for many notebooks, double-click the Mouse icon in the Control Panel window to access the settings.

If you've never used a touchpad before, read on. Experienced laptop users, feel free to skip this section.

Lightly drag your finger (whichever one feels the most natural) across the touchpad surface to move the onscreen cursor. Drag to the right, and the cursor moves right. Drag up, and the cursor goes up. You get it.

To move the cursor more than a short distance, simply lift your finger when it starts to go off the touchpad, put it back down on the touchpad, and drag again. Repeat until the cursor is where you want it to be.

Some netbook touchpads have what looks like a blunt sewing needle printed on the pad. This is a visual clue that the touchpad supports scrolling. If there's an up-and-down sewing needle, vertical scrolling is supported, and if there's a right-to-left sewing needle, horizontal scrolling is supported. That means if you drag in the touchpad scrolling area, you can control programs that display a vertical (and/or horizontal) scrollbar. Drag up to scroll up. Drag down to scroll down. Drag left to left scroll. Drag right to right scroll.

If you're so inclined, you can always plug a USB or wireless mouse into your netbook and use it instead of the touchpad.

Figuring out Function Keys

The top, first row of keys on your netbook are the *function keys* — sometimes called *F keys*. These keys allow you to quickly control different hardware components on your netbook. In addition to the key labels (such as F1, F2, and so on), these function keys also have small icons printed on them that give you a clue to their purpose — or depending on what the icon looks like, simply confuse you.

Function keys' functions vary from one netbook to another, but here are some general things holding down the function key (often labeled *Fn*) key and then pressing the appropriate F or symbol key can do:

✔ Turn the wireless card on and off.

✔ Turn Bluetooth (if built-in) on and off.

✔ Increase and decrease the screen brightness.

✔ Turn off display backlighting.

✔ Control the internal speaker volume.

✔ Control display output. (For example, when the netbook is connected to an external monitor or projector, this key toggles among showing only the netbook screen display, both the netbook and external monitor display, or just the external monitor display.)

✔ Turn the touchpad on and off.

✔ Put the netbook in sleep state (and wake it up).

Not to sound like a broken record, but refer to the user manual for a list of your netbook's function keys and what they do.

Exchanging Data with Your Primary PC

Because there's a good chance your netbook won't be your main computer, you'll likely want to exchange data between it and your primary computer. You can do this in a number of different ways, some simple, some complex. I mention four of my favorite options that don't require a lot of techno-savvy.

Using USB flash drives

In the old days, you used floppy disks to move files between computers — fondly called a *sneaker* (as in shoes) net. I can't remember the last time I saw a floppy disc drive on a new computer, and now the media of choice for getting files from Computer A to Computer B is a USB flash drive. These inexpensive and versatile drives are a must for quick backups and transferring files. To use them, simply follow these steps:

1. **Insert the flash drive in Computer A's USB port.**

2. **Using Explorer, copy files to the drive — dragging works well.**

3. **Remove the drive.**

Don't forget to use Window's Safely Remove command in the taskbar before removing the drive.

4. **Insert the drive in Computer B's USB port.**

5. Use Explorer to copy the files from the flash drive — again, dragging and dropping.

That's all there is to it. I give you more information about these flash drives in Chapter 14.

Keep files you'll be working on with different computers on a single USB flash drive. Plug the flash drive into your netbook when you want to edit a file and make your changes. If you want to work with the file on your desktop PC, do the same. This avoids any version control problems with multiple copies of files floating around. Just be sure to keep backups of the files in case you misplace your flash drive.

Don't forget about your SD card reader. Many newer laptop and desktop PCs can read SD cards just like your netbook, and you can also use this media for transferring files.

Making the most of Windows file sharing

If you've set up a home network or are using your netbook with a work network, you can easily exchange files with Windows file sharing. If both your netbook and desktop PC (or laptop) are connected to the same workgroup, you can use shared folders to move files back and forth. I provide full details on file sharing in Chapter 6.

Making sense of online storage

Online storage is turning into a big deal these days. In the next decade, an estimated 70 to 75 percent of all PCs will be using some form of online storage. In fact, some manufacturers are even providing free secure online storage with the purchase of certain netbook models.

Online storage makes exchanging data between computers a snap. All you need to do is sign up with a storage service and then connect to a Web site and upload and download your files. (Some netbooks come with online storage programs installed, so be sure to check your user manual.) I discuss this option more and provide a list of popular online storage services in Chapter 17.

If you're considering using online storage, check out a Web site called Backup Review (www.backupreview.info), which provides information and ratings on many online storage services.

A simple, Net-centric way of getting files between computers is by sending a file as an attachment to your Web e-mail account. You can then open the e-mail from another computer and save the attachment. This works if you need to transfer only a few files. Also remember that most Web mail providers place limitations on attachment size — you may have trouble with a file that's 1GB or larger.

Be careful when storing documents with personal or financial information online — social security numbers, credit card numbers, bank account information, and so on. Although online storage Web sites may advertise all sorts of security measures, there's always the risk a server could get hacked, the company could go out of business, or some other disaster could befall your data. If you're going to store sensitive information online, encrypt it first. I give you tips on using encryption in Chapter 9.

Synchronizing with Briefcase

Although it's easy to copy files or folders between computers by dragging and dropping, you may be faced with the problem of duplicate named files. If there's already a file or folder with the same name, Windows politely asks if you're sure you want to replace it. Although the file size and last modified dates are shown to help you determine whether it's an older or newer version, it's still a hassle — especially if you're dealing with a significant number of files.

You can skip this headache and those annoying Confirm File Replace dialog boxes with a nifty Windows file synchronization feature called Briefcase. The following sections tell you how it works.

Making a Briefcase

Say you have some word processing and spreadsheet files you want to transfer to your netbook. (Or perhaps you have these files on your netbook and you want to move them to your desktop PC — it doesn't matter, the process is the same.)

First you need to create a Briefcase:

1. **On an empty part of the Windows desktop, right-click to open a pop-up menu.**

2. **Choose New➪Briefcase.**

    A Briefcase icon named New Briefcase appears on the desktop. You can rename it if you like.

That's all there is to it.

Packing the Briefcase

Just like going on a trip, the next step is to pack the little case. This means copying any files you want to exchange with the other computer into the Briefcase. The Briefcase acts just like a folder — double-click to open it. You can then copy and paste files into the Briefcase just like you would with a folder.

Transferring the Briefcase

After you've copied any files you want to transfer to Briefcase, it's time to copy the Briefcase to your netbook. Here are the steps:

1. **Make sure any files you've copied to the Briefcase are closed.**

   For example, if you have a Word document you want to transfer, don't be working on it in Word.

2. **Double-click the Briefcase (if it's not already open).**

3. **Click either the Update All Items button or the Update All button.**

   This step ensures Briefcase has the most recent versions of the files.

4. **Copy the Briefcase to your netbook.**

   You can use a USB flash drive, an SD card, or a network connection. (If you're using a flash drive or memory card, make sure you have enough room to copy the Briefcase. You can right-click the Briefcase icon and click Properties in the pop-up menu to see how big the Briefcase file is.)

Working with the Briefcase

After the Briefcase is on your netbook, treat it like a folder. Leave any files you want to exchange with your desktop PC in it — programs treat Briefcase just like a folder when you use the File⇨Open or File⇨Save as menu commands.

When you want to transfer the files back to your desktop PC, follow these steps:

1. **Copy Briefcase from your netbook to your desktop PC.**

2. **Double click Briefcase to open it.**

3. **Click the Update All button (or select the files to synchronize).**

4. **Click Update.**

   Any modified files are now synced up. Repeat the process as needed.

Part II
Using Your Netbook

"I just can't keep up with the cosmetics industry. That woman we just passed has a makeup case with a screen and keyboard."

In this part . . .

A netbook is certainly not just meant to be looked at fondly and admired. You most certainly want to use your little laptop, and that's what this part is all about.

I start with a chapter that puts the net in netbook — more specifically, it includes everything you need to know about networking and connecting to the Internet.

In the work department, I discuss various productivity software suites (both traditional software like Microsoft Office and the latest online services such as Zoho). I also devote a chapter to netbook security issues — both physical and networked. You definitely need some playtime to balance out the work, so I tell you what you need to know about listening to music, watching videos, and playing games on your netbook.

Social networking (using sites such as Twitter, Facebook, and MySpace) is big these days, and a netbook makes keeping in touch from just about anyplace a snap. If you haven't tried Web-based social networking, I tell you what you need to get started — as well as some tips for getting the most out of instant messaging and Skype.

I wrap up with information about GPS and how to turn your netbook into a nimble navigator.

Chapter 6

Netbook Networking

- -

In This Chapter

▶ Understanding 802.11 (Wi-Fi) networking

▶ Using 3G modems

▶ Considering Bluetooth

▶ Checking out wired Ethernet connections

▶ Browsing with Firefox

▶ Picking a netbook e-mail strategy

▶ Using Ultra VNC to remotely connect to a computer

▶ Sharing files on a Windows network

- -

This chapter puts the *Net* in netbook — or maybe the *book* in netbook, take your pick. What I mean is that I cover everything you need to know about doing some serious networking with your netbook.

That of course includes wireless connectivity of all types (802.11, 3G, Bluetooth, and WiMAX) as well as the more old-school Ethernet cable way to connect to the Internet.

In addition to telling you about the basics of getting connected, I provide netbook-specific pointers on Web browsers and e-mail clients, how to use remote control desktop software, and the art of sharing files on a Windows network.

Your netbook was born to network, so what are you waiting for?

Wireless Wanderings

When you buy a netbook, you'll undoubtedly want to use its wireless capabilities — that's what the netbook is designed for, after all. In the following sections, I walk you through all the wireless radio wave wizardry options you have available for getting connected.

802.11

If you have experience connecting to the Internet with a wireless laptop, you can skip this section — you never know, though; you might discover something new. If you've never connected to the Net with a laptop, I tell you what you need to know to get started.

Wi-Fi basics

IEEE (Institute of Electrical and Electronics Engineers) *802.11,* better known as *Wi-Fi* or *WLAN* (wireless local area network), is a set of wireless standards for connecting to networks (most commonly, the Internet). Your netbook has a built-in wireless card and antenna that allow you to connect to the Net wherever there's a nearby wireless router or access point (AP) — such a place is known as a *hotspot.* Wireless routers and access points access the Internet through a high-speed, wired connection and share this connection with computers via radio waves.

If the Wi-Fi hotspot is publicly accessible (doesn't require a password), Windows happily connects to it, and *voilà,* you're on the Internet.

Wireless routers cost between $35 and $100 (depending on the model). Because they're cheap and easy to install, many people connect them to their DSL or cable modems to create a wireless home network. If you do this, be sure to enable WPA security on the router. If you don't, it's possible for someone to "borrow" your wireless Internet connection — and rack up a big download bill if your bandwidth is metered.

Making a wireless connection

Windows is usually configured so it automatically connects to a nearby, *open* (with no security) access point. If your netbook doesn't automatically connect (or if you want to see whether any networks are available), here's what you need to do:

1. **Right-click the wireless icon in the Windows taskbar and choose View Available Wireless Networks from the pop-up menu.**

   If you left-click the icon, a status dialog box appears and shows information about the current wireless connection.

2. **Select a wireless network you want to connect to in the dialog box and click the Connect button. (A connected network is shown in Figure 6-1.)**

   If a lock icon is shown beneath the network name, that means the network uses encryption and is secured. You need to enter the correct password to access the network.

802.11 alphabet soup

A veritable alphabet soup of letters has been tagged on to 802.11. Here's what all those extra letters (which have to do with specific protocols) mean:

- **802.11a:** This standard has a maximum data rate of 54 Mbps and a range of 35 meters. It broadcasts in the 5 GHz frequency range, which reduces the chance of interference but decreases its penetration. (Walls and other solid objects can absorb the radio waves.)

- **802.11b:** This was the first widely adopted wireless standard and has a maximum speed of 11 Mbps with a range of 30 meters. Most 802.11b access points and routers used a security method called WEP, which isn't very secure.

- **802.11g:** The next step in wireless standards evolution was G. This version features increased speed (54 Mbps) and range (100 meters) compared with the older B standard. The 802.11g routers and access points also have beefed up security known as WPA.

- **802.11n:** This new standard is expected to be finalized and released in 2010 — that hasn't stopped some manufacturers from already releasing 802.11n products, though. It's considerably faster at 108 Mbps with an expanded range of 300 meters.

Many wireless cards (and netbooks) can operate with several of these protocols — the system software automatically switches the protocol depending on whatever the router/access point is using.

However, just having a speedy new 802.11n card in your netbook doesn't mean you're going to have a super-fast Internet connection. Even though you have 802.11n, if you're connecting to an 802.11g access point, you get 802.11g speeds. As soon as the N standard becomes finalized, expect hotspots to replace their older routers and access points with newer, faster models.

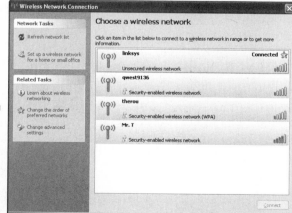

Figure 6-1:
The Wireless Network Connection dialog box.

The signal strength bars are useful for determining how good the connection is. Typically, the more bars, the better and faster the connection.

Windows provides you with some status information as it tries to connect to the selected network and then tells you whether the connection was successful.

That's it in a nutshell. It's relatively straightforward — check your user manual for additional information. If you do run into problems, I recommend reading through this Microsoft troubleshooting guide: `http://support.microsoft.com/kb/870702`.

You can turn off the wireless card to increase battery life. Also, you should turn off the wireless card while flying on a plane where wireless might interfere with the aircraft's instruments — or so they say.

The 802.11b and g wireless cards and access points transmit and receive 2.4 GHz radio waves. The problem with this frequency is that baby monitors, Bluetooth devices, certain cordless telephones, and microwave ovens also emit radio signals in the same general range. That means when you pop some popcorn in the microwave, there's a possibility your Net connection will temporarily go snap, crackle, pop while the oven is on, depending where your netbook, microwave, and access point are located.

3G networks

Whenever you hear the term 3G (as in Third Generation), it refers to Internet access through cellular phone networks. It works like this:

You subscribe to a data plan through a cellular phone provider (or a combination voice and data plan). If you have a relatively current cell phone, you probably know what I'm talking about in that you can check e-mail and browse the Web from your phone. However, you can also use a 3G modem connected to your netbook (or laptop) to access the Net.

Unlike a Wi-Fi network, where you need to be near a wireless access point, with a 3G network you can be anywhere in the cellular network's data coverage area to access the Internet. Speed is decent (especially if you're stationary), but isn't as fast as a good 802.11 wireless connection.

Some higher-end netbooks come with built-in 3G modems. If your netbook doesn't have a 3G modem, you can add this type of wireless connectivity several different ways.

✔ **USB:** This 3G modem plugs into a USB port on your netbook, as shown in Figure 6-2.

✔ **ExpressCard:** A few netbooks come with an ExpressCard expansion slot — this is a smaller version of a PC Card. Several manufacturers offer ExpressCard 3G modems.

Figure 6-2:
A plug-in
USB 3G
modem.

You can get a 3G modem through your cellular provider (or a compatible version from a retailer). Prices range between $100 and $200 depending on the model. But hold onto your hats because some providers are now offering discounted netbooks and modems when you sign up for a data plan — and if this marketing gimmick takes off, there may come a day in the future when carriers start giving away subsidized, no-frills netbooks for free like they do with phones.

Check with your cellular provider to get more information about its 3G services and compatibility with your netbook.

Before you sign up for 3G service, try to get some feedback about how the service is in your area — check out user forums such as www.howardforums.com or http://cellphoneforums.net. Although a cellular carrier may claim coverage over a large area, some places may have faster and better connectivity than others.

WiMAX

WiMAX stands for Worldwide Interoperability for Microwave Access. It's an up-and-coming Fourth Generation (4G) communications standard — officially known as 802.16. The 4G services promise to give you wired broadband speeds on mobile devices — they're designed primarily to move data and not voice like the earlier generation standards. WiMAX also allows a provider to offer literally blanket Internet coverage: With 802.11, you need to be within 100 to 300 feet of an access point; compare that with WiMAX, which has up to a 30-mile range.

Like 3G services, you subscribe to a data plan and use a plug-in USB modem to access the Net. At the present, companies like Clearwire (www.clearwire.com) have just started to roll out WiMAX networks in limited parts of the United States. Computer manufacturers are bullish on WiMAX and have announced plans to start offering laptops and netbooks with built-in 4G modems.

WiMAX isn't the only horse in the 4G race. A competing technology known as LTE (Long-Term Evolution) is favored by telecommunications companies, but as of 2009, it isn't out of the gate yet — and likely won't be available for another several years.

Keep your eye on 4G technologies. It's what your netbook will likely be using (as well as your desktop PC, mobile phone, and maybe even your toaster) in the not-so-distant future.

Bluetooth

A fair number of netbooks tout Bluetooth in their feature lists. But what exactly does that mean for you? Here's the lowdown:

Bluetooth is a wireless protocol for exchanging data over short distances — up to 10 meters or around 32 feet if you're metrically challenged. A device sends out a 2.4 GHz radio signal, another device receives the signal, and the two devices start talking to each other.

Bluetooth is named after Danish King Harald "Bluetooth" Blaatand. No, Harald didn't invent the wireless protocol — that would have been some mean trick since he died in 985. Actually, the good king was known for unifying Denmark, Norway, and Sweden. Because the inventors of Bluetooth saw the standard as a unifying communications protocol, they decided to honor King Harald. By the way, those symbols on the Bluetooth logo are the king's initials in Nordic runes.

Bluetooth is a way to replace cables. There are Bluetooth-compatible printers, headphones, keyboards, mice, PDAs, cell phones, and GPS receivers. None of them require cables. One of the biggest uses of Bluetooth is synchronizing contact and calendar information among PDAs, laptops, and cell phones. If you don't have an Internet connection but you do have a Bluetooth-compatible phone and netbook, it's also possible to wirelessly connect to the Net through the cell phone.

Keep in mind that Bluetooth transfers data at a rate of 1 Mbps. That's about three to eight times faster than the average speed of parallel and serial ports (which it aims to replace), but considerably slower than an 802.11 wireless connection — you're not going to be using Bluetooth for your everyday Internet connection.

The next generation of Bluetooth, version 3.0, will amp up the protocol's speed to a zoomy 24 Mbps. In addition to the speed increase, Bluetooth devices will also get improved power management capabilities so they'll run more efficiently and longer on batteries.

What does all of this have to do with netbooks? Simple: If you use a Bluetooth device such as a cell phone, headphones, or a GPS receiver (or are planning on purchasing such a device in the future), be sure your netbook has Bluetooth so you can take advantage of it. (If you don't need Bluetooth, you can save a few bucks on a model without it.)

If your netbook lacks Bluetooth but you want to join the party, you can get an inexpensive (around $20) Bluetooth adapter that you plug in to one of your USB slots — you may need to install driver software, but Windows might automatically do this for you. I talk more about Bluetooth adapters in Chapter 15.

Before using Bluetooth in Windows, you need to configure it, which you can easily do with a configuration wizard by just following the steps. You need to choose what types of services the computer will offer, such as file transfer, personal information manager (PIM) synchronization, headset, and so on, as shown in Figure 6-3.

Figure 6-3:
During Bluetooth configuration, you can specify services that your computer will offer.

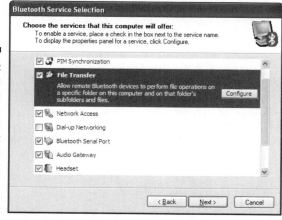

When you're finished with the configuration, Windows places a My Bluetooth Places icon on your desktop. By clicking the icon, you open a window, which is where you control all your Bluetooth connections (including searching for nearby devices) and settings. A Bluetooth icon is also installed in the taskbar for quick access.

Check your netbook's user manual for more details on using Bluetooth.

If you have Bluetooth built into your netbook, you can turn it off to save on battery drain. Press a function key or use a menu command (check your user manual) to turn it on and off.

Easy Ethernet

All netbooks have an RJ45 jack located somewhere on the case. It looks like what you'd plug a landline telephone into but is a bit larger — if you try to plug a phone cord into it, it won't fit.

The RJ45 jack is the key to wired network access because, behind it, your netbook contains a 10/100 Ethernet card. Plug one end of a cable with RJ45 connectors (commonly called a CAT5 or Category 5 cable, shown in Figure 6-4) into your netbook and the other end into a router, switch, or wall network port, and you're ready to go.

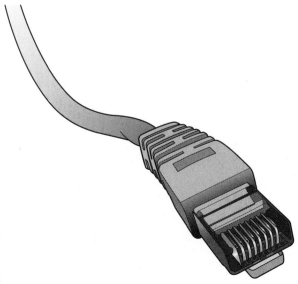

Figure 6-4: A CAT5 Ethernet cable with RJ45 jack for wired Internet connections.

If the router or switch you're connecting to uses DHCP (Dynamic Host Configuration Protocol), Windows does everything for you and automatically connects to the Internet. It's as easy as plugging in the cable and having Internet access in a matter of seconds.

Most networks use DHCP, but some use static Internet Protocol (IP) addresses. In these cases you'll need to get an IP address from your system administrator and configure Windows to use it. Your administrator will provide you with instructions on how to do this.

If a wired Ethernet connection is available, here are a few things to consider:

- ✔ A wired connection is faster than a wireless connection — unless it's a 4G network, which I discuss in the previous wireless section.

- ✔ A wired connection uses less power than a wireless connection.

- ✔ A wired connection isn't susceptible to radio wave interference.

- ✔ A network status icon appears in the Windows taskbar — it looks like two computer monitors, side by side. Move the mouse over the icon to check whether you have a wired connection. If you do, the connection speed is shown.

You don't need to turn off your netbook's wireless card when you're using a wired connection. Windows is smart enough to handle two types of network connections at once. If you start getting odd networking errors though, consider turning off the wireless card.

Internet Instructions

After you connect to the Internet, I'm going to make a bold assumption you already know what to do — if I'm wrong, I suggest picking up a copy of *The Internet For Dummies* by John R. Levin, Margaret Levine Young, and Carol Baroudi (Wiley Publishing, Inc.).

Instead of telling you what a browser is and how to use e-mail, I give you various useful Net-related tricks that I've gleaned from using netbooks over the past several years.

I discuss social networking sites as well as Twitter and Skype in Chapter 10.

Browsing the Web

If you purchase a Windows netbook, it's going to come preinstalled with Microsoft's Internet Explorer (IE). If you're like most users, you'll start using IE to browse the Web and think nothing more of it.

That's cool, but I want to make a pitch for downloading and trying Firefox (www.mozilla.com/firefox), a popular, free, open-source browser with versions that run in Windows, Macintosh OS X, and Linux. The browser, running on a netbook, is shown in Figure 6-5.

Figure 6-5:
The Firefox browser on a netbook.

If you've been using IE for awhile, you'll notice that Firefox is very similar. There are a few interface differences that are explained on the following site (a no-pressure sales pitch is also included): www.mozilla.com/en-US/firefox/switch.html.

Firefox features

Most browsers share basic functions and generally work the same, but if you've never used Firefox before, I want to mention some features that make it my browser of choice on a netbook (as well as other computers):

✔ **Built-in spell checking:** No matter what Web site you're on, as you type words that aren't in the browser's spelling dictionary, they're underlined in red. This prevents many embarrassing typos when you're composing Web e-mail.

- ✔ **Enhanced security:** I used to do quite a bit of computer security work, and still dabble in it, and quite honestly Firefox is the most secure Web browser for Windows. You'll find phishing and spyware protection, easy private data clearing, and prompt update releases when security vulnerabilities are discovered.

- ✔ **Multiple search engine support:** Type a term in the toolbar and then select which search engine you'd like to use, such as Google, Yahoo!, Wikipedia, eBay, and others.

- ✔ **Pop-up blocking:** Firefox can automatically block annoying (and sometimes malicious) pop-up windows.

- ✔ **RSS reader:** Get RSS (Really Simple Syndication) feeds, such as blog postings, news headlines, and Web site updates from inside the browser.

- ✔ **Session restore:** If your computer crashes while Firefox is running (or you shut it down), the browser remembers and loads all the Web sites you had open the next time it runs. You can also elect to save all your open tabs when you quit — they automatically open the next time Firefox runs.

- ✔ **Speed:** Firefox is quick, even on netbooks with their small amount of memory and not-exactly-speedy processors.

- ✔ **Add-ons:** These are small programs for extending Firefox's functionality. I provide more extensive coverage on these useful mini-programs in the next section.

- ✔ **Tabbed browsing:** Firefox pioneered the use of tabs versus separate windows for browsing, and it has a number of different options for maximizing tabbed Web surfing.

Microsoft has been playing catch-up with Firefox and has copycatted some of the preceding features in the latest release of IE. The Firefox developers aren't sitting still, though, and are incorporating new, innovative features at a much faster rate than the Redmond giant.

I could go on listing more features, but instead, why don't you start using the browser and discover all it has to offer? To read more about browsing the Firefox way, visit the official Web support site at http://support.mozilla.com or check out the forums at http://forums.mozillazine.org.

Using Firefox add-ons

Other browsers have add-ons (small programs that provide additional functionality to the browser) but a big advantage Firefox has over the competition is the large number of free add-on programs and themes.

Add-ons come in three different types:

- ✔ **Extensions:** Small programs designed to extend the browser's functionality

✓ **Languages:** A feature that changes the language of the user interface

✓ **Themes:** Code that alters the browser's user interface

Add-ons tend to be relatively small (measured in kilobytes) and don't take up a lot of disk space — which is important if disk space is at a premium on your netbook.

They are also very easy to install. The Firefox add-ons Web site (`https://addons.mozilla.org`) contains descriptions, links, and reviews of over 1,000 available add-ons. Installation is a matter of clicking a few buttons.

To get you started with add-ons, here are a few of my favorites that you may want to try:

✓ **Adblock Plus:** Blocks Web site advertisements, which is especially useful on a netbook with its smaller screen: `https://addons.mozilla.org/firefox/addon/1865`.

✓ **Forecastfox:** A slick little weather add-on that gets forecasts from Accuweather.com and displays them in the status bar: `https://addons.mozilla.org/en-US/firefox/addon/398`.

✓ **NoScript:** If you're concerned about Java and JavaScript security, use this add-on to execute scripts from only the sites you trust: `https://addons.mozilla.org/en-US/firefox/addon/722`.

✓ **Video DownloadHelper:** Saves YouTube and other online videos to your drive: `https://addons.mozilla.org/en-US/firefox/addon/3006`.

Have fun with add-ons. With the large number of available add-ons, you can spend hours browsing through the add-on database, reading reviews and descriptions, and downloading different versions.

Add-ons take up memory and processor cycles, so if you go crazy installing a lot of them, Firefox's performance will begin to suffer. If this happens, just start removing the add-ons you've installed.

Maximizing screen real estate

In Firefox, you have a number of ways to deal with a netbook's reduced size screen viewing area. Try one or more of the following:

✓ **Hide the Windows taskbar.** Right-click the taskbar at the bottom of the screen and choose Properties. Then select the Auto-Hide the Taskbar check box.

✓ **Hide Firefox toolbars.** From Firefox's View menu, choose Toolbars. Then deselect the Navigation Toolbar and Bookmarks Toolbar check box.

✓ **Hide the Firefox status bar.** On the View menu, deselect Status Bar.

> ✔ **Use a Firefox add-on.** Several available add-on themes can maximize screen space. They include
>
> - *miniFox:* This theme maximizes space between interface elements: `https://addons.mozilla.org/en-US/firefox/addon/607`.
> - *Tiny Menu:* Replaces the default menu with a reduced size version: `https://addons.mozilla.org/en-US/firefox/addon/1455`.
> - *Compact Menu:* Provides several ways of compressing the menu: `https://addons.mozilla.org/en-US/firefox/addon/4550`.
> - *Full Fullscreen:* Starts Firefox in full-screen mode and hides the toolbars: `https://addons.mozilla.org/en-US/firefox/addon/1568`.

You can find other add-on themes for netbook screens besides the ones I mention here. Visit the Firefox add-ons site (`https://addons.mozilla.org/firefox`) and do a search for *compact.*

Exchanging e-mail

If you're like most people and use your netbook as a secondary computer, e-mail has the potential to become a royal pain in the you-know-what. Whenever you access your e-mail with a traditional e-mail client (such as Outlook or Thunderbird), messages are downloaded from a remote mail server to the inbox on your hard drive. After the message is successfully downloaded, it's removed from the mail server — unless you set an option to keep it there.

So far, so good. The problem with traditional e-mail clients is that when you access mail on your primary laptop or desktop PC, messages are stored there, and when you check your mail on a netbook, messages are saved there too. Soon you have lots of e-mails scattered between your primary computer and your netbook. Good luck trying to keep all the messages on the two computers organized!

There are ways to synchronize inboxes between two computers, but instead I recommend the simple approach of using a Web mail account. They're free, convenient, easy to use, and you don't need to worry about e-mails stored on multiple computers — because messages are stored and managed remotely.

There are lots of free Web mail services available on the Net, but here are the biggies:

- ✔ **Gmail:** Google's e-mail service (`http://mail.google.com`).
- ✔ **Hotmail:** Microsoft's e-mail service (`www.hotmail.com`).

 ✔ **Yahoo! Mail:** The Yahoo! e-mail service (http://mail.yahoo.com).

 ✔ **AOL Mail:** The America Online e-mail service (http://mail.aol.com).

If you don't have a free account with one of these services, you can create one on the preceding login Web pages.

For a great comparison of features that the different Web e-mail services offer, visit http://blogs.swebee.com/e-mail-service/free-webmail-services-comparison/2008-05-01_69-1.html.

If you plan to exclusively use your netbook for accessing e-mail, I suggest you use a free e-mail program called Thunderbird (www.mozilla.com). It's brought to you by the same people who provide the Firefox Web browser and is an excellent traditional e-mail client. Standalone e-mail programs have more features than Web-hosted mail systems, and Thunderbird is especially versatile because you can use it with a Web mail account.

Connecting remotely with Ultra VNC

Speaking of the Internet, I have to mention a very cool and useful tool that's popular with geeks but is mostly unknown outside of techie circles. It's a Windows version of a program and communications protocol called VNC (Virtual Network Computing). Here's the general idea:

Say you're on the road with your netbook and need something on your primary computer back home — maybe it's a spreadsheet file you forgot or perhaps you need to get some information out of a database you don't have installed on your netbook. Through the magic of the Internet, how would you like the desktop of your primary PC to appear on the netbook's screen and then be able to transfer the file you need or run the database program on your home computer? You can do this with a free program called Ultra VNC (www.uvnc.com).

Installing Ultra VNC

Here are the basic steps to get rolling with Ultra VNC:

1. **Download the Ultra VNC software and install it on your primary computer — not your netbook. Specify you want the *server* files during the installation.**

2. **Download and install a copy of VNC on your netbook. Have the installation program install the *viewer* files.**

3. **Run the Ultra VNC server on the primary computer.**

   It's best to have a DSL or cable modem Internet connection, and always leave your primary computer running so you can access it anytime.

The configuration dialog box automatically appears, as shown in Figure 6-6.

4. **Configure the server.**

   Among settings you need to provide is a password, which you can enter in the Authentication area in the VNC Password text box. This password prevents anyone from logging onto the computer. Don't let the complicated dialog box intimidate you. Unless you want to use some of the advanced features of Ultra VNC, just enter a password and leave the other default settings alone.

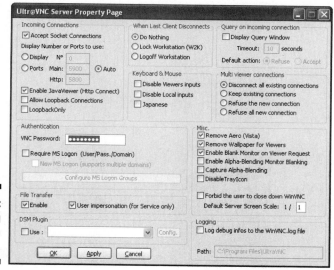

Figure 6-6: Configuring the Ultra VNC server.

If you're using a router or firewall on your primary computer, you need to change settings to allow Ultra VNC to send and receive data on a certain port — the technical term for this is _port forwarding_.

Go to www.youtube.com and search for _Ultra VNC_ to view video tutorials and demonstrations of Ultra VNC in action. The Ultra VNC home Web site also has documentation and tutorials.

Using Ultra VNC

When Ultra VNC is running in server mode on your primary computer (which is connected to the Internet), here's how to access the server:

1. **Run Ultra VNC in Viewer mode on your netbook.**

2. **Connect to your primary computer using its IP address.**

   You need to determine the IP (Internet Protocol) address of the server computer so that you can connect to it. A number of free Web sites can return the IP address of a computer that visits them — for example, www.ip-adress.com and http://whatismyipaddress.com.

   Most Internet service providers provide dynamic versus static IP addresses. This means if your Internet service is temporarily interrupted, such as with a power outage, your computer may be assigned a new IP address. This can create problems connecting with Ultra VNC which relies on a current IP address. The solution is to use a free dynamic DNS (Domain Name System) service — I personally like DynDNS. After installing a program on your computer, instead of using a numeric IP address to access a remote computer, you can use a hostname such as *mycomputer.ath.cx.* If the dynamic IP address ever changes, it's no big deal. Check out www.dyndns.com for more information.

3. **Enter the server password.**

Ultra VNC now shows the desktop of your primary computer in a separate window, as shown in Figure 6-7.

When you move or click the mouse in the window (or type), it sends those commands to your primary computer. In effect, you're remotely controlling the other computer (including running programs on it) and watching the results in the Ultra VNC window.

Figure 6-7:
This netbook is running Ultra VNC remotely running a program on another computer.

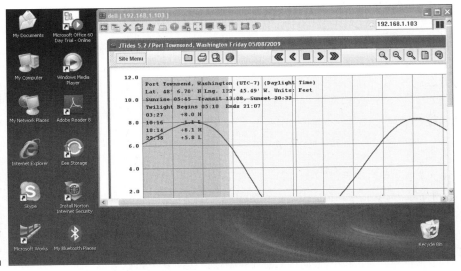

A series of icon commands appears at the top of the screen. Here you change different options, initiate file transfers between the two computers, and close the connection.

The main downside to using Ultra VNC (or any remote desktop program; there are other free and commercial versions available) is the screen-size disparity between your larger-screen primary computer and smaller-screened netbook — you'll need to scroll to see the full screen.

If you often find yourself playing computer technical support for less-savvy friends and family members, Ultra VNC is a great tool for remotely troubleshooting their problems.

Sharing files on a Windows network

A router (or switch) allows a single broadband Internet connection to be shared by multiple computers. You hook up the router to a DSL or cable connection, and it provides other computers with access to the Net — either with plugged in Ethernet cables or wirelessly, depending on the router type. Routers also offer essential security against outside intruders serving a hardware firewall.

In addition to accessing the Internet, multiple computers connected to a router can communicate with each other in a local area network (LAN), which makes it easy for computers running Windows to share files and even printers.

A Windows network is very useful for netbooks because you can transfer files between your primary computer and print files — all via the network.

I want to give you a synopsis of what's involved in sharing files over a Windows network, but I don't have the space for it. Entire books have been written on the subject, so I'm just going to provide a brief overview. For more details, check out Microsoft's extensive collection of tutorials and guides for XP networking at www.microsoft.com/windowsxp/using/networking/default.mspx.

For networking with Windows 7, which as I write this hasn't been released, check out the main product page at www.microsoft.com/windows/windows-7/default.aspx.

For starters, Microsoft uses a Network Setup Wizard that makes it fairly painless to get a home network up and running. You can find the wizard by clicking Network and Internet Connections in the Windows Control Panel.

All computers in the network need to have the same workgroup name. By default, Microsoft uses the name *workgroup.* You can change the workgroup name by right-clicking the My Computer icon on the Windows desktop and choosing Properties. Then click the Computer Name tab. If you change the workgroup or computer name, you need to restart the computer.

After you have your network configured, here's what you need to do to share a folder on a Windows network. (This applies to a netbook or any other PC running Windows XP on the network.)

1. **Right-click the Start button and choose Explore.**

2. **Right-click the folder you want to share and choose Sharing and Security.**

   A folder Properties dialog box appears, as shown in Figure 6-8.

3. **Select the Share This Folder on the Network check box and click OK. (You can optionally give the folder a different shared name in the Share Name text box.)**

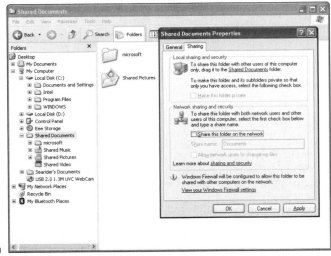

Figure 6-8:
Setting up a folder to be shared in a Windows network.

A hand icon appears on the folder, indicating it's shared. Any computer on the network can now access the folder. Here's how:

1. **Click the My Network Places icon on the Windows desktop.**

   A window with computers connected to your Windows network appears.

2. Double-click a shared folder you want to access.

A list of files and folders inside the folder appears (as shown in Figure 6-9). You can double-click a file to open it or copy files to your hard drive by dragging and dropping.

Figure 6-9: Accessing a shared folder in a Windows network.

One of the biggest challenges to getting a Windows network working properly can be software firewall settings. A firewall can block a computer within the network from sending and receiving data packets from other computers. If shared computers don't show up in My Network Places, the first place to check is your firewall settings — make sure LAN traffic is allowed.

Chapter 7

Netbooks at Work

*N*etbooks are nifty productivity tools. Because of their size, they're perfect for business trips, presentations, or anytime you need to work but don't feel like lugging around a traditional laptop or sitting down to a desktop PC.

Because most netbooks run Windows, it's a snap to use many familiar business-related Windows programs — as long as you abide by the terms of the license agreement, of course.

In this chapter, I get down to work with netbooks. I'm guessing you already know about Microsoft mainstays Word, Excel, and PowerPoint (which I briefly discuss), but you may not know much about Microsoft Works (which often comes preinstalled on many netbooks) or OpenOffice (a free, open-source alternative to Microsoft Office).

In addition to these traditional software packages that you download or install from a CD-ROM or DVD, you can also find and make use of some very slick, Web-hosted productivity alternatives such as Google Docs and Zoho.

So grab a cup of coffee and pull up a chair as I survey different ways to put your netbook to work.

Working with Microsoft Works

Microsoft Works is the kid-brother to Microsoft Office: It's smaller, cheaper, and doesn't have as many features. Because some netbooks come bundled with Works, I spend a little time telling you about this consumer-grade productivity suite.

Works comes with a word processor, spreadsheet, database, calendar, and dictionary.

Over the years, manufacturers have bundled Microsoft Works on PCs of all shapes and sizes. In the old days, all the Works programs ran in the same window and used the same interface. However, with Works 2000, Microsoft switched over to a more familiar, modular approach, where each program runs in its own window. (As I write this, the current release of Works is version 9.)

When you run Works, you're greeted with a task launcher page (shown in Figure 7-1). Click a program icon on the left side of the window to run that program.

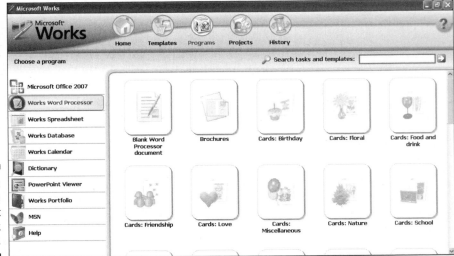

Figure 7-1: The Microsoft Works task launcher.

When you load Works, Microsoft Office program icons may be displayed. If they are, these are trial versions of the Office programs and will work for only 60 days or a limited number of file opens — after that, you need to purchase a registered version. Works itself is not a trial version, though.

When you run a Works program, you're prompted as to whether you want to open a blank document or use a template (shown in Figure 7-2). Templates allow you to easily create professionally formatted newsletters, greeting cards, invoices, schedules, and other forms.

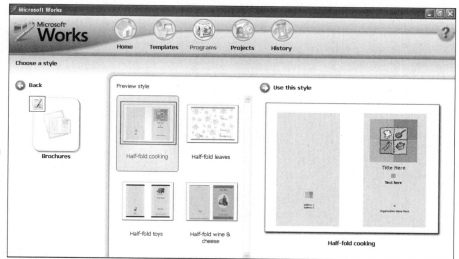

Figure 7-2:
Microsoft Works has a variety of document templates.

Older versions of Microsoft Works often got a bad rap for using a proprietary document format that wasn't compatible with any other applications — including Microsoft Office programs. That's changed with the most recent releases, and you can import and export all the common Office file formats. A file created with Microsoft Word is shown opened in Works in Figure 7-3.

You can still hear people on the Internet grousing about Works and how other better, free alternatives are available — and that's true. OpenOffice (more on that coming up in this chapter) and AbiWord (a free word processor down-loadable from `www.abisource.com`) have many more features. However, the current release of Works isn't that bad, and I have a feeling many of the complaints came from those who used older versions.

If you're looking for a basic, easy-to-use collection of productivity programs and if Works came preinstalled on your netbook, give it a try and see what you think. (However, I wouldn't run out and purchase a copy of Works, because of the free alternatives I mention here.)

You can find out more about Works directly from the Microsoft source at `www.microsoft.com/products/Works/default.mspx`.

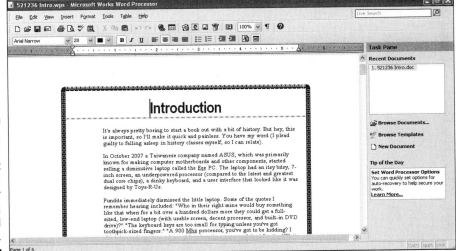

Figure 7-3:
The
Microsoft
Works word
processor
is showing
an imported
Word file.

If Works was preinstalled and you decide to remove it to save disk space, it might not be easy to restore the program after you've uninstalled it. Many netbook manufacturers don't include a separate install program for Works — you have to do a full system restore from a recovery disc or drive partition to get the program back.

Managing Microsoft Office

I'm not going to spend a lot of time discussing Microsoft Office. The productivity suite is pretty much the de facto standard in the business world, and if you've used a Windows computer in the past, I'm guessing you've been exposed to the ubiquitous Word (shown in Figure 7-4), Excel, and PowerPoint.

From a netbook standpoint, Office works just like it does on a traditional laptop or desktop PC — although the performance isn't as zippy due to the netbook's underpowered processor and limited memory. If you use Office on your primary computer, it's nice to have the same interface and file compatibility on your netbook.

Some netbooks come with a trial version of Microsoft Office. This free demo lets you evaluate the software for a limited period of time. To use the trial version, you need to activate the software the first time you use it — if you don't, the program runs in Reduced Functionality mode, which means you can view documents but can't edit, save changes, or create new documents.

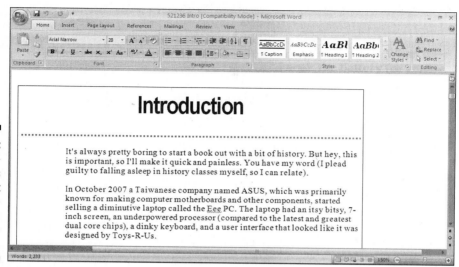

Introduction

It's always pretty boring to start a book out with a bit of history. But hey, this is important, so I'll make it quick and painless. You have my word (I plead guilty to falling asleep in history classes myself, so I can relate).

In October 2007 a Taiwanese company named ASUS, which was primarily known for making computer motherboards and other components, started selling a diminutive laptop called the Eee PC. The laptop had an itsy bitsy, 7-inch screen, an underpowered processor (compared to the latest and greatest dual core chips), a dinky keyboard, and a user interface that looked like it was designed by Toys-R-Us.

Figure 7-4:
The ubiquitous Microsoft Word running on a 10-inch netbook.

When you run one of the Office programs for the first time, follow the prompts to activate the software — an Activation Wizard contacts Microsoft over the Internet and does the rest.

When the trial period is over, Office returns to Reduced Functionality mode — any documents you created or edited will still be there, but you can view them only with the Office programs on your netbook. (You can edit the documents if you move them to another computer running a registered version of Office.) You need to purchase a license to restore the full functionality of Office, which you can get either online or from a retail outlet.

For more information on Office activation, go to `http://us20.trymicro softoffice.com/faq.aspx`.

My biggest complaint with Microsoft Office is that, like many other software packages, it has become increasingly bloated over the years. On an underpowered netbook, performance can get pokey if you're working with large documents or have a number of files open — and please, don't even attempt to run complex spreadsheet models unless you want to wait forever.

I've found that older versions of Office (specifically the 1997, 2000, and XP versions) are less resource-intensive and better performers — you should still avoid complex spreadsheets, though. If you have an old, licensed copy lying around, consider running it on your netbook instead of Office 2003, 2007, or later.

It sounds like Microsoft may be planning a trimmed down version of Office for netbooks with the next release of the product — dubbed Office 2010. During a technology conference in the spring of 2009, without giving away any details, the president of Microsoft's business division said the company would be incorporating netbooks into its overall plans for Office. In addition to the traditional software, also look for an online version of the productivity suite called Office Web Apps.

To get more information about Office, visit `http://office.microsoft.com`.

Because netbooks don't have built-in DVD drives like many other PCs, what do you do if you've purchased a copy of Office and want to install it on your netbook? The friendly folks in Redmond make it easy. With your netbook connected to the Internet, go to `www.getmicrosoftoffice.com`. There you can download the installation files directly to your netbook — you'll need the 25-digit product key found in the software package. When the download is finished, install Office, and you're ready to go.

Considering the OpenOffice Option

OpenOffice is an office application suite of programs. The legally correct name is *OpenOffice.org,* but most people refer to it as *OpenOffice.* Think of it as a free, open-source Microsoft Office alternative (with a few more features, actually).

OpenOffice started life in the late 1990s as StarOffice, a commercial office application suite. Sun Microsystems (which was in a pitched battle with Microsoft at the time) purchased the software from a German company and then made it available for free. In 2000, Sun released the source code, and OpenOffice became an open-source project. Over the years, it has evolved from a slightly clunky collection of programs to a full-featured, viable alternative to Microsoft Office.

StarOffice, which is preinstalled on some netbooks, has most of the same programs and interfaces as OpenOffice.

OpenOffice (the startup screen is shown in Figure 7-5) comes with several programs, including

- **OpenOffice Base:** A database application similar to Microsoft Access

- **OpenOffice Calc:** A spreadsheet program similar to Microsoft Excel

- **OpenOffice Draw:** A vector graphics program with features comparable to early versions of CorelDRAW

✔ **OpenOffice Impress:** A presentation program similar to Microsoft PowerPoint

✔ **OpenOffice Math:** A utility for creating and editing mathematical equations (similar to Microsoft Equation Editor)

✔ **OpenOffice Writer:** A word processor (shown in Figure 7-6) that has a set of features similar (and a similar look and feel) to the Microsoft Word features

Figure 7-5:
OpenOffice
startup
screen.

One program that OpenOffice doesn't come with is an e-mail/scheduling application like Microsoft Outlook. You need to download and install open-source Thunderbird and Sunbird to get this functionality.

For the most part, OpenOffice is compatible with Microsoft Office format files. That means you can copy a Word file from your PC onto a USB flash drive, plug it into your netbook, and work on the document with OpenOffice. And when you get back to your main PC, Word can happily read all the edits you made on your netbook.

You will likely run into compatibility troubles if your Microsoft Office documents have complex graphics, fancy fonts and formatting, nested tables, complicated macros, and embedded OLE objects.

OpenOffice programs can save files in Adobe Acrobat PDF format, so you don't need commercial or free conversion applications.

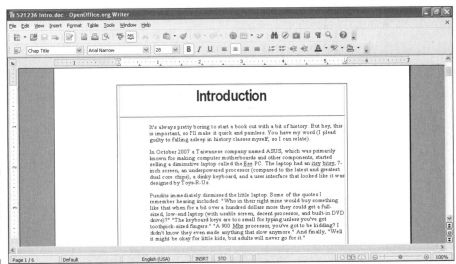

Figure 7-6: The OpenOffice Writer word processor.

Versions of OpenOffice are available for Windows, Linux, and Mac. To find out more about OpenOffice or to download a version visit www.openoffice.org.

If you want to give OpenOffice a try without installing it on your hard drive, check out this portable version: http://portableapps.com/apps/office/openoffice_portable. It runs on a USB flash drive or an SD card with about 250MB of free space available. After you install it, just plug in the drive or card and run OpenOffice on any Windows PC.

OpenOffice Internet resources

If you're an OpenOffice user or a potential one, consider checking out some of the many resources available on the Internet to get more information about the suite. Here are some of my favorites:

✔ **OpenOffice main support page:** http://support.openoffice.org

✔ **OpenOffice Wiki:** http://wiki.services.openoffice.org/wiki/Main_Page

✔ **OpenOffice User Guides Authors documentation project:** http://documentation.openoffice.org/manuals/oooauthors2/index.html

✔ **Tutorials for OpenOffice:** www.tutorialsforopenoffice.org

✔ **OpenOffice community forums:** www.oooforum.org

Going Online with Google Docs

Google Docs (`http://docs.google.com`) is a free, online suite of office programs, including a word processor, spreadsheet, and presentation application. Instead of the conventional approach of using standalone programs installed on your netbook (or any other PC for that matter), Google Docs lets you create, edit, and store documents online by using a Web browser and an Internet connection. The Google Docs interface is shown in Figure 7-7.

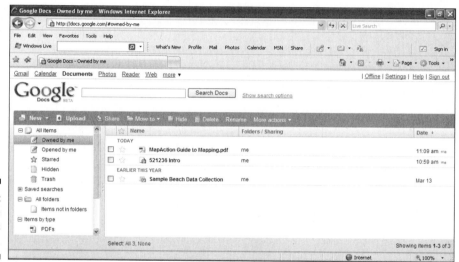

Figure 7-7: The Google Docs interface.

You need a free Google account to use Google Docs. Either sign in with your existing account information or create a new account.

Some of Google Docs' features include

- ✔ A simple, easy-to-use interface
- ✔ The ability to save documents in PDF and other common formats
- ✔ The ability to import Microsoft Office and OpenOffice documents (An imported Word document is shown in Figure 7-8.)
- ✔ Collaboration options that allow documents to be shared, opened, and edited by multiple users at the same time
- ✔ The ability to publish documents as Web pages

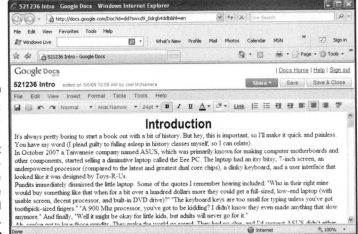

Figure 7-8:
You can
upload a
Microsoft
Word docu-
ment to the
Google
Docs word
processor.

New features are regularly added to Google Docs. To keep up with the latest, check out the Google Docs development team's blog at `http://google docs.blogspot.com`.

Storing your documents online and working on them from anywhere you can get an Internet connection is pretty appealing — especially with a go-anywhere netbook. However, before you start putting all your eggs in the Google Docs basket, you should be aware of a few catches:

- **Internet connection required:** No Net means no access to documents. Google Docs does, however, allow you to save documents directly to your netbook.

- **Basic features:** The word processor, spreadsheet, and presentation programs have basic features. If you need advanced functions and features, you should turn to a conventional office program like Microsoft Office or OpenOffice.

- **Document size and total storage space:** Google Docs puts limitations on how large a single document can be as well as the total number of documents that you can store online. See the "Google Docs limitations" sidebar for more.

- **Theoretical security issues:** There are some theoretical security and privacy issues with using Google Docs. Not to be overly paranoid, but I personally wouldn't use it to work on a document that contains sensitive information.

I've just scratched the surface on Google Docs, and there's a lot more to discover, so pay a visit to `http://docs.google.com/support`.

Google Docs limitations

Aside from needing an Internet connection to use the Google Docs applications, you should be aware of a few other limitations to the online service.

You have a limited amount of storage space with each Google account:

✔ **Docs:** Each doc can be up to 500K, plus up to 2MB per embedded image.

✔ **Spreadsheets:** Each spreadsheet can have up to 256 columns, 200,000 cells, or 100 sheets — whichever is reached first. There's no limit on rows.

✔ **Presentations:** Files in PowerPoint formats (.ppt and .pps) can have a maximum size of 10MB or 200 slides. Files uploaded

from the Web can be up to 2MB. E-mailed files can be up to 500K.

✔ **PDFs:** You can store up to 10MB per PDF from your computer and 2MB from the Web in your Docs list. You can have up to 100 PDF files.

Google Docs also has the following limitations:

✔ Files can only be uploaded or downloaded one at a time.

✔ Older Web browsers aren't compatible with Google Docs.

Google is always tweaking its services, and some of these limitations may change in the future.

Getting in the Zoho Zone

Another option in the online productivity suite department is an amazing collection of programs available from Zoho (www.zoho.com). Like Google Docs, you dispense with traditional office software installed on your hard drive and do everything over the Net instead. Figure 7-9 shows the Zoho desktop interface. (In case you're curious, the name Zoho is a deliberate misspelling of SOHO, an acronym for Small Office/Home Office.)

Starting out with only an online word processor about four years ago, Zoho has added a wide array of products to its application suite. The company's Web services are extremely popular with around 1.5 million registered users and 500,000 unique monthly logins.

Zoho caters to individuals as well as organization and small-to-medium-size businesses. Online applications are free for individuals, but the company charges subscription fees for some of the business-oriented services.

If you've never checked out Zoho, you'll be surprised at the number of programs that are available. Here's what's currently offered in the way of productivity software:

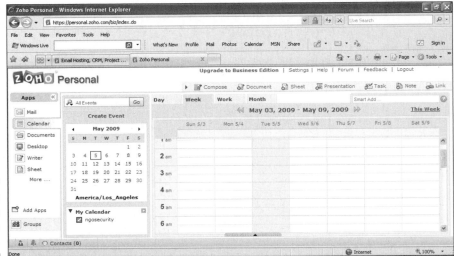

Figure 7-9:
The Zoho
user inter-
face.

- ✓ **Zoho Chat:** You can embed this chat application into pages or blogs. Zoho Chat also supports private instant messaging and can integrate with many popular chat clients.

- ✓ **Zoho Mail:** This Web-based collaboration program includes e-mail, calendar, and document, task, and contact management features. It also integrates with Zoho Sheet, Show, and Writer.

- ✓ **Zoho Notebook:** A tool for organizing information similar to Microsoft OneNote or Google Notebook. You can include text, images, video, and audio in a "notebook" and optionally share the notebook or its individual pages over the Net.

- ✓ **Zoho Planner:** It's just what it sounds like: an online planner with a calendar, to-do lists, pages, and reminders that's similar in functionality to Google Calendar and Microsoft Outlook. You can share the information with other people.

- ✓ **Zoho Share:** It's a service for sharing content of all types. Think of it as a cross between Microsoft SharePoint and YouTube.

- ✓ **Zoho Sheet:** Every productivity suite needs a spreadsheet, and this is Zoho's. It's compatible with Microsoft Excel file formats.

- ✓ **Zoho Show:** This online presentation application allows users to create or import Microsoft PowerPoint or OpenOffice presentations.

- ✓ **Zoho Wiki:** This program acts as a simple wiki and Web page–creation tool.

- ✓ **Zoho Writer:** The suite's word processor supports most common document formats as well as multiuser collaboration. (See Figure 7-10.)

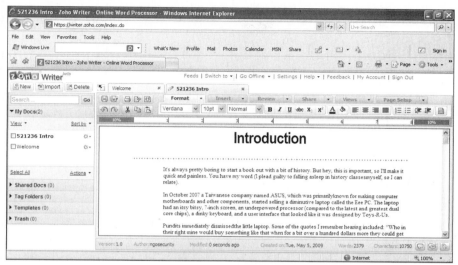

Figure 7-10:
The Zoho
Writer word
processor.

To stay current with Zoho happenings, check out the official blogs at `http://blogs.zoho.com`.

In addition to productivity applications for individuals, Zoho has a series of business-oriented applications that include

- ✔ **Zoho Creator:** A database-creation tool. Picture an easy-to-use Microsoft Access (with basic features), only online. Use drag and drop tools to create custom forms.

- ✔ **Zoho CRM:** CRM stands for Customer Relationship Management. This application helps a business manage sales leads, accounts, campaigns, forecasts, and activities.

- ✔ **Zoho Invoice:** An online invoice generator and tracking program. With it, you can create, send, and track estimates and invoices.

- ✔ **Zoho Meeting:** A Web conferencing application that supports audio, video, and presentation display.

- ✔ **Zoho People:** A human resources program for handling recruitment, common organizational forms and charts, and more.

- ✔ **Zoho Projects:** A classic project management application that supports tasks, task ownership, deadlines, milestones, Gantt charts, and everything you need to track a project.

- ✔ **Zoho Reports:** An online database and reporting program.

In addition to applications included in the productivity and business suites, Zoho offers tools such as Zoho Challenge (an online test and evaluation program), Zoho Polls (a survey application) and Site 24x7 (a Web site statistics service). New applications and tools are frequently introduced, and existing versions are often updated.

It's hard to do justice to Zoho in words alone, and I encourage you to go to www.zoho.com and try the applications for yourself. In my opinion, some of the features and functionality beat the competing Google services.

Chapter 8

Netbook Fun and Games

*I*n addition to checking e-mail, browsing Web sites, and using productivity software, a netbook is also one sweet little portable entertainment center. With it, you can listen to music and radio stations, watch movies, and play games.

This chapter is all about fun and games. Here I tell you everything you need to know about listening to music, podcasts, and streaming audio on your netbook. I then cover watching DVD movies and streaming videos, and I explain how to watch movies if your netbook doesn't have an external DVD drive. I wrap things up with a discussion of playing games on your netbook and a description of the limitations that might stymie a hardcore gamer.

Remember, all work and no play makes a dull netbook.

Music to My Ears

No, I'm not advocating you ditch your MP3 player or cell phone and start listening to music exclusively on your netbook — I've yet to see someone with a netbook strapped to their arm or tucked in a front shirt pocket. That would be crazy.

Instead, I want to clue you in to different aspects of using your netbook to groove to tunes. It's nice to listen to music while working or browsing the Web, and because you're already using your netbook, you may as well plug in some headphones and rock (or chill out with a calm instrumental if need be).

Most MP3 player headphones should fit your netbook's audio output jack.

Using an MP3 player is pretty simple, but if you want to turn your little laptop into a mobile jukebox, you should know a few things. Don't press Fast Forward, but keep on reading.

MP3 mania

If you don't know it, MP3 stands for Moving Picture Experts Group-1 Audio Layer 3 — which is a mouthful to say. It's arguably the mostly widely used format for storing digital music. If you copy an MP3 file to your netbook and double-click it, there's a very good chance Windows Media Player (or some other program) will start, and if you have the speakers turned up, a song will begin playing.

If you copy more than one MP3 file to a folder on your netbook, you can have the music player program play all the songs in the folder, one after another — or randomly shuffle through the entire collection. Check your media player's online help file for instructions on how to do this.

Other common digital music formats you should know about are WMA (Windows Media Audio, used by Microsoft); AAC (Advanced Audio Coding, used by Apple); and OGG (Ogg Vorbis, an open-source format — you've got to love geeks and their weird naming sense). If you see a file with any of these extensions, it's digital music or sound.

Although Windows Media Player plays MP3 files and other sound formats, many people who listen to music on their netbooks use some other music playing software. There's nothing wrong with Windows Media Player — it's just that there are better options available. Here are some top picks:

✔ **iTunes:** If you have an Apple iPod, you already know about iTunes and likely have installed it on your netbook. iTunes is a proprietary media player that can play and organize digital music and video files. The program also manages music on Apple iPods and iPhones. In addition, if you're connected to the Internet, iTunes can access the iTunes Store, where you can purchase and download music — as well as videos, games, audiobooks, and other media. iTunes itself is free, and you can download it from `www.apple.com/itunes`.

Music downloaded from the iTunes Store has traditionally been encoded with copy protection — the music can play only on the computer that downloaded the song (or the iPod the music was copied to). In January 2009, Apple announced it would eventually stop selling music with digital rights management (DRM) restrictions, which means it will be easier to copy tunes to your netbook.

✔ **Songbird:** If you don't like to be locked into proprietary media players from Apple or Microsoft, I have one word for you: *Songbird* (see Figure 8-1). Songbird is somewhat like Firefox and Internet Explorer — the little guy is up against the 800-pound gorilla, which in this case is iTunes. Songbird shows a lot of promise and is turning into a mature and feature-rich program for playing and managing your music. Check it out at `http://getsongbird.com`.

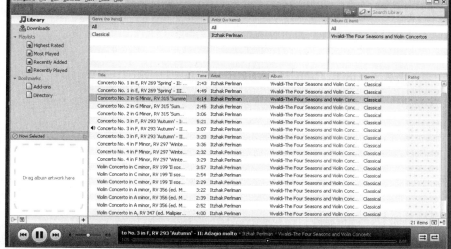

Figure 8-1: The Songbird music player and organizer.

✔ **WinAMP:** Last but not least is the granddaddy of music playing programs, WinAMP, which was released way back in 1997. I have to mention this software for nostalgic reasons as well as recommend it as a simple, no-frills music player that just plain works — particularly the pre-5.0 versions, which don't take up a lot of system resources. One of the other benefits to WinAMP is the large number of add-ons and *skins* (files that customize the appearance and user interface) that are available. You can download the current version of WinAMP at `www.winamp.com` or older versions at `www.oldversion.com/Winamp.html`.

In addition to playing MP3s, your netbook can record MP3 files. By using the netbook's built-in microphone (or plugging in an external mic for better sound quality), you can record lectures, immortalize your baby's first words, or prove to your spouse that he indeed does snore in the middle of the night. Instead of using the Windows sound recorder accessory program, download a copy of Audacity (`http://audacity.sourceforge.net`), a free and powerful sound editor.

Music ripping

Your netbook probably doesn't have a CD-ROM/DVD drive, so how do you listen to your music CD collection? (Even if you do have an external drive, it may be almost as big as your netbook, which doesn't make for a very portable music solution.)

To take your tunes on the road, you need to *rip* your music CD. This means putting the CD in a computer (that has a drive capable of reading CDs) and running a program that copies the music tracks onto the hard drive, saving them in the MP3 file format or another format of your choice. When you're done, copy the files to your netbook and listen away.

My favorite Windows CD ripper is a free, open-source program called CDex (`http://`

`cdexos.sourceforge.net`). It's been around forever but provides everything you need. The MP3 format supports a series of tags that provide information about the file — such as music type, artist, track number, and so on. When you rip music with CDex, you need to manually enter this information. (You don't have to, but your media player uses the tag information to display information when the song plays as well as for searching and sorting.)

Just remember to respect the copyright holder and not give away copies of the ripped tunes to your friends — either in person or over a peer-to-peer (P2P) network.

Streaming audio

Most people know they can play MP3 files on a computer. But you might not be aware of the large number of podcasts (a downloadable audio broadcast) and radio stations that stream music, news, and commentary over the Internet. An example of a streaming radio station is shown in Figure 8-2.

Unlike downloading a music file where you have to wait until the file finishes downloading to play it, *streaming* works by sending a continuous stream of data to your music player. After a certain amount of data is saved to disk (a process called *buffering*), the audio starts to play.

The player continues to download the audio stream, buffering as necessary, until the program is finished. Streaming audio is an efficient way of providing a large amount of data to many people at once. In most cases, the complete audio program isn't permanently saved on your hard drive — a temporary file may be saved but usually is automatically deleted after you quit the music player program.

The cool thing about many of these podcasts and radio stations is they have an international reach — as well as a unique voice outside the typical homogenized corporate media you typically hear on your car radio. If you have a Net connection and live in Heartland America, you can easily tune in to Radio Netherlands to get a European view of world events.

Figure 8-2:
Listen to the music: A radio station streams audio on a netbook.

Try dialing in your netbook to some of the following free Internet radio sites or directories of online stations and podcasts. In most cases, it's just a matter of pointing your Web browser to a site, clicking, and then sitting back and listening.

✔ **Live365,** www.live365.com

✔ **Radio Tower,** www.radiotower.com

✔ **Pandora,** www.pandora.com

✔ **SHOUTCast,** www.shoutcast.com

✔ **Radio Locator,** www.radio-locator.com

✔ **BBC Radio,** www.bbc.co.uk/radio

✔ **National Public Radio (NPR),** www.npr.org

✔ **Podcast Directory,** www.podcastdirectory.com

✔ **Podcast Alley,** www.podcastalley.com

If you're learning a foreign language, international Internet radio stations are a great resource for practicing your listening skills. News programs are a good place to start because the broadcasters speak a little more slowly and really articulate their words.

Remember your netbook's limited memory and processing speed. If you're working on too many things at once, taxing the memory and processor, your music will likely pause and stutter. There's nothing wrong with your netbook. You're just doing more than it can handle at one time.

Viewing Videos

As the old Buggles song goes, "Video killed the radio star." Faster processors and more memory; high-speed Net connections; compressed video formats; peer-to-peer file-sharing networks (legitimately used, of course); and cheap DVD drives have made video on computers as common as rain on a picnic.

Your netbook is no exception, especially considering it's roughly the size of a portable DVD player and can serve double duty as a computer and a movie viewer. The following sections give you the lowdown on viewing videos on your netbook.

DVDs

Even with the advent of high-speed Net connections, a significant number of people still watch movies at home or on the road the old-fashioned way — with a DVD. And you can certainly do this with your netbook, turning it into an inexpensive, personal home theater.

Of course, because your netbook probably doesn't have a built-in DVD drive, you'll need to buy one. I discuss purchasing external DVD drives in Chapter 14.

After you have that little detail taken care of, you can go to the movies! Here's how:

1. **Plug in the external DVD drive into one of your netbook's USB ports — your netbook should be powered on, by the way.**

2. **Insert a movie into the DVD drive.**

3. **Watch the movie (as shown in Figure 8-3).**

Windows should automatically recognize that a movie has been inserted into the drive and will start up Windows Media Player (or whatever your default player is) to play it.

If Windows Media Player won't play the DVD, there's a good chance you're missing a codec that supports DVD viewing (see the "Codec connection" sidebar nearby). You can either download the codec you need, or use another media player that already has the proper codec — my favorite is VLC, which you can download for free at www.videolan.org.

Watching a movie on an external DVD drive drains batteries faster than normal, so consider keeping your netbook plugged in to an electrical outlet during show time if you have the choice.

Figure 8-3:
Big screen on the small screen: watching a DVD movie on a netbook. The experience will make you feel *Spirited Away.*

Most netbooks aren't up to the task of watching Blu-ray and high-definition (HD) movies and streaming TV shows. The little laptops just don't have the graphics horsepower to display the real-as-life videos. Newer netbook models are becoming available with faster graphics processors, though. If HD is a big deal for you, shop around for a netbook that's rated (and reviewed) to handle high definition.

Ripping movies

If you own a movie on a DVD but don't have an external DVD player for your netbook, it's still possible to watch the movie on your little laptop. This involves a technique known as *ripping*. Ripping is the process of copying a movie from a DVD and then converting it to a compressed file that can be stored and played on a computer. (DVD rippers are different from the CD rippers I describe in the "Music ripping" sidebar in this chapter — you typically need separate programs to rip music and movies.)

A movie DVD contains a number of different audio and video files. The primary tasks of a ripping program are copying the appropriate files and then combining them into a single compressed file that you can watch on your computer.

To rip a movie on a DVD, you need the following:

✔ **A computer with a DVD drive:** The faster the processor and more memory, the better.

✔ **A ripping program:** Free options include Handbrake (`http://hand brake.fr`) and AutoGK (`www.autogk.me.uk`, shown in Figure 8-4). You run the ripping program on the computer with a DVD drive. (Even if you have an external DVD drive for your netbook, I still recommend ripping on a computer with a faster processor and more memory unless you want to wait for a very long time.)

Most DVD movies are protected with an encryption scheme to prevent piracy. Many DVD-ripping programs attempt to bypass the copy protection to create an unprotected file that can be played on any computer. However, in some cases, you may not be able to make a copy of a movie due to the protection scheme.

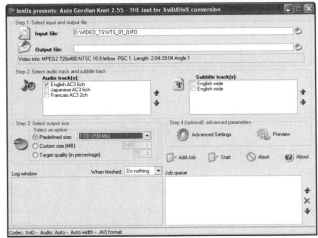

Figure 8-4: The AutoGK ripping program for copying DVD movies to your netbook.

When you've ripped the movie, copy it to a USB flash drive and then move it to your netbook for viewing. You can use Windows Media Player or another player — my favorite is VLC, which you can download for free from `www.videolan.org/vlc`. If the movie doesn't play correctly, you're likely missing a codec. See the "Codec connection" sidebar for more information.

Ripping copyrighted material for personal use isn't considered a crime in many countries. However, if you rip a movie and give a copy to a friend, that is an illegal copyright violation — unless you live in a country that permits it.

Codec connection

If you rip a movie and it doesn't play (you get sound but no video or video and no sound), there's a good chance an associated codec isn't present on your netbook. A *codec* (which stands for coder-decoder or compressor-decompressor) is a program (or file with instructions for a program) that compresses or decompresses digital audio and video. Depending on how the video was encoded, you may need to install a specific codec to view it.

One of the most common file extensions for ripped movies is AVI (Audio Video Interleave). An AVI file is a container that can store different types of encoded videos — such as DivX or Xvid formats. Although most media players can play AVI files, if the appropriate codec hasn't been installed (for example, one that decodes an Xvid video), you won't be able to watch the movie.

If you have an Internet connection, some media players will attempt to download and install the required codec. The easiest solution is to download the K-Lite Codec Pack from `http://codecguide.com`. This is a free collection of just about every codec you'll ever need to watch videos — currently around 15MB in size. Follow the instructions for installing the latest version of the pack, restart your media player, and then break out the popcorn and enjoy the movie.

There's a lot more to DVD ripping than I have the space to describe. The best place to get all the information is `www.doom9.org`. There you can find a full set of tutorials and various useful programs to download.

Movies ripped by other people are available on the Net, and you can find them readily on popular BitTorrent sites. However, in many countries (such as the U.S.), downloading these videos is illegal because it violates copyright laws. Know the laws in your own country and understand that prohibited downloading may result in legal action, a fine, your Internet provider canceling your account, or all of the above.

Streaming video

Streaming video is just like streaming audio (check out the earlier "Streaming audio" section for a general discussion on streaming) with video data added to the audio. You typically don't need a separate program to watch streaming video — just point your Web browser at a site, click, and then sit back and start munching some popcorn. (There's a small chance your Web browser may need a plug-in installed before you can view the video.)

The Net has lots of streaming video content these days, but here is a collection of Web sites I recommend for getting your video fix:

- **YouTube:** (www.youtube.com) This is the original "anyone can be a filmmaker, post your own videos" site. Aside from all the amateur content, some of which is pretty good, YouTube has started to add TV shows and movies in a new Shows section.

- **Hulu:** (www.hulu.com) This Web site provides commercial-supported streaming video of TV shows and movies from NBC, Fox, and other networks and studios. (Figure 8-5 shows Hulu in action.)

- **Joost:** (www.joost.com)An innovative Internet TV service from the founders of Kazaa and Skype.

- **Crackle:** (www.crackle.com) A Sony Pictures Entertainment site featuring free movies and TV shows.

- **Netflix:** (www.netflix.com) If you have a Netflix account, don't forget you can view a number of movies online in addition to getting DVDs through the mail.

- **Surf the Channel:** (www.surfthechannel.com) This site doesn't stream TV shows but is a search engine for finding sites that do stream your favorite shows.

- **TV.com:** (www.tv.com) This CBS-owned Web site is starting to offer streaming videos similar to content on Hulu.

Figure 8-5: You can watch old TV shows on a netbook with Hulu. Everybody needs a vice (specifically, a *Miami Vice*) or two.

If you're a TV junkie, many networks are offering streaming videos of their shows directly from their main corporate Web sites — for example, www.nbc.com.

Flash dance

This section is about streaming video, but this sidebar isn't a link to the old Jennifer Beals movie — sorry. Instead, I want to talk a little about Flash Video. Quite a lot of the video you watch on the Net these days is delivered in Flash Video (FLV) format — YouTube is an example. Most Web browsers come with an Adobe Flash Player plug-in, which allows you to watch a video inside your browser.

The Web server streams the video, and Flash Player saves incoming video data *(buffering)* and plays it. If you've ever had a video abruptly stop and then restart, it's because the player is waiting for more data to continue; otherwise, enough of the video hasn't been buffered yet.

Most streaming video Web sites don't offer you an option of saving the video to your hard drive. If you want to watch it again, you need to connect to the Net and revisit the Web site. However, because of the way Flash Video works, you can save video from some sites directly to your netbook.

The Flash Player creates a temporary file as the video is streamed. It's possible to rename this file and have a video you can open and watch whenever you like. A number of Web sites make this process simple — you can do a Google search for *YouTube flv* to find some such sites. You supply a link to a video (such as from YouTube), and the Web site saves the FLV file to your hard drive.

Another approach to saving Flash videos is to use a browser add-on program — I like DownloadHelp for Firefox. With these add-ons, whenever a Flash video is shown in your browser, you can click a menu item to save the file. Check your browser's add-on page to find an FLV utility — for Firefox, go to `https://addons.mozilla.org`.

Web sites that offer commercial videos (such as Hulu.com) stream Flash in a way that a temporary file isn't saved to disk — mostly as a form of copy protection. In these cases, you're out of luck if you want to save a video. A few products on the market claim to be able to save protected videos, but new protection schemes are then quickly introduced to thwart the programs.

Instead of using a Net connection to watch TV, you can go retro and pluck television signals from the airwaves and view shows on your netbook. I discuss TV tuners in Chapter 15.

Both Hulu and YouTube Shows currently restrict viewing to computers in the United States. With a little technical know-how and a proxy server, it's possible for international viewers to watch U.S. only video content. Use Google to find out more.

Some Internet providers are starting to charge by the amount of bandwidth used. That means you can upload and download only a fixed number of gigabytes each month based on a subscription level. If you exceed the amount, you pay more. (This is similar to cell phone plans where you have a set number of minutes.) If your Net provider is metering your service, keep in mind streaming video can consume a lot of bandwidth.

Shall We Play a Game?

I need to talk to you about games. I don't mean Solitaire and Minesweeper, but action games like Crysis, Half-Life 2, or Counter-Strike: Source. If these names don't ring a bell, consider this section optional reading.

If you just got a netbook and are a gamer, you're probably dying to load up your favorite games and start playing. But hold your horses: You need to know a few things before you can start blasting away with your plasma rifle.

Bonus points if you can name the movie this section heading refers to. Give up? It's *War Games* (1983), starring Matthew Broderick as a student who saves the world from a war-gaming super-computer. It was actually nominated for a couple of Academy Awards and was one of the first hacker flicks to come out of Hollywood.

Netbook limitations

First off, a netbook is not a game machine. Yes, it's a computer and runs Windows, so it should theoretically run popular Windows games. But there are five things going against a netbook when it comes to playing games.

These limitations apply to graphics-intensive, 3-D commercial games or multiplayer Internet games. A netbook can easily handle less-resource-intensive games like Tetris, Solitaire, and other popular time wasters.

The five limitations are

- **Screen size:** A 10-inch (or less) screen just doesn't cut it with some games — either in terms of usability or game requirements; for example, some games require 1024 x 768 resolution. There's not much you can do about this without hooking up an external monitor.

- **Processor:** The Atom processor isn't what you'd call a rocket ship, and you'll experience considerable lag on some games compared with playing games on laptops or desktop PCs equipped with faster chips.

  The more the chip has to work, the hotter the netbook gets. I've found some games can get a netbook case uncomfortably warm when it's perched on my lap.

- **Graphics chipset:** This is the biggest stumbling block for playing modern 3-D games. Many best selling computer games require a cutting-edge graphics card that supports 3-D animation to present realistic video. Currently, most netbooks have graphics chipsets more suitable for business or basic home PCs, not full-on game computers — a few are starting to appear with decent graphics processors, though.

✔ **Memory:** The more memory the better, and although netbooks sporting 1 or 2GB of RAM are usable, more is always preferred — but you're stuck due to Microsoft's licensing stipulation that states netbooks running XP can have a maximum of 2GB of RAM. The same limitation will likely exist with Windows 7.

✔ **CD/DVD player:** If you don't have an external DVD drive to install the game, you're stuck.

It's sometimes possible to get around a missing DVD drive with a little trickery. On a PC with a DVD player, use a DVD copy program to create an ISO image of the entire DVD. Copy the ISO file to your netbook's hard drive and then use version 3.47 of Daemon Tools (www.oldversion.com/Daemon-Tools.html) to mount the ISO file. Daemon Tools emulates a CD-ROM drive, and the installer will think you have an optical drive and that the game DVD is inserted.

It might seem like I've painted a bleak picture for gaming on a netbook. You really need to accept a netbook's hardware limitations and try not to turn the little laptop into something that it's not.

Don't give up hope, though. Lots of games can run on a netbook. For example, if you have any older games lying around the house gathering dust like Half-Life 2, Starcraft, and Diablo, give them a try. A screen from the original Call of Duty is shown in Figure 8-6. On most netbooks, the oldie-but-goodie games run fine, and because you probably haven't played them in awhile, it will be just like getting a new game — with a bit of déjà vu.

Figure 8-6: Older games like Call of Duty work fine on most netbooks.

Internet resources for netbook gamers

Instead of playing test pilot (or crash-test dummy as the case may be) and spending a bunch of time seeing whether a favorite game works on your netbook, I suggest you save possible frustration and first check whether anyone else has had success. The Internet is perfect for this, and the resources that I mention in this section can help.

Because of the hardware similarities among netbooks, if someone reports having success getting a game to play on one particular brand and model of netbook, there's a pretty good chance it will work on a different brand, too. In other words, if you have an Acer netbook, don't immediately think because I list an ASUS Web site here that it doesn't provide useful information.

✔ **Gameeer.com:** (www.bourdeaux.net/eeepc) The ASUS Eee PC site has an extensive list of games that work and don't work on an Eee PC 900 20G running Windows XP.

✔ **EeeUser.com Forum:** (http://forum.eeeuser.com/viewforum. php?id=28) Check the gaming section of this popular Eee PC user forum for an extensive list of games — as well as tips and hints for getting games working.

✔ **Acer Aspire One User Forums:** (www.aspireoneuser.com/forum/ viewforum.php?f=21) This site has a game-related forum for Acer users.

✔ **MyDellMini Forums:** (http://mydellmini.com/forum/list-of-games-that-play-on-the-mini-t639.html) Here you find a list of games that work, don't work, or sort of work on Dell Minis.

✔ **Freeware Windows XP games:** (http://home.comcast. net/~SupportCD/XPGames.html) You can find many Windows XP–compatible games out there, including some very good free ones. Although I can't promise that all the games listed on this Web site will work with every model of netbook, it's still a worthwhile reference.

Chapter 9

Better Safe than Sorry: Security

*T*his chapter is about netbook security. "Ho, hum," you probably say. "He's going to rehash all that stuff I've already heard about scary viruses, programs called firewalls, and other things that frankly I find boring."

Actually I'm not. After spending a whole lot of years advising corporations, organizations, and government agencies on computer security, I'm tired of using fear, uncertainty, and doubt (FUD) to get people to adopt more secure computing practices. So I'm not telling you evil-hacker, boogieman stories or top-ten reasons why you should use security software. You're already bombarded with enough of that stuff in the media as it is.

Instead, how about if I treat you like a grown-up who's going to make his or her own decisions about how much and what types of security to use? No scolding, threats, or browbeating. Sound like a deal? If so, great, because in this chapter, I dispense with the hype and boil down what you need to know about basic netbook security practices, including antivirus software, spyware detection programs, personal firewalls, encryption, and locks for physically securing your netbook. You might even find out something new, so read on.

Glossary of gotchas

Here's a collection of computer-security terms you may have read or heard about. I'm guessing you're aware of at least half of them. If you recognize more than that, give yourself a gold star for being security savvy:

- ✔ **Adware:** A program that displays advertisements after the software has been installed or while it's being used — typically without your knowledge or permission.

- ✔ **Botnet:** As in ro**bot net**work. A collection of zombie computers (see *zombie* in this list) that's used for malicious purposes such as spamming or *denial of service attacks* (where a Web site is bombarded with traffic, preventing use).

- ✔ **Malware:** As in **mal**icious soft**ware**. A term that encompasses Trojan horses, viruses, worms, and other software meant to harm you or your computer.

- ✔ **Rootkit:** A program or collection of programs designed to hide the fact that someone has broken into a computer. For example, certain system files that could reveal that a computer has been compromised might be replaced by rootkit files to hide the attack or provide a backdoor for future unauthorized access.

- ✔ **Spyware:** A program installed on a computer without your knowledge to covertly collect information on you, your computer, or how you use the computer.

- ✔ **Trojan horse:** Just like in the old Greek story, a program pretends to be something else while concealing a more nefarious purpose — in other words, beware of geeks bearing gifts.

- ✔ **Virus:** An up-to-no-good program that can copy itself and infect your computer without your knowing about it.

- ✔ **Worm:** A self-replicating program that sends copies of itself to other computers on a network. Unlike a virus, worms don't attach themselves to a program but still perform varying degrees of mischief.

- ✔ **Zombie:** A computer that is secretly under the remote control of someone else — again, typically for malicious purposes.

Keeping Viruses at Bay

Brush your teeth after meals, clean your plate, wear clean underwear, and always run antivirus software. Yeah, yeah, yeah. I said I wasn't going to be your mother when it comes to computer security, and I mean it.

You already know about viruses and that you should be running some kind of antivirus program — especially if you have a Windows netbook. Little laptops running Linux are much more immune to getting bad infections.

Let me start by saying that many netbooks come with trial subscriptions of commercial security products. These programs provide you with updated virus and malware protection for a set period of time and then require you to purchase the services after the initial trial (or future subscription period) ends. It's usually a fairly nominal fee, and many computer users automatically break out the credit card for peace of mind.

That's your choice, but personally I'm not overly enamored with these security suites. They tend to be big and consume a bunch of memory and processor cycles — both of which are at a premium in a netbook.

If you don't feel like shelling out hard-earned bucks after a trial period, or if you don't appreciate the system performance slowdowns security suites often cause, or if your netbook doesn't come preinstalled with antivirus software, here's what I suggest: There are three free Windows programs that provide you with real-time virus protection — the software runs in the background and is always on the lookout for viruses. These programs all offer basic virus protection, and you can get for-pay versions of the programs with more advanced features. Coincidentally, all the software names start with the letter *A*:

- **avast!:** (www.avast.com) avast! is a very popular, free antivirus program that hails from the Czech Republic. It first came out in 1988, and as of the spring of 2009, it has over 50 million registered users worldwide. The software has a number of different features that protect you from all sorts of malicious threats. Download the free version and get more information at the avast! Web site.

- **AVG:** (http://free.grisoft.com) AVG is another widely used antivirus application from the former Czechoslovakia. (Do the Czechs know viruses or what?) avast! has a few more features and a cleaner interface in my opinion.

- **AntiVir:** (www.avira.com) No, not another Czech security program. This one is from German company Avira and is well-suited for netbooks because of its low system requirements — it also gets good marks from users and reviewers.

I recommend downloading and evaluating all of these programs to see which one works best for you.

The three free antivirus programs I mention in the preceding section certainly aren't the only game in town. You can also find a slew of other commercial and free alternatives. Even Microsoft is aiming to get into the free antivirus game — the Redmond giant has announced a product tentatively called Microsoft Security Essentials, which will likely be available by the time you read this.

Online antidotes

Viruses, Trojan horses, and other related ilk have grown considerably more sophisticated over the years. A good virus (good for the virus writer, bad for you) can detect that antivirus and other security applications are running and then attempt to circumvent the good-guy programs.

If you think your netbook is infected with a virus that has somehow managed to beat your security software, don't panic. Several free virus utilities can work over the Internet through your Web browser. They can detect and often remove any nasties that may have breached your defenses. Point your browser to one of the services listed here and follow the instructions:

✔ **TrendMicro HouseCall,** `http://house call.antivirus.com/`

✔ **Symantec SecurityCheck,** `http:// security.symantec.com/`

✔ **McAfee Virusscan Online,** `http:// us.mcafee.com/root/mfs/ default.asp`

An online antivirus program should never replace its standalone cousin because it doesn't perform real-time scanning and it requires a Net connection. However, it's a great supplementary security tool and is perfect if you ever need to provide technical support over the phone to a friend or family member who is suffering from mysterious netbook problems that may be virus-related.

The main downsides to these online antidotes are they can be a bit slow and some services run only with Internet Explorer.

Instead of giving you a laundry list of software, I suggest you check out some independent online resources that list and rate antivirus packages. That way you can pick a solution that you like the best. My top information sources are

✔ **Virus Bulletin,** `www.virusbtn.com/index`

✔ **AV.Test,** `http://av-test.org`

✔ **AV Comparatives,** `www.av-comparatives.org`

Your netbook's startup time increases when you use antivirus software that provides real-time protection. More system resources are also used because the program is always running. An alternative is to use the open-source ClamAV utility (`www.clamav.net`). ClamAV searches for viruses and Trojan horses only when you run the program (which means no real-time protection). If you have a low risk of picking up a virus, use this program to scan your drive every week or so to check for infections.

Zapping Spyware

If you didn't read the "Glossary of gotchas" sidebar near the beginning of this chapter, *spyware* is a general term that relates to any ill-intentioned, eavesdropping program or file that is installed on your PC without your knowledge. Spyware is designed to take control or monitor your computer — without your permission.

Spyware can be covertly installed on your computer when you run a program or visit a Web site. It's very pervasive these days (especially targeted at Windows PCs), but the good news is that a number of free and commercial utilities can detect and remove unwanted snooping pests. The following sections discuss several free ones.

Call me paranoid, but I have all three of the following programs installed on my netbook. In the past, there have been times when I've found that one utility can detect and deal with something malicious that the others missed.

Ad-Aware Free

Ad-Aware Free started out as a utility for alerting users to advertising Web sites that were secretly tracking your visits. Since then, the program has evolved into a complete spyware detection and removal tool. It identifies dialers (programs that make long distance phone calls and you get the bill), Trojan horses, keyloggers (programs that monitor what keys you press), browser hijackers, and other privacy-violating malware. For more information and to download the program, visit `www.lavasoft.com`.

Spybot-S&D

Spybot-S&D (for Search and Destroy) is the granddaddy of spyware detection and removal programs. Although it's been around forever, it's still a valuable tool to have in your protection arsenal. You can find out about it at `www.safer-networking.org`.

CCleaner

CCleaner (the first C stands for Crap) really isn't a dedicated spyware detector per se. Instead, it cleans up temporary files, browser histories, cookies, and unused registry entries. Although spyware can hide data in some of these places, CCleaner is even more indispensable on a netbook with a small drive because it gets rid of unneeded files that take up valuable space. To download the utility, go to `www.ccleaner.com`.

Focusing on Firewalls

Most home and business computer users connect to the Internet through routers and switches. In addition to allowing multiple computers to share to a single Internet connection (DSL, cable, T1 line, and so on), these hardware devices also serve as firewalls to the Internet — keeping you safe from hackers trying to break into your computer.

But what about when you connect to the Internet with your netbook in a coffee shop, park, fast food restaurant, or other place? Heck, you have no idea how secure the hotspot connection is and what security measures are being used. Me, I don't like cowering in fear when I use my netbook, so a software firewall is always running when I'm on the Net on the road.

Firewall programs (often called *personal firewalls*) control network traffic coming into and going out of your computer. You permit or deny certain types of traffic based on rules you establish — for example, you could create a rule that allows incoming and outgoing Internet traffic for your Web browser. If network traffic occurs that doesn't conform to a rule, the firewall notifies you, and you have the option of blocking the connection.

Even if you're protected by a hardware firewall such as a router or switch, it's cheap insurance to run firewall software. Besides being a redundant system, firewall software packages often include additional security features to help you keep the bad guys out.

What firewall would I recommend? I'm glad you asked.

Windows Firewall

Windows XP comes preinstalled with a firewall. The problem is this firewall is a little like using Paint — it's free, comes with a computer, and has limited functionality. What I don't like about the Windows firewall is it doesn't identify or allow you to control outbound connections. That means if a malware program somehow gets onto your netbook and tries to covertly phone home (connect to a server over the Internet to send eavesdropped or stolen data), the Windows firewall isn't going to alert you. This is not a good thing, especially because just about every commercial and free firewall program lets you set up rules for allowing and disallowing outgoing Net connections.

If you're using the Windows firewall, I suggest you download and install one of the alternative programs I list in the following section and then turn off the Microsoft firewall and let the other firewall assume guard duty.

The firewalls that come with Vista and Windows 7 protect you against potentially harmful outbound connections and include a number of more advanced features. In other words, if you're running Vista or Windows 7 on a netbook, you should be fine with the default firewall.

Firewall alternatives

If you want a more substantial firewall than the one that comes with Windows XP, and I recommend that you should, you have many choices. The market is filled with free and commercial offerings.

Your netbook may have a trial version of a security suite that comes with a firewall. If you read the previous section on antivirus software, you know I'm not a big fan of security suites because they tend to eat up system resources like memory and processor cycles. Instead, I recommend an *à la carte* approach, using individual security programs of your own choosing,

By now, you should have a pretty good idea that I'm value-minded — or a cheapskate, take your pick. Considering that, here are three free firewall programs you should consider:

- **Comodo Internet Security,** `http://personalfirewall.comodo.com`
- **PC Tools Firewall Plus,** `www.pctools.com/firewall`
- **Online Armor Personal Firewall,** `www.tallemu.com/free-fire wall-protection-software.html`

After you've installed a personal firewall, it needs a little training. That means a dialog box will pop up every now and then, asking whether it's all right that a program you're running is connecting to the Internet. This is normal, and your responses teach the firewall each time so it won't be constantly bugging you. If you want to get advanced, you can also create a list of rules for the firewall to allow or disallow certain programs or connections via certain ports (with network protocols). An example of this is shown in Figure 9-1 with the Comodo firewall.

PC pioneer Steve Gibson offers a free Web service called ShieldsUP! that tests how much protection your current firewall and security configuration provide against Net no-good-niks. Check it out at `www.grc.com`.

Windows firewalls rated

My favorite resource for making sense of the large number of free and commercial Windows firewalls on the market is Matousec, an independent security firm that provides firewall ratings. Matousec cuts through the advertising hype, applying a set of rigorous tests to see which firewalls cut the mustard — and which are full of hot air.

The results may surprise you. To check out the ratings (and other detailed information), visit `www.matousec.com/projects/fire wall-challenge`.

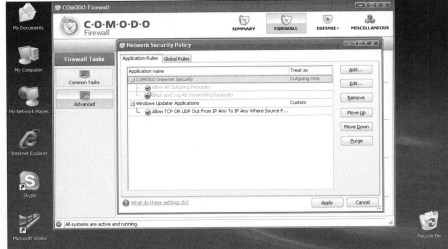

Figure 9-1:
The Comodo firewall rule set for allowing and disallowing network access.

Evading Evil (with Encryption)

One of the biggest benefits of a netbook is also one of its main vulnerabilities. Because a netbook is so small and light, it's easy for someone to snatch it if you leave the laptop unattended or if you aren't paying attention. Plus, its diminutive dimensions put the netbook at risk for accidental loss. It's not as bad as a cell phone, but you can still easily slip it out of a bag or leave it behind at the local coffee shop.

If one day your netbook disappears, never to be seen again, you'll be out the replacement cost. But a bigger concern is what's on your netbook — you do back it up on a regular basis, don't you?

Aside from backing up the Great American Novel you're working on and your favorite MP3s, you should think about backing up any personal or financial information that resides on your netbook. Identity theft is a big deal, and if you have any files that contain your Social Security number, credit card numbers, or other sensitive and personal information, there's always a chance it could fall into less-than-honest hands. (Okay, I promised not to tell any scary stories, but I just couldn't help myself.)

Even using a password when Windows starts up may not keep files safe from prying eyes. If someone with basic hacking skills has physical access to any password-protected Windows netbook, there's a good chance he or she will be able to defeat the login security and get at the files.

Most netbooks don't enable Windows startup password protection by default. To turn it on, in the Windows Control Panel select User Accounts. A somewhat more secure way of password protecting a netbook is to use a BIOS password, which I discuss in Chapter 21.

The way to protect critical documents is with encryption. In simple terms, *encryption* means employing a program that scrambles the contents of a file so only a person who knows an associated password can access the information. I spend a little time telling you about one of my favorite Windows encryption programs. It's called TrueCrypt, and it's a powerful (and free) way to keep your files safe.

Finding out about TrueCrypt

TrueCrypt is a free, open-source program that allows you to secure your files. This is industrial-strength encryption that even those three-letter-acronym government spy organizations would have difficulty cracking.

Before launching into specifics, you should know the two types of encryption programs:

- **File encryption:** An individual file is scrambled. (See the "File locker" sidebar.)
- **Disk encryption:** An entire volume is scrambled.

TrueCrypt is a disk encryption program. You can use it three different ways:

- Create an encrypted *virtual volume* — a file container that can be mounted and used like a storage device (such as a USB flash memory drive or hard drive).
- Encrypt an entire partition or storage device.
- Encrypt a system disk partition or volume where Windows is installed.

File locker

I recommend using file encryption anytime you're storing sensitive files on the Internet. Although online storage sites may tout strong security procedures, you should shoulder the ultimate responsibility for your own file security. In addition, you may want to use file encryption if you have only a few sensitive files on your netbook and don't need a disk encryption solution like TrueCrypt.

When it comes to file encryption, I recommend giving potential snoopers the axe — the AxCrypt, to be precise.

AxCrypt is an easy-to-use shareware encryption program. It integrates with Windows Explorer, so it's simply a matter of right-clicking on a file and selecting Encrypt from the AxCrypt context menu. Enter a password or passphrase and *voilà,* the file is encrypted. (Use the reverse procedure to decrypt a file.)

You can download AxCrypt from www.ax antum.com/AxCrypt.

The University of Delaware has a simple tutorial if you'd like to find out more: www.udel.edu/ pnpi/tools/encrypt/win/axcrypt/ index.html.

In the following sections, I cover creating and using encrypted virtual volumes. Because many people don't know about TrueCrypt, I go into step-by-step detail on a few of the basics. Read the documentation that comes with the program (you can download it from www.truecrypt.org) to find out how to encrypt partitions and use other advanced TrueCrypt features.

Creating a TrueCrypt volume

First, download and install TrueCrypt. Versions are available for Windows, Linux, and the Mac, so no matter what operating system your netbook is running, you should be able to use the program.

Here's all you have to do:

1. **Run TrueCrypt.**
2. **Click the Create Volume button.**

   This starts the TrueCrypt Volume Creation Wizard.
3. **Make sure the Create a File Container radio button is selected and click Next.**
4. **Select the Standard TrueCrypt Volume radio button and click Next.**

5. **Click the Select File button.**

6. **Create a file container, specifying the filename and location. Click Next to continue.**

7. **Select the encryption and hash algorithm types and click Next. (See Figure 9-2.)**

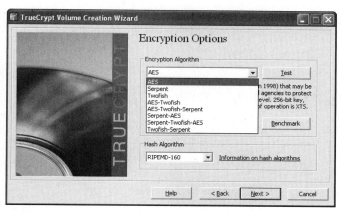

Figure 9-2: Specify the encryption algorithm when creating a TrueCrypt volume.

TrueCrypt supports a number of different encryption algorithms. The default is AES, a strong encryption method standardized by the U.S. government. The default hash algorithm is RIPEMD-160. Use the default settings — unless you're a techie and have a good reason not to. You can find out more about these algorithms by clicking the information links in the dialog box.

8. **Enter the size of the file container and click Next.**

Make sure the container size will be big enough to store all the files you want to encrypt. You can specify a size in either K (kilobytes) or MB (megabytes).

9. **Enter a password (twice for confirmation) and click Next.**

Use a strong password when creating a TrueCrypt volume. A weak password (such as one that is easy to guess, short in length, or contains only alphabetic characters in the same case) can render a strong encryption algorithm useless. Your password should be a combination of numbers, letters, and punctuation marks — the longer and harder to guess, the better. Combine multiple words or use an easy-to-remember phrase.

10. **Enter information about the volume format and then click Format button.**

You can use the default settings. Move the mouse randomly inside the dialog box to generate random numbers for the encryption algorithm to use.

A window informs you that the volume has successfully been created.

11. **Click Exit to return to the main TrueCrypt user interface.**

You're now ready to add files you want to encrypt to the volume you just created.

Opening a TrueCrypt volume

Before you can copy files to an encrypted TrueCrypt volume or access files that you have stored in that volume, you need to open the volume. Here's how:

1. **Run TrueCrypt.**

2. **In the large text box, select a free volume letter.**

Such as X:, Y:, or Z:.

3. **Click the Select File button.**

4. **Choose the file container you previously created and click Open.**

5. **Click the Mount button.**

6. **Enter the password you associated with the volume and click OK.**

Information about the volume now appears in the list. For example, if you selected Z: as the volume, the file container name, size and encryption algorithm appear next to Z: (as shown in Figure 9-3).

TrueCrypt interacts with the operating system and Windows treats the file container just like a folder or hard drive.

Accessing files in a TrueCrypt volume

After you've opened and mounted a TrueCrypt volume, it behaves exactly like a hard drive or USB flash drive does under Windows (as shown in Figure 9-4):

✔ In Explorer (right click Start and select Explore), drag and drop files to copy or move them to and from the volume.

✔ Double-click a file on the encrypted volume to open it.

✔ From inside a program, access a file with the Open command in the File menu.

As long as a TrueCrypt volume is mounted, it's business as usual when it comes to accessing files.

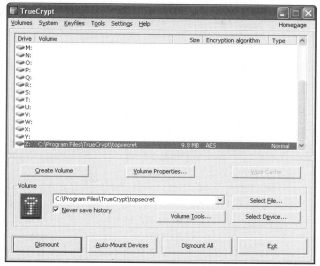

Figure 9-3:
A TrueCrypt
file
container
mounted as
volume Z:.

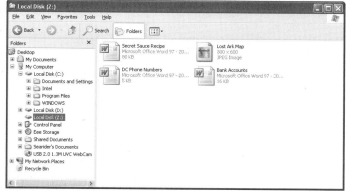

Figure 9-4:
A mounted
TrueCrypt
volume is
just like
any other
Windows
volume
when you're
working
with files.

Be sure to delete the original file after you copy it to the TrueCrypt volume. If you don't, theoretically, someone could access the original, unencrypted version.

Technically speaking, even after you move a file into the Windows Recycle Bin and empty it, the file still exists on the hard drive. Some file recovery programs can restore the contents of a deleted file. To eliminate this vulnerability, use a secure erasing program — my favorite is Eraser, which you can download for free at www.heidi.ie/eraser. These programs overwrite the contents of files before they're deleted. If someone uses a file-recovery utility on a securely erased file, he's out of luck in viewing the original contents.

Closing a TrueCrypt volume

When you're finished accessing files in the encrypted volume, it's time to lock them up. Here's the procedure:

1. **Make sure all files in the volume you've been working with are closed.**

2. **Select the volume you want to close in the TrueCrypt volume list.**

3. **Click the Dismount button.**

This closes the volume — file container information no longer appears next to the volume letter. In addition, this volume is no longer available to Windows.

The only way anyone can access the documents in the file container is if he runs TrueCrypt, selects the container file, and mounts it with the correct password. This means if your netbook takes a hike, either accidentally or with a thief, you don't have to worry about any sensitive documents falling into the wrong hands.

Keying in on Kensington Locks

Most laptop cases, and netbooks are no exception, have a small slot molded into the side or back for attaching a security cable. The idea is you can secure your computer to some big, relatively immovable object (desk, table, chair, fence, park bench, and so on), so if you temporarily need to leave your netbook unattended, it will be there when you get back. Here's the scoop on this antitheft system.

The Kensington Security Slot has been around since 1990. Kensington Computer Products, which makes accessories for computers, sold a group of computer manufacturers on the idea of providing a simple way of securing laptops, monitors, desktop PCs and other electronic equipment. By incorporating a small, metal-backed slot in the case design, security-conscious users could purchase a patented cable lock from Kensington. "That makes sense," the manufacturers said because adding a slot wouldn't be a big expense. And thus a standard was born.

Kensington locks (one is shown in Figure 9-5) feature a plastic-coated cable with a lock on one end and a loop on the other. The lock is simple to use.

1. **Find some difficult-to-move object (park bench, table, pipe, Congress, and so on).**

2. **Thread the lock end of the cable through the loop end and secure the cable to the object.**

   Just make sure the cable can't be easily slipped off whatever you attach it to. Don't do something like secure the cable to a table leg if the table could be easily lifted and the loop slid down the leg.

3. **Insert the lock end into your netbook's security slot.**

4. **Lock it up.**

That's it. You can now wander off, safe in the knowledge that your netbook is secure — however, be sure to read the "Pros and cons" sidebar.

Kensington offers several different models, featuring two types of locks: one that uses a key and another that employs a combination lock. If you shop around, expect to pay around $40 for a Kensington lock.

Other manufacturers make similar locks, but Kensington models tend to get the highest user ratings.

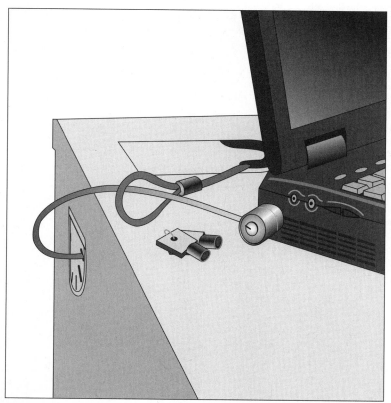

Figure 9-5:
A Kensington lock for securing your netbook.

Pros and cons

I know a guy who happens to know a guy who knows a guy who knows a thing or two about locks. Let's just say he's been locked up a time or two for getting caught doing things to locks he shouldn't have. His name is Spike, and I recently paid him a visit to get his professional opinion on Kensington-type lock systems. Here's what he had to say.

"Let me put it this way. And I'm just talking in theoretical terms, okay? Certainly not from practical experience. There are three weaknesses to these kinds of locks.

"First, the computer case. It's plastic right? You don't have to be a gorilla like me to grab a locked-up laptop, start yanking on the computer really hard, and rip the lock out of the case. Yeah it may leave a big, jagged hole, but you just tell people it's a manufacturer's defect, which is the reason you're selling it so cheap. Heh, heh.

"Number two, the cable. If the bad guy has the time and not too many people are around, he can just whip out a little pocket saw. You want the thickest cable available to slow down cutting.

"And last, the lock. You have your choice of a tubular lock or a combination lock. Some people think because I bench press 300 pounds, I'm a brute force kind of guy. *Au contraire*. I prefer finesse over muscle, and some of these locks are very easy to defeat by manipulation. You don't believe me? Try searching YouTube for *Kensington lock*. The proof is in the videos. Word on the street is the lock company made some improvements, but I can't personally vouch for that.

"I want to say one more thing before time is up and I need to go back to my cell, uh, I mean *temporary domicile*. This kind of lock works great for keeping honest people honest — seeing an unattended netbook securely cabled to a table greatly reduces the temptation of someone walking by, picking it up, and strolling away with it. But if it were me, I would never leave my netbook all by its lonesome — locked up or not. Well, got to go now, pal. Enjoy life on the outside; I'll look you up in a couple years."

Chapter 10

Staying in Touch: Twitter, Social Networking, IM, and Skype

The bring-anywhere, do-anything nature of a netbook makes it ideal for a number of popular Internet social networking and communication services. Wherever there's a Wi-Fi connection, you can use your netbook to stay in touch with friends, family, and co-workers — and I'm not talking about e-mail. E-mail is so old school.

Using the Internet as a foundation, many innovative ways of communicating electronically have appeared. Social networking sites such as Twitter, MySpace, and Facebook and programs like Skype and instant messaging clients have all redefined how people interact.

This new generation of communication tools is especially well suited to netbooks, and if you're not already using some of these Web sites and programs, it's worthwhile to find out more.

In this chapter, I tell you what you need to know about these tools so you can try them out. I provide a general introduction, how to get started using them, and where to go for more information. (If you're an experienced social networker, feel free to skim this chapter. You never know though — you might find out something new.)

Social networking defined

You hear the term *social networking* used quite a bit these days, but what exactly is it? Social networking refers to Internet services that are used to build online communities. These communities consist of people who share similar interests or activities. Social networking Web sites provide a way for people to interact — through forums, e-mail, instant messaging, and blogs.

Social networking isn't new and can be traced back to bulletin board services (BBSs), USENET (Internet newsgroups), and e-mail listservs — all of which emerged in the 1970s and '80s.

However, it wasn't until the World Wide Web took off in the 1990s that social networking really blossomed. Web sites such as Geocities, Tripod, and Classmates.com were early pioneers, followed by hugely successful sites including MySpace, Facebook, and LinkedIn.

Social networking is often associated with *Web 2.0* — another buzzword that refers to the next generation of Web site development and design. Whereas first-generation Web sites mainly provided information, Web 2.0 is all about communication, facilitation, sharing, and collaboration.

Of Twitter and Tweets

Twitter is all over the news these days. It's the latest hot Internet-related thing. Oprah tweets with celebs (it took awhile, but she finally figured it out), the CDC tweets about flu, Lance Armstrong tweets about training and bike racing, and everyday people tweet about everyday stuff. Just what's up with all this tweeting and exactly what is Twitter?

Twitter (www.twitter.com) is a free *microblogging* Web site — it's been around since 2006. You probably already know about *blogging* — Web logging, where someone posts an online journal. Twitter is the same idea except a posted message can be no more than 140 characters — these posts are called *tweets*. People, known as *followers,* subscribe to tweets. You have the option of limiting who your tweets go out to (such as friends and family who subscribe), or you can open up subscriptions to anyone.

People seem to either love Twitter or hate it. The service's critics view the majority of tweets as time wasting, ego-driven, stream-of-conscious ramblings. Twitter fans argue that the service is a valid form of modern-day expression and communication and good tweets are informational and useful — in addition, following some of the less-useful tweets is a nice diversion from reality.

I say give Twitter a try and then make up your own mind. The following sections cover some basics to get you started.

Before you can subscribe to tweets or have your own adoring followers, you need to sign up for a free Twitter account. It's painless, and you can do so at www.twitter.com. Pick a simple name that's similar to your own, upload a picture of yourself (or something cool), fill in the bio, and you're ready to go.

Following tweets

The best way to get a taste of Twitter is to play follow the leader. In this case, you'll be following (reading) someone else's tweets.

If a friend or family member tweets, that's a good place to start. If not, after you log in to your Twitter account, go to the top of the page and click the Find People link. This link takes you to a screen where you type in someone's first name, last name, or Twitter username, and see whether he or she is tweeting.

Try typing **obama**, **mccain**, **oprah**, or **cnn** as examples. Figure 10-1 shows the results if you typed **CDC** (Centers for Disease Control). The agency uses Twitter to get the official word out regarding swine flu and other health emergencies — a useful example of tweeting, in my opinion.

Twitter found a number of CDCs. Click the first link to display a list of recent tweets for that Twitterer (another name for a tweeter). What you get is shown in Figure 10-2.

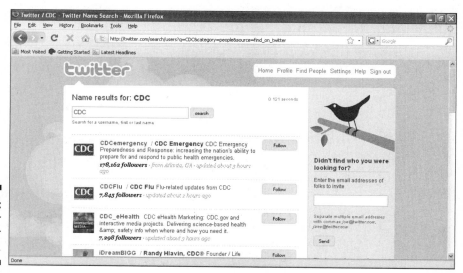

Figure 10-1: A Twitter search for CDC.

The Follow button

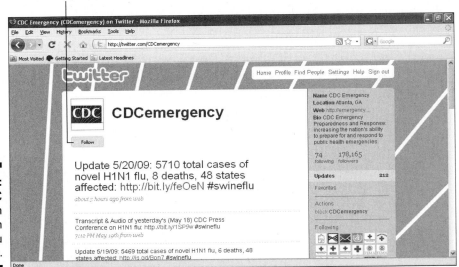

Figure 10-2:
The CDC
tweets with
information
on flu
outbreaks.

Clicking the Follow button subscribes you to that Twitterer's future tweets. Your Twitter home page displays any tweets you've subscribed to.

You can easily delete a tweet subscription by clicking the Following link on your Twitter home page. Choose the subscription to delete and click the Remove button.

Searching is fine, but sometimes it's easier to see categorized tweets. Use a Twitter directory Web site such as WeFollow.com (`http://wefollow.com`) to check out tweets organized by categories.

As a follower, you can reply to a tweet either publicly or privately. Unless the tweets are going out to a relatively small number of people, it's a good idea not to expect a reply, though — especially with famous and not-so-famous Twitterers with legions of followers. But you never know who you might get a response from.

Some Twitterers use automated programs to post their tweets. With some tweets, you do the math and tell me whether anyone could possibly be churning out such a high volume of messages by hand. In addition, although some celebrity tweeters do post their own messages, others rely on ghost-tweeters or PR services to do most of the work.

Twitter.com or not

Although you can certainly use the Twitter. com Web site to send and follow tweets, it's much easier to use a standalone program that accesses the Twitter feeds. The friendly folks at Twitter released an API (Application Programming Interface) that allows anyone to write a program that will work with the Twitter service. These programs are quicker to use and provide additional functionality.

Here are several Windows programs you might consider installing on your netbook:

✔ **MadTwitter:** (www.madtwitter.com) Based on the popular Twitterrific for the Mac, this application installs in the desktop system tray and alerts you of incoming

tweets. Click the icon to bring up a window to send tweets of your own.

✔ **Feedalizr:** (www.feedalizr.com) An Adobe Air desktop application for interfacing several social networking sites, including Twitter, Facebook, and Flickr.

✔ **TweetDeck:** (www.tweetdeck.com) Another Adobe Air application that offers extended features for Twitter users not found on the Twitter Web site.

For more applications (including Twitter programs for Macs, Linux PCs and cell phones), visit http://twitter.pbworks.com/Apps.

Sending tweets to followers

Sending a tweet out to your followers is simple. On your Twitter.com home page, type up to 140 characters in the "What are you doing?" text box and click the Update button. The tweet is sent winging its way out to your loyal followers.

Better yet, use one of the Twitter applications I mention in the "Twitter.com or not" sidebar to send out your tweets.

There are lots of Web sites, forum posts, and blog articles devoted to Twitter etiquette, including do's and don'ts. Google them if you're interested, or just apply some common sense.

Twitter makes use of special characters at the beginning of a tweet to do different things. For example, if you want to send a private message to someone, type **d** and then the person's Twitter username. For example, the following statement would send a message only to a user named renaldo_moon:

```
d renaldo_moon was that a fat cat or what?
```

Check the Twitter online help for information on all the text commands.

Shrinking links

Because tweets are limited to 140 characters, you want to be brief and terse. This can be a challenge if you're including a Web site address in the tweet — especially a long one.

The secret is to use a free Web service that provides a short Web address that redirects to the longer one. For example, you could turn a long Web address like `www.dummies.com/store/product/GPS-For-Dummies-2nd-Edition.productCd-0470156236.html` into a short one like `http://tinyurl.com/qgo52v`.

Here are some free services that put bloated Web site addresses on a crash diet:

- TinyURL (`www.tinyurl.com`)
- bit.ly (`www.bit.ly`)
- is.gd (`www.is.gd`)
- Snipurl (`www.snipurl.com`)

Getting the word out

Knowing how to tweet to followers doesn't do you much good if you don't have any followers, does it? Here are a few tips for attracting followers:

- **Make yourself easy to find by choosing a Twitter name that's close to your real name.**
- **Click the Find People link on your Twitter home page and then click the Invite By E-Mail link.** You can enter one or more e-mail addresses to tell people that you tweet.
- **Include your Twitter account name in e-mail, on Web sites, business cards, advertisements, wherever.**
- **Include useful or interesting information in your tweets.** Unless you're famous, most people couldn't care less what kind of pickle is on your sandwich.
- **Be engaging.** Don't make it a one-way conversation.

Unless it's friends and family (who tend to be captive audiences), you need to put some work into retaining followers. The best way to do this is by following different people and understanding what makes a good (and bad) Twitterer.

Practical applications

I'm a practical kind of guy, and personally don't see the value in knowing when a celebrity is walking her toy poodle or in getting 24/7 updates on what my best friend is doing or thinking. But hey, if you like that kind of thing, that's cool.

In my opinion, Twitter is a great tool for quickly communicating time-sensitive information and keeping people updated on significant stuff. Aside from the entertainment value (everyone needs guilty pleasures), here are some practical applications for Twitter:

- ✔ Quick updates to distant friends or family
- ✔ Brand building (developing a loyal base of followers)
- ✔ Marketing (driving traffic to Web sites)
- ✔ Stock tips and financial news
- ✔ Asking questions (If you have a large enough group of followers, collective wisdom can often be much faster than searching the Web.)
- ✔ Breaking news stories
- ✔ Critical emergency information (disasters, flu pandemics, fires)
- ✔ Advertising (special sales, discounts, and so on — just don't spam)

You could make the argument that anything you can do with Twitter you can do with e-mail, instant messaging, or blogs. That's very true, although Twitter forces you to be brief and doesn't seem to be as time consuming — unless you're following lots of people.

It's too soon to tell whether Twitter is just another fad with its popularity driven by novelty or whether it will have legs and become a mainstay of the Net like e-mail or Web sites. Time will definitely tell.

There's much more to Twitter than I have the pages to cover. To come up to speed, check out the Help section at www.twitter.com. In addition, lots of Web sites and blogs are devoted to Twitter. Google is your friend when it comes to finding out more.

Social Networking "Friend" Sites

You've probably heard and read about MySpace (shown in Figure 10-3) and Facebook. These two Web sites (www.myspace.com and www.facebook.com) are currently the biggest players in the Internet social networking scene. If you already have a MySpace or Facebook account, this section is going to be old news for you. If not, read on to see what all of the buzz is about.

Figure 10-3:
Even
the U.S.
president
is on
MySpace.

For starters, social networking sites share common characteristics:

- ✔ **Web-centric:** You use a Web browser to access the site. Also, unlike building a traditional Web site, which requires varying degrees of technical knowledge and skill, social networking sites feature easy-to-use tools for creating a Web presence.

- ✔ **Free:** Most social networking sites are supported by advertising and don't cost anything to join. (A few sites cost money to join or provide premium services for a fee.)

- ✔ **Communication-oriented:** Blogs, messaging, and photo and music hosting are just a few of the internal tools that sites offer their users for staying in touch with each other.

- ✔ **Profile-based:** Social networking sites rely on user-created profiles. You provide various bits of information about yourself in a profile that other users can see. Profiles are searchable so people on the network can find you.

- ✔ *Friend*-**focused:** Part of a social network presence includes a list of other people in the network who are your "friends." (The definition of *friend* ranges broadly. At one end is a stranger who's hoping you'll reciprocally list her as a friend, and at the other end is your mother. Because your total number of friends is always displayed, some people go for quantity versus quality.)

Younger Internet users were the early adopters of social networking Web sites. When the ball got rolling in the mid-2000s, MySpace was viewed primarily as a place for teenagers (and even younger kids) to hang out. When Facebook (see Figure 10-4) debuted, it was targeted toward college-age users.

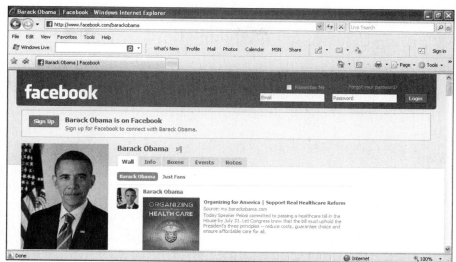

Figure 10-4:
The U.S.
president
is also on
Facebook.

Since then, older users have flocked to both sites (often to the dismay of the original younger generations), and social networking has gone mainstream. Professionally oriented sites such as LinkedIn (www.linkedin.com) are seeking to tap into the growing adult interest in social networking.

According to a Pew Internet survey, at the beginning of 2009, about 35 percent of adult Net users use social networking sites. Compare that to around 65 percent of online teens ages 12 to 17 and roughly 75 percent of Net users between 18 and 24 who use social networking sites. Only 7 percent of Net users 65 and older can be found on the sites, but I suspect that number will rise.

Should you participate in a social networking site? That's up to you. They do offer a great way to stay in touch with friends and family members and to share what's going on in your life. Check out a social networking page that belongs to someone you know and see what you think. If it looks interesting, sign up for an account and give it try. If you don't like the experience, you can always stop participating and delete the account.

Employers and prospective employers are increasingly checking out MySpace and Facebook to see what kind of presence employees or potential future employees have. (In fact, some employers are even requesting Facebook URLs from prospective employees instead of traditional resumes.) The lines between personal and professional life are becoming increasingly blurred. Yes I know, you have a right to self-expression. Just realize that anything you say (and post) on the Internet may be held against you — even 5, 10, or 15 years down the road.

MySpace and Facebook differences

In a nutshell, here are the differences between MySpace and Facebook:

MySpace:

- ✔ Younger demographic

- ✔ Users tend to use aliases

- ✔ Offers more creative options for custom layout designs

- ✔ More focused on entertainment and music

Facebook:

- ✔ Older demographic

- ✔ Users tend to use real names

- ✔ Standardized layout designs

- ✔ More professionally oriented

MySpace long was the top social networking site, but in the spring of 2009, it was surpassed by Facebook's higher growth rate and hit counts. Many analysts believe Facebook will take a commanding lead and dominate the social networking market in the coming years.

 All online networking sites have extensive online help that covers all aspects of using a site — in addition, the Internet is filled with tutorials, guides, and how-tos for social networking sites. Or if you're old school, visit your local library or friendly bookstore and pick up a copy of *MySpace For Dummies* by Ryan Hupfer, Mitch Maxson, and Ryan Williams, or *Facebook For Dummies* by Carolyn Abram and Leah Pearlman, both published by Wiley Publishing, Inc.

Going inside Instant Messaging (IM)

Instant messaging (commonly known as IM or *chat*) is a way to have a real-time text conversation with one or more people. You run an IM program on your netbook (which needs to be connected to the Internet) then type a message to someone else who's online. The text appears on his screen, and he replies. Then you reply. And so on.

The technology isn't exactly cutting edge, but if you've never done instant messaging before and want to try it out on your netbook, read on.

IM networks

Instant messaging works through a series of servers connected to the Internet. You connect to a server with an IM program (more on that coming up). The server notifies other users that have added you to their address books that you're online. They can then send you messages, or you can send them messages. The IM servers handle all the traffic passing back and forth. When you're done, you either finish the conversation or log off the network.

Before you can instant message, you need a free account on an IM network, which houses the servers. A number of IM networks are available. Here are Web addresses for the most popular services where you can register for an account:

- ✔ **AIM,** www.aim.com
- ✔ **Google,** http://mail.google.com/mail/signup
- ✔ **ICQ,** http://web.icq.com/register
- ✔ **MSN,** http://registernet.passport.com
- ✔ **Yahoo!** http://edit.yahoo.com/config/eval_register

Skype also features IM capabilities. I discuss Skype later in this chapter.

IM clients

When you have an account on an IM network, you need an IM program (in geek-speak, a *client*). This is a program that connects to the IM network over the Internet and allows you to send and receive messages — as well as perform other IM housekeeping tasks.

Generally, each IM network has a specific client program that works only with that network. For example, if you sign up for an account on the AIM (AOL Instant Messaging) network, you would use the AIM client program. You can freely download the client software from the Web site where you registered for the IM network account.

Most networks also let you IM through a Web page on the network's Web site (listed in the preceding section). This is handy if you're on a computer that doesn't have the client software installed — or you're too lazy to load it on your netbook.

Your Windows netbook should come with MSN Messenger already installed. Depending on the manufacturer, other IM programs may also be present.

My favorite IM client is a free, open-source program called Pidgin (www. pidgin.im). Pidgin is a multiprotocol client (you can use it on a number of different IM networks, as shown in Figure 10-5) that has many nifty features.

Figure 10-5:
With the
Pidgin
client, you
can use
multiple IM
networks.

For a thorough comparison of IM clients and more, check out this About.com URL: http://im.about.com.

IM basics

Entire books have been written on instant messaging, and there's a lot to know, but I want to give you a very quick rundown on some basic information to get you going:

- ✔ **IM client software has a search feature for finding people that have an account on the IM network.** Use the search feature to find people you want to chat with — or better yet, ask a friend or family member ahead of time for his or her IM account name; be sure to tell them yours.

- ✔ **IM programs have address books (also known as *buddy lists*) where you store the network account names of people you frequently chat with.** An icon typically appears next to an account name to let you know whether a person is online and available to chat. (To avoid spamming, most networks require a user to approve or deny adding their name to someone else's address book.)

- ✔ **While your IM program is running and connected, if someone wants to chat with you, a sound is played or an icon flashes.** Because of this, many users keep their IM program running in the background; just remember, this taxes your netbook's memory and processor a bit.

✔ **If you're away from your netbook (or too busy to chat), you can set your status to "away from desk"** so people won't try to ring you up.

✔ **You can include emoticons (smiley and other faces) in a message** to add a little more feeling to the text.

✔ **Some IM clients offer more than just text chatting.** For instance, your IM client might include features such as video conferencing (with a webcam), sending messages when someone is offline, encryption, and file transfer.

✔ **IM tends to favor speedy typists and people who communicate better with written versus spoken words.**

The main IM network Web site, as well as the online help that comes with your IM client, tells you everything else you need to know.

IMing can be a huge time-sink, especially if you keep your client running in the background and feel obligated to chat with everyone who rings you up. At first it's kind of fun, but it can easily become a productivity hit if you let it get away from you — both initiating and receiving chat sessions.

Getting the Scoop on Skype

How would you like to talk with someone across the country without paying expensive long distance bills or burning up precious cell phone minutes? You can, using the Internet and a popular free program called Skype. There's a good chance it's already installed on your netbook, but if not, you can get it from www.skype.com. If you've never used Skype, this section tells you what you need to know.

Skype was originally known as "Sky peer-to-peer" or Skyper. Because someone already had the Skyper Web domain, the developers decided to drop the *r,* and Skype was born.

Skype, and other programs like it, use a protocol designed for sending and receiving digitized voice over the Internet (the technical term for this is *Voice over Internet Protocol* or VoIP). When you speak into your netbook's microphone, your words are converted into data packets that are sent to the computer of whomever you're having the conversation with. The data is then reconverted, and the person on the other end hears your voice. It's just like a normal phone conversation, with the same level of voice quality, but everything is done over the Internet without a traditional phone company involved.

Skype is free if you're calling someone else who has a Skype account or that person is calling you. If you want to use Skype to call a landline or mobile phone (or take an incoming call from someone on a landline or mobile phone), you need to pay for an additional service — which is usually cheaper than most long distance plans.

To get started running Skype, you need an account. If you don't have an account, you can sign up for one directly from the program — that's a hint to run it now if you're following along. Select a Skype name and password, enter your e-mail address, fill in your profile, and you're ready to go. The main Skype program window is shown in Figure 10-6.

You have the option of automatically loading and running Skype whenever your netbook starts. Just remember, the more programs that are running in the background, the bigger a performance hit your little laptop will take.

Skype allows you to search for other Skype users based on information in their profiles — specifically the user's Skype name, full name, or e-mail address. As I write this, over 440 million Skype accounts are in existence, so there's a good chance someone you know is using Skype.

Figure 10-6:
The Skype window is ready to do your bidding.

When you find out someone's Skype account name (whether by searching the Skype network or simply by asking), you add that name as a contact. After you've added a contact, you can give that person a ring by double-clicking her Skype name in the main program window. You can tell whether she's available by an icon that appears next to her name — a gray icon with an X means unavailable. (With newer versions of Skype, the person needs to approve you before you can add her name to your contact list.)

Before calling someone, I suggest you double-click on the Skype Test Call contact. This is a handy feature that makes a test call to ensure your microphone and speakers are configured correctly.

Skype will let the person know you're calling, she answers, and then you have a conversation just like you were talking on the phone — speaking into your microphone and listening to your speakers. In addition to making voice phone calls you can also instant message, video conference (using your webcam), and transfer files with another user.

Instead of using your netbook's built-in speakers and microphone when you're using Skype, I suggest you invest in a headset. I discuss selecting headsets in Chapter 15.

Check the Skype online help to find out more or watch one of the many tutorials available on YouTube. Or, if you're old-fashioned, pick up a copy of *Skype For Dummies* by Loren Abdulezer, Susan Abdulezer, Howard Dammond, and Niklas Zennstrom (Wiley Publishing, Inc.).

Chapter 11

Netbook Navigators

*I*t's not everyday I get a chance to talk about two of my favorite subjects, GPS and netbooks. You might not know it, but these two recent technological innovations go together like apple pie and vanilla ice cream. Combine the two, and you get a delicious netbook navigator.

You may be wondering in these days of cheap car GPS units and maps on your cell phone, why would you need GPS on your netbook? Simple: A netbook gives you a lot of navigation power in a small package. Lots of the free and low-cost map software available can run circles around your cell phone or car GPS unit. Load a program or two onto your take-anywhere netbook, connect a GPS receiver, and you'll never be lost again — at least as long as the battery lasts.

In this chapter, I bring you up to speed on using GPS with a netbook. I briefly explain what GPS is, describe different types of GPS units you can use with your netbook (and how to connect them), and recommend map programs for various uses.

It's time to set a 270 degree course heading and shove off, matey! Steady as she goes.

GPS in a Nutshell

There's a lot to know about GPS, and entire books have been written about the subject (more on that in a minute). But I keep it short and sweet and just tell you the absolute basics:

- ✔ **GPS stands for *Global Positioning System*.** It's a series of satellites that transmit radio waves down to earth. A GPS unit receives the signals from three or more satellites and mathematically determines your location — anywhere in the world.

- ✔ **GPS was originally developed by the U.S. military but is freely available to anyone who has a GPS receiver.** There are no annual subscription fees to use the service.

- ✔ **GPS works best if you have a clear view of the sky.** Heavy forests, tall buildings, and parking garage interiors can all block GPS signals so an accurate position can't be determined. Newer GPS receivers use high-sensitivity chips for better signal reception.

- ✔ **GPS units report your location in latitude and longitude.** It looks something like this: 48.14417, – 122.75522. They also provide information about time, speed, distance, and elevation.

- ✔ **When you save a location on your GPS unit, it's called a *waypoint*.**

- ✔ **GPS is typically accurate anywhere from 10 to 100 feet — these days more like in the 10-to-30-foot range.** Satellite signal strength and the number of satellite signals available impact accuracy.

- ✔ **GPS units can be connected to netbooks and other personal computers and interact with programs and digital maps**. For example, your current position appears on a map that moves as you do.

That's a super-encapsulated explanation of the nuts and bolts of GPS. There's a lot more to discover, so here's a shameless plug for another *For Dummies* book I wrote called *GPS For Dummies* (Wiley Publishing, Inc.). Enough with the sales pitches and back to netbooks.

Surveying GPS Receivers

I assume you already have a netbook (or plan to get one). If so, you're about halfway there in turning your little laptop into a personal navigator. The next thing you need is a GPS receiver that will work with your netbook. As I write this, a few manufacturers have announced netbook models that will come with built-in GPS receivers. However, if you don't have one of these new geo-smart netbooks, the following sections tell you about the types of GPS units you can use with any netbook.

Minimum netbook navigator requirements

You can turn just about any netbook into a netbook navigator (one is shown in Figure 11-1), but I strongly recommend the following for your minimum requirements:

✔ **10-inch screen:** The more screen real estate to display the map and program controls, the better.

✔ **Hard disk drive:** Lots of maps take up lots of space. Although a solid state drive is fast, most don't have enough capacity to store a large number of maps — I'm talking gigabytes of data for a decent size collection of maps.

✔ **Windows operating system:** You can find a few Linux map programs out there, but many more Windows programs are available — I discuss some of the best coming up.

✔ **External power source:** If you're using your netbook in a car, truck, or boat, you'll want some type of an external power supply, such as a cigarette lighter adapter or inverter. I tell you everything you need to know in Chapter 13.

✔ **External DVD drive:** Some map software packages require a DVD drive to install the program and data. Check the software requirements before you purchase or download a map program.

Handheld GPS receivers

Handheld GPS receivers are traditionally used for hiking and other outdoor activities. They're compact, run a long time on AA batteries, and often display maps. Most models can also connect to a computer to provide your netbook with real-time location data. The big advantage to a handheld GPS receiver is you can use it by itself (for hiking, biking, boating, whatever) and then connect it to your netbook whenever you need to.

When it comes to handheld GPS units, I prefer Garmin (www.garmin.com) products, like the one shown in Figure 11-1. They tend to be easy to use, well built, and reliable. Good battery life, the availability of many free maps that can be uploaded to the unit, and ease of connecting to a netbook via a USB cable are also big pluses.

Other handheld GPS manufacturers to consider include DeLorme (www.delorme.com), Lowrance (www.lowrance.com), and Magellan (www.magellangps.com).

Handheld GPS receivers generally are priced between $100 and $500 — the higher the price, the more features. An expensive consumer GPS unit is generally no more accurate than a budget model — in most cases a basic or mid-ranged model will serve you just as well as a top of the line model.

If you have a GPS unit in your car, keep in mind that most automotive GPS receivers aren't designed to interface with a computer. Sorry.

Mouse GPS units

GPS receivers that don't have a display screen but connect to a computer with a USB cable are often called mouse receivers because they sort of look like a computer mouse — one is shown in Figure 11-2. A mouse GPS receiver acts as an input device for your netbook and sends only satellite data that it's currently receiving.

There is a product that incorporates a GPS receiver into a real computer mouse — personally, I think it's a little cheesy.

Mouse GPS receivers are about half the size of the smallest handheld GPS receivers, but even so, they still have good satellite reception with open skies. Depending on the model and type, a mouse GPS receiver can be powered by a cigarette lighter adapter, rechargeable batteries, or from the USB port of the computer it's plugged into.

Figure 11-2:
A USB mouse GPS receiver.

Mouse GPS products are usually under $100. A number of companies that offer street map programs optionally bundle a mouse GPS receiver with t heir software. Garmin (www.garmin.com), DeLorme (www.delorme.com), and Microsoft (www.microsoft.com) are among some of the popular manufacturers.

You can also find *tailless* mouse GPS receivers. These are GPS units that plug directly into your netbook's USB port — there's no cable. The downside to these products is you can't position the GPS receiver in an optimal location because it's attached directly to the netbook. If your netbook doesn't have a good view of open skies, you may get weak satellite signals.

Bluetooth GPS

Bluetooth GPS units (one is shown in Figure 11-3) get rid of cable clutter by wirelessly sending location information to your netbook. If your netbook supports Bluetooth (see Chapter 6), it's just a matter of installing some software, configuring your netbook, and turning on the Bluetooth GPS unit. Just like magic, GPS data is wirelessly transmitted.

Bluetooth GPS receivers are pretty slick because of what they *don't* do:

- **They don't rely on the netbook's batteries for power.** They have their own power source and will run from 6–10 hours when fully charged, depending on the model.

- **They don't use up one of the netbook's USB ports.**

- **They don't need cables that can become a tangled mess.** Bluetooth devices have about a 30-foot range, and the GPS receiver can be placed in an optimal position on a car's dashboard to receive satellite signals.

Place your Bluetooth GPS receiver (about the size of a mouse GPS receiver or smaller) anywhere with an open view of the sky, and it will broadcast GPS data to your Bluetooth-enabled netbook.

Some Bluetooth models serve dual duty and also allow you to connect the GPS receiver with a USB cable.

Many Bluetooth GPS receivers are on the market these days. Your best bet to find out more is to do a Google search for *bluetooth gps*.

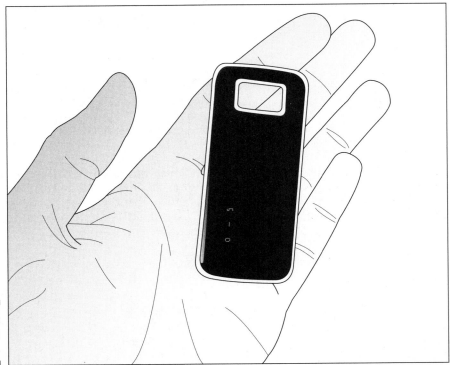

Figure 11-3:
A Bluetooth GPS unit.

SD card GPS

In addition to USB and Bluetooth GPS receivers, some GPS units that are available can be inserted into your netbook's SD card reader. This might sound like a good idea, but I'm not too keen on these products for a few reasons:

✔ If you're not connected to an external power source, GPS receiver cards can run down your netbook's battery fairly quickly.

✔ They take up your only SD card slot.

✔ Because they're inserted into your netbook, you can't position the receiver for optimal satellite reception.

Opt for a USB mouse or Bluetooth GPS receiver instead.

Selecting Map Software

After you have a netbook and a suitable GPS receiver, you need some mapping software. Before I make recommendations on what to get, you should know there are three ways to use a GPS-enabled netbook. With it, you can

✔ **See where you're currently located.** The GPS unit reports your current location, and the mapping software displays your location on a map. The location point on the map moves, and the map itself scrolls as the GPS unit moves. With street map programs, you enter a destination, and the program gives you turn-by-turn directions on how to get there, whether the directions are listed onscreen, are announced with a synthesized voice, or both.

✔ **See where you've been.** A GPS receiver stores information about where it's been — see the "Making tracks (and waypoints)" sidebar. You can transfer this information to your netbook and use a map program to display it.

✔ **Exchange data.** Map programs allow you to download other data from your GPS unit (such as waypoints) to your netbook or upload data (waypoints and maps) from your netbook. Most GPS receivers come with basic software for exchanging and saving data.

Manufacturers use proprietary map formats for displaying maps on handheld and automotive GPS units. Unless map software comes from the manufacturer, you won't be able to copy a digital map you see on your netbook to a GPS receiver. (There are few exceptions to this rule. For example, hackers successfully reverse-engineered Garmin's map format, and now a number of utilities are available for creating Garmin-compatible maps.)

Making tracks (and waypoints)

GPS receivers support a feature called *tracks.* A track is a location where you've been — think of it as an electronic breadcrumb. Whenever the GPS unit is turned on, it dutifully collects and stores a *track point* — the latitude and longitude, data and time, and elevation. You specify how often track points are collected, either by a set amount of time or distance.

When you connect a GPS receiver to a netbook, you can download the track file. Then you run a map program, load the track file, and presto, a record of your travels appears overlaid on the map.

Another GPS term you should be familiar with is *waypoint.* This is information about a known location, including coordinates and a name. Say you wanted to mark a favorite fishing spot. You'd create a waypoint for the location with your GPS unit and give it a short name. The waypoint is stored in a list in the GPS receiver's memory. When you want to go back to where the fish are biting, you display the waypoint list and instruct the GPS unit to go to that point. It happily calculates the distance and uses an arrow to show you how to get there. If your GPS receiver can display a map, an icon appears at the waypoint's location.

Oh, if only Hansel and Gretel had a GPS unit with them, that poor misunderstood witch might still be around today.

You can spend a little or a lot on map programs — commercial, shareware, and free programs are available. Because so many different types of maps exist, you can find programs that are specialized for one particular use or another — such as street map program, hiking map program, and so on.

The following sections give you a quick rundown on some suitable map software candidates for your netbook, organized by type.

Street maps

Street map programs help you navigate paved roads, highways, and byways. If you've used a car GPS unit, street map programs provide the same functionality — with more features and a bigger screen.

One of the more popular street map programs is DeLorme's Street Atlas USA, shown in Figure 11-4. This program displays roadmaps of the United States, Canada, and Mexico; finds addresses; and creates routes between two or more points. Check out a few of the program's other useful features:

✓ **POIs:** All street navigation programs contain extensive databases of POIs. POIs refer to Points of Interest such as restaurants, hotels, parks, gas stations, and other locations you might be interested in while traveling. Street Atlas USA has a POI database that contains over four million businesses, services, and organizations.

- ✔ **Voice support:** Street Atlas USA can give you voice instructions when you need to turn to reach your destination. You can also use a voice recognition feature to give Street Atlas USA commands instead of using a keyboard or mouse.

- ✔ **Routable roads:** A big issue that all map companies face is ensuring that their road data is accurate — this is challenging considering the number of new roads that are built every year. Street Atlas USA has a feature that allows you to draw in roads that are missing on a map. After you create a road, Street Atlas USA can use it when calculating routes.

- ✔ **Netbook interface:** Street Atlas USA offers a UMPC (Ultra Mobile PC) mode during installation that configures its interface for a smaller-screen netbook.

- ✔ **Aerial photos:** You can purchase and download aerial photos and then overlay streets and POI information on top of the bird's-eye view.

- ✔ **Customizable maps:** Street Atlas USA has an extensive collection of drawing tools for customizing maps with symbols, shapes, and text annotations.

Street Atlas USA has many more features than I can cover in the space of this section (such as downloadable maps, distance measuring, and trip planning that takes fuel consumption as well as the number of hours spent driving into consideration). To find out more about all of the features, visit www.delorme. com. The program's suggested retail price is under $40.

Microsoft also makes a popular street and roadmap program appropriately named Streets & Trips. Find out more about it at www.microsoft.com/ Streets/en-us/default.aspx.

If you want to run street map software on your netbook, you need an external DVD drive to install the program and maps.

At this point, there aren't any free street map programs that match the features of commercial road navigation programs. That may be changing in the future with a slick open-source project called OpenStreetMap. To find out more, visit www.openstreetmap.org.

Topographic maps

Topographic maps show land features and are primarily used for hiking and other outdoor activities. If you visit the TerraServer-USA Web site (http:// terraserver-usa.com), you can view topographic maps of different scales for the United States; these official maps are produced by the United States Geological Survey (USGS).

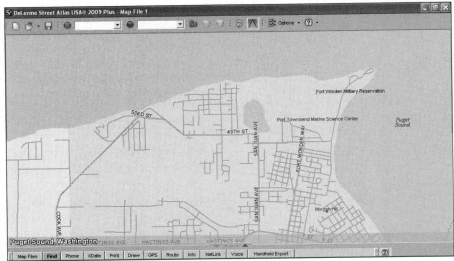

Figure 11-4:
DeLorme
Street Atlas
USA running
on a
netbook.

Doug Cox, who is a retired airline pilot turned Windows programmer, leverages this map data in an elegantly small, powerful-yet-easy-to-use program called USAPhotoMaps (`http://jdmcox.com`). Use it to

✔ Display USGS topographic maps and aerial photos.

✔ Zoom in and out on map features.

✔ Support user-defined text labels.

✔ Print and save user-selected areas as JPG format files.

✔ Interface with a GPS receiver for real-time tracking.

✔ Import and export GPS waypoints, routes, and tracks.

The cool thing about this program is it caches all the map data to your hard drive. That means after you initially view an area, you don't need an Internet connection to display the maps again. You can be out in the middle of nowhere, with no wireless or Net connection for miles, and USAPhotoMaps will show you where you're located. (See Figure 11-5.)

Cox updates the program regularly and has added a variety of new features over the years. It's free (including the C source code), but if you like it, give him a tip of the hat with a PayPal donation.

DeLorme (`www.delorme.com`), Maptech (`www.maptech.com`), National Geographic Maps (`www.natgeomaps.com`), and TopoFusion (`www.topofusion.com`) all make commercial topographic map programs for Windows and are worth checking out.

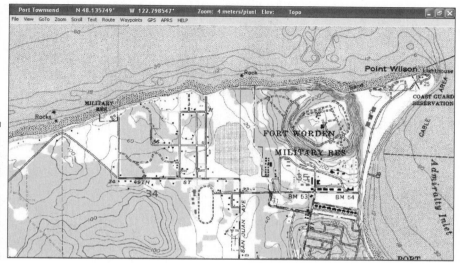

Figure 11-5:
USAPhoto-
Maps
displays U.S.
topographic
maps and
aerial
photos.

Some topographic map programs can display maps in 3-D. But be prepared for a potentially long wait because most netbooks don't have the graphics or processor horsepower for this kind of work.

Satellite images

Google Earth has to be one of the slickest free pieces of software to come around in years. The program is a virtual globe with color satellite imagery of the entire world. You simply rotate the globe to a location you're interested in and then zoom in to see more detail.

In addition to showing satellite imagery (an example is shown in Figure 11-6), Google Earth can also overlay data onto its bird's-eye views. With a click of a button, you can see roads, storm fronts, cities, borders, Wikipedia entries, user-submitted photos, and more.

Between satellite images and layers, this is a huge amount of data. It would be impossible to include all of this on a few DVDs, so Google keeps the data online on some serious, industrial-strength servers. The program uses an Internet connection to download data you're interested in seeing. When you scroll or zoom, Google Earth gets new data from the servers and displays it.

Google Earth caches data to your hard drive. This means if you've previously viewed an area, you won't need to have an Internet connection to see it again — that is, unless the cache (up to 2GB) is written over by new places you visit.

Figure 11-6:
Google
Earth
displays
satellite
images of
the world.

Google offers a for-pay version of the program called Google Earth Plus that incorporated several advanced features such as the ability to interface with a GPS receiver. Recently, the company decided to add GPS functionality to the free version of the program. That means you can have satellite image moving maps with your netbook when you connect a GPS unit. James Bond has nothing on you — well, the Google images aren't real time, sorry 007.

To download Google Earth and find out more about the program, visit `http://earth.google.com`.

Charts

A *chart* is the official term for a map that covers navigable waters — such as coastal waters and the oceans. A netbook makes a handy-dandy boating companion (for vessels with cabins) when coupled with digital charts and a GPS receiver.

Although you can find many commercial Windows navigation programs on the market (they vary considerably in price), if you're just getting your feet wet with electronic navigation, I suggest you start the low-budget (as in *free*) route.

If you live in the United States, reclaim some of your hard-earned tax dollars by downloading free nautical charts — noncitizens can, too. In 2005, the National Oceanic and Atmospheric Administration (NOAA) began making all of its digital charts available on the Internet for free. Just point your browser to `http://nauticalcharts.noaa.gov` and follow the directions. You want to download Raster Navigation Charts (RNCs). These are scanned versions of paper charts, sometimes referred to as BSB charts; the name of the proprietary format back when they weren't free.

After you've downloaded a few free charts, you need a program to use them. The navigation software packages on the market cost anywhere from $50 to $1,000 or more. These programs let you view and print charts. If you have a netbook hooked up to a GPS receiver, you can see where you are on the chart in the comfort of your boat's cabin while motoring or sailing.

I want to point you in the direction of a great Windows navigation program that's free. It's called SeaClear (shown in Figure 11-7), and you can download it from `www.sping.com/seaclear`. SeaClear is a powerful and easy-to-use program that works great with NOAA RNC charts. It's in use all over the world and is frequently updated by its creator. A netbook (SeaClear isn't system-resource intensive), free NOAA charts, and an inexpensive GPS receiver give you a bargain-basement navigation system.

A number of other free or demo programs are also available for viewing and printing charts. NOAA provides a convenient list of software, including Web links, at `http://nauticalcharts.noaa.gov/mcd/Raster/resources.htm`.

Making the Connection

You have a netbook, GPS receiver, and some mapping software. Great! Now there's just one more thing I need to tell you about: getting them all to talk to each other.

When consumer GPS receivers first hit the market in the 1990s, users connected them to a computer with a serial cable — one end plugged in the GPS unit, the other into the PC's serial port. Getting the two devices to communicate was sometimes a challenge and required tweaking a number of different settings like baud rates, parity, and stop bits — those were the dark ages, believe me.

Fortunately, serial ports have mostly gone the way of the dinosaur, and USB is now the way to easily connect peripherals and other devices. However, when it comes to GPS receivers, it's not always as simple as plugging and playing. Read on to find out why.

Protocols

A *protocol* is a way for two devices to successfully talk with each other. Think of a protocol as a language with a strict set of rules. When one device sends a message to another device, it expects a certain response back. This structured, back-and-forth chit-chat takes place until one device sends a message that states the conversation is over. Like, "Gotta run, catch you later."

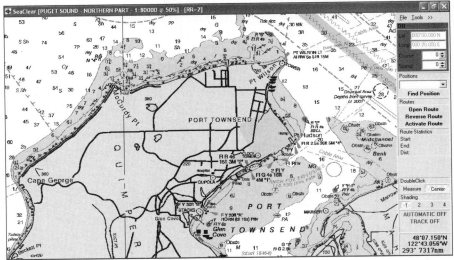

Figure 11-7:
SeaClear
maritime
navigation
software
running on a
netbook.

Likewise, when you connect a GPS receiver to a computer, a certain protocol is used to transfer data between the two devices. You need to ensure that the same protocol has been selected for both devices. If two different protocols are used, it's like the GPS receiver speaking Navajo to a netbook that understands only Aleut.

The protocols typically used with GPS receivers are

- ✔ **NMEA:** The National Marine Electronics Association came up with the *NMEA 0183* standard, which is a protocol for transferring data between marine-related electronics, such as GPS receivers, autopilots, and chart plotters. Most GPS receivers support the NMEA 0183 standard, which uses widely documented text messages. Typical NMEA data includes latitude, longitude, time, and satellite status.

    NMEA comes in several different versions, including 1.5, 2.1, 2.3, and 3.01. Make sure that this version number matches both the GPS receiver and the map program that you're using.

- ✔ **Proprietary:** Some GPS manufacturers have proprietary protocols for communicating with a GPS receiver. These protocols send additional data (for example, altitude, speed, and position error) that isn't included in the NMEA standard.

NMEA is the de facto standard for getting a GPS receiver to talk to a computer. However, if you have a choice between NMEA and a proprietary protocol (for example, the Garmin protocol used with Garmin GPS receivers), select the proprietary protocol because it can supply richer data to a program. Some Garmin GPS units don't support NMEA, and in that case you need to use the Garmin protocol. The popularity of Garmin products has prompted most map programs to support Garmin's protocol.

Virtual serial ports

Most USB-compatible GPS receivers come with special driver software that creates a virtual serial port (a serial port is also known as a COM port) that's associated with the GPS unit. You install and configure the driver software (which comes with the receiver on a CD-ROM or DVD or is downloadable from the manufacturer's Web site). When you plug the GPS unit into your netbook with a USB cable, the software emulates a serial port connection. This allows mapping software that needs to communicate with a GPS unit through a serial port to successfully do so even though it's a USB connection (which uses a different protocol). Check your GPS unit's user manual for more information.

If you plug in a USB GPS receiver that doesn't have an associated driver installed, the Windows Found New Hardware wizard should fire up and step you through the installation process. No driver means no interfacing the GPS unit with your netbook.

Always make sure you have the latest USB driver, the latest version of the mapping software (that supports your receiver), and the latest version of the GPS receiver firmware. For the driver and firmware, visit the GPS unit 's manufacturer Web site.

Putting it all together

After you have the driver software for the GPS receiver installed on your netbook and know what protocol to use, it's time to put everything together and test out your netbook navigator.

Here are the general steps for interfacing your netbook with a GPS unit with a USB cable. (If you have a Bluetooth GPS receiver, see the instructions that came with the GPS unit.)

1. **Connect the GPS USB cable to your netbook and to your GPS unit.**

   Your netbook should be running.

2. **Turn on your GPS receiver.**

   If you're plotting your current location with a map program, the GPS receiver needs to get a satellite fix (receive signals from at least three satellites) before it can provide your present position. This process can take a matter of seconds or minutes. A GPS receiver will get a fix faster if it's stationary and not moving.

3. **Run the map program.**

4. **Ensure that the protocols and settings on both the GPS receiver and the map program are the same.**

   Some map programs automatically search all of the available COM ports for a connected GPS unit. If your GPS receiver doesn't seem to be talking to your netbook, try manually specifying a different COM port setting — they're numbered, such as COM1, COM2, and so on.

If you successfully connect (if you don't, the map program will tell you), you can then

✔ Select the type of data (waypoints, routes, or tracks) and upload it to the GPS receiver from your netbook — or download it from the GPS receiver to your netbook.

✔ Upload a map to the GPS receiver that was created with a GPS manufacturer's mapping program.

✔ Have the GPS receiver start providing location data to the program for real-time mapping.

Check the map program's user manual or online help for specific instructions on transferring data between your GPS receiver and a computer. If you're still having difficulties, post a message in one of the netbook forums I list in Chapter 22.

Happy navigating!

Spanner

When it comes to using my netbook with software that doesn't directly support a Garmin handheld GPS unit, I use Spanner. Spanner is a free Windows program that reads current GPS coordinates from Garmin's proprietary data transfer protocol and translates the coordinates into NMEA 0183 format. You can download it from the support section of the Garmin Web site (www.garmin.com).

This utility was originally designed for Garmin's USB mouse GPS product, so the receiver could interface with other navigation programs (such as Microsoft Streets & Trips, DeLorme Street Atlas, and Ozi Explorer) that use real-time NMEA data to display moving maps. Spanner also works with a number of other Garmin receivers and allows you to use your handheld GPS unit with a netbook and navigation software.

Spanner version 2.1 (the most current release) doesn't work with several newer Garmin handhelds. An alternative is to use a commercial product called GPSGate. You can find more information about it at http://franson.com/gpsgate.

Part III
Netbook Add-On Accessories and Hardware

The 5th Wave   By Rich Tennant

"Yes, it's wireless, and yes, it weighs less than a pound, and yes, it has multiuser functionality...but it's a stapler."

In this part . . .

Despite being such small and affordable laptops, netbooks come with quite a number of hardware features. However, if you're like most people, you want to purchase some accessories and hardware add-ons to jazz up your netbook's usability and functionality. If that's what you're interested in, you came to the right part.

I start by describing netbook carrying cases — you'll be surprised at all the choices. I then tell you about powering your netbook and include information on spare batteries, car chargers, and how to make your batteries last longer. In the remaining chapters in this part, you find out about expanding storage with various types of drives and how to connect a variety of different peripherals to your netbook (including monitors, keyboards, modems, Bluetooth, and more).

Chapter 12

Carrying Your Netbook

. . . .

In This Chapter

▶ Selecting a sleeve

▶ Choosing a soft carrying case

▶ Finding out about rugged cases

▶ Making your own carrying case

. . . .

"*A*n entire chapter devoted to carrying around your netbook? Doesn't that seem a bit much?" you say. A netbook is so light and small, it's easy to carry around in your hand or tuck inside a bag or a large purse. So what's there to know?

Actually there's a surprising amount to know. For starters, I recommend always using some type of case when it's time for your netbook to leave the house or office. A case . . .

✔ Offers added protection from bumps, scratches, and drops.

✔ Isn't as likely to slip out of your hands.

✔ Can provide much-needed room for your wall charger, spare battery, and other accessories.

After you decide you need a case, you have all sorts of choices — from simple neoprene sleeves to high-end carrying cases to do-it-yourself carriers. It's worth knowing about all these options (and more), and that's what this chapter is all about.

Case in Point

You decided to take my advice about cases, and now you're in the market for something you can use to carry your netbook around. Good for you — you won't regret it.

Before I go into specifics, here are some tips to get you started:

- ✓ **When shopping for a case, the first thing you should do is write down the dimensions of your netbook.** Knowing the dimensions makes it easy to narrow down your choices because cases list their own dimensions and what size of laptops and netbooks they fit.

  If you're using an extended battery (bigger than what came standard), don't forget to factor it into your measurements.

- ✓ **Don't feel obligated to purchase a case sold by your netbook manufacturer.** Lots of cases are available, and brand loyalty will likely end up costing you a little more — often without much gain.

- ✓ **Check out Web forums devoted to your netbook.** What people use to carry their netbook is a popular topic, and you frequently can find pages of product recommendations along with photos.

- ✓ **Shop around.** There are lots of deals to be had online — never pay manufacturer's suggested retail price for a carrying case.

The next few sections describe the types of cases available.

Who needs a case if you have the right type of clothes? If you really want to go for Gucci geek look, check out a SCOTTEVEST at www.scottevest.com.

Sleeves

The most basic type of carrying case is called a *sleeve*. This is several pieces of cushiony neoprene (the material used for wetsuits) sewn or glued together. Your netbook slides inside the sleeve, and then you put the protected netbook in a backpack, book bag, purse, or whatever. Some netbook models come with sleeves, but most don't. A sleeve is shown in Figure 12-1.

Sleeves come in different sizes. Your netbook should fit snugly into a sleeve — not so tight that it's difficult to insert or remove, and not so loose that it slides around inside. You want a Goldilocks "just right" fit.

Figure 12-1:
A neoprene
sleeve
protects
your
netbook.

Basic sleeves are simply constructed like a pillowcase. However, many varieties on the market have more features, including

- ✔ Handles
- ✔ External pockets
- ✔ Zippers
- ✔ Colors other than black (Some sleeves have two layers of colored neoprene and are reversible.)

If you're not going to carry your netbook around in a padded carrying case designed expressly for a netbook, I strongly recommend purchasing a sleeve. Sleeves are generally priced between $10 and $25. Do a Google search for *netbook sleeve* for online sources.

Sleeves designed for portable DVD drives tend to be cheaper than laptop sleeves, and many models are sized for netbook dimensions.

Beware of inexpensive neoprene sleeves in the $5 or under range. They may be made from a cheap grade of rubber that has a distinctly bad smell. The odor usually goes away after a few days, but in the meantime, phew.

Soft carrying cases

A sleeve works great if you're stashing your netbook in a bag, pack, or sack without padding, but many people opt for a soft, padded carrying case instead. Carrying cases are fitted with shoulder straps and usually offer extra room for carrying netbook accessories — as well as sunglasses, notebooks, pens, cell phones, and other stuff you use on a daily basis.

Friendly frequent fliers

If you do a lot of air travel with your netbook, consider a checkpoint-friendly carrying case design. In 2008, the Transportation Safety Agency (TSA) invited case manufacturers to produce bags that would allow passengers to pass through airport security checkpoints without having to remove laptops from their bags. Some of the TSA criteria included

✔ A laptop-only section that unfolds and lies completely flat on the X-ray conveyor belt

✔ Easy access to the laptop in case an officer needs to examine it

✔ A full view of the laptop in its dedicated compartment — no emblems, metal snaps,

pockets, zippers, or seals on top of or underneath the compartment

✔ No more than 30 inches in length when opened, so X-ray machines can display the bag's contents in one image

Checkpoint-friendly bags should help speed up the screening process as well as protect your netbook from bumps and scratches as it rides on the conveyor belt.

TSA has trained its screeners to recognize these bags, and they'll be labeled as such by the manufacturer.

What's the point of buying a sub-3-pound netbook if you're going to fill your bag up with everything but the kitchen sink? What you carry around is your business, but personally I'm a fan of packing light.

Cases come in a variety of sizes, shapes, colors, designs, and materials (leather, lightweight and heavyweight nylon, neoprene, plastic, and combinations thereof). Aside from picking one that fits your netbook, select something that's aesthetically pleasing to your eye. Use your favorite search engine and type in *netbook case* to see what's available.

Netbook and laptop cases

When shopping for a netbook case, it's logical to start looking at products designed specifically for netbooks (and small laptops) — one is shown in Figure 12-2. Lots of small and large companies make all manner of computer carrying cases. They typically feature

✔ Padded compartment for the laptop

✔ Shoulder strap or carrying handle

✔ Pockets of different sizes

I look for several things in a good netbook case:

- ✔ Decent level of padding in the computer compartment
- ✔ Plastic lining to keep rain and moisture off the netbook
- ✔ Adjustable strap to provide a secure fit in the computer compartment
- ✔ Comfortable, padded shoulder strap
- ✔ Good closures on flaps and pockets so they don't come open
- ✔ Durable materials (I personally like Cordura and ballistic nylon.)

You can spend anywhere from $25 to several hundred dollars on a netbook case. Inexpensive, mass-produced cases are fine if you infrequently carry your netbook. If your little laptop goes everywhere with you, I recommend investing in a better quality carrier — expect to spend between $50 and $100.

Figure 12-2:
A netbook
case.

DVD cases

My favorite low-budget way to protect and carry a netbook is with a case designed for a portable DVD player. The dimensions of many netbooks happily match the size of different types of travel DVD players. Because of the popularity of these players, you can find a lot of nice, padded cases on the market that don't cost an arm and a leg — it's easy to find something under $20. I personally like the Case Logic brand. These products can be had for under $20 — an example is shown in Figure 12-3.

Figure 12-3:
A DVD
case makes
a good,
low-budget
netbook
carrier.

Other padded cases

In addition to cases primarily designed for electronic devices, it's worthwhile to check out other types of padded cases that can safely hold a netbook, such as the following:

- ✔ **Camera cases:** A number of excellent 35mm camera bags on the market offer a perfect fit for netbooks. (See Figure 12-4.)

- ✔ **Messenger bags:** Messenger bags are shoulder bags originally designed for bike messengers. More and more models, large and small, are featuring padded compartments for netbooks and laptops.

Expect to pay between $50 to $150 for these types of cases.

If a case is a little skimpy on the padding, don't hesitate to beef it up. Fabric stores sell different types of foam you can install to add more shock absorbing properties. With a little glue, custom-cut foam, and patience, you can even turn an unpadded bag or case into a suitable carrier.

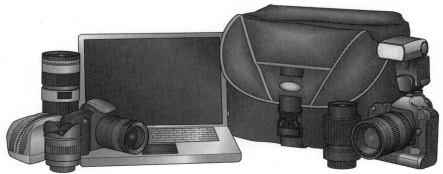

Figure 12-4:
A camera
case
suitable
for netbook
carry.

Hard cases

If you're venturing off the beaten track and bringing your netbook with you while you climb Everest, sail around the world solo, ride a dog sled to the arctic (before it melts), or blog about the war in Afghanistan, you'll want something a little more rugged than your standard-issue, soft carrying case.

Perhaps I can interest you in a little waterproof number that's shock resistant and can be driven over by a truck without crumpling whatever is inside. Yes? Ah good, step this way. I have just what you're looking for.

When the going gets tough, the tough turn to plastic. Not cheap plastic, mind you, but a strong and durable material called copolymer polypropylene — an example case is shown in Figure 12-5. Two companies dominate the market for very rugged, plastic cases for carrying all manner of precious things (including netbooks):

- ✔ **Pelican:** Pelican (`www.pelican.com`) is the big name in rugged, water-proof, shock-resistant cases. These cases receive rave reviews from militaries, governments, and other professional users. The case in Figure 12-5 is made by Pelican.

- ✔ **OtterBox:** OtterBox (`www.otterbox.com`) has focused on building tough, waterproof cases for electronics devices — they also make some smaller cases similar in design to Pelican cases.

You can't go wrong getting a case from either of these manufacturers. Just because the cases are made of plastic, that doesn't mean they're cheap. Depending on the size and features, expect to spend as much as you would on a conventional laptop case.

Unconventional cases

Think outside the box (or in this case, the bag)! Many cases and containers not designed specifically as netbook carriers fit the little laptops like a charm. You can usually score one of these unconventional cases for cheaper than a case sold specifically for netbook use. Plus, they're the ultimate in low-profile stealth — who would expect you're packing a computer in one of the following:

✔ Hardware store tool bag

✔ Bible case (from Christian bookstores)

✔ Padded lunch sack

✔ Military surplus gas mask or map bag

✔ Nintendo Wii soft carry bag

✔ Rectangular candy tin (with glued in padding)

That should give you some ideas to be on the lookout for other unconventional cases. Don't be afraid to find something unique that matches your personality.

Figure 12-5:
A Pelican case offers hard shell protection for your netbook.

Because many hard cases have carrying handles, it's possible to use smaller models as bulletproof (not literally), daily carry briefcases — a pair of hand-cuffs attached to the case and your wrist makes a nice accessory.

What's with the valve on Pelican cases, you may ask? This has nothing to do with netbooks, but here's the story: This is a pressure-relief valve. If the case is shut and sealed at a low elevation and then taken to a very high place (or travels in an un-pressurized aircraft), the ambient pressure outside the case drops. If a large enough drop occurs, a normal case would start to bulge, blow a gasket, and would no longer be waterproof, or even pop open. The relief valve on the Pelican case prevents this from happening. Unless you have this specialized need, as the military does, forget about the valve. For most people, it will never serve its purpose.

For the Do-It-Yourselfer

If you're on a tight budget (and who isn't these days?), instead of shelling out bucks for a commercial carry case, how about making one of your own? If you're handy or know someone who is, give one of these inexpensive projects a try. After all, you don't necessarily need to be a lawyer to make your case.

Sew it yourself

If you have a sewing machine and someone who knows how to use it, it's easy to make your own custom netbook carrier or sleeve. To get you started, here's a great illustrated tutorial for making your own netbook carrying case out of fabric: http://forum.eeeuser.com/viewtopic.php?id=13300.

This is for an Eee PC, but it's easy enough to adapt the pattern to your own netbook.

Modify an old planner

If you have an old, zippered binder planner (like a Day-Runner) lying around that isn't getting much use, see whether the dimensions fit your netbook. It takes about five minutes of minor surgery with a pair of pliers to remove the interior metal 3-ring clip. When the clip is removed, slide your netbook in, zip it up, and you're ready for the road. (See Figure 12-6.)

Check out this Web page from Instructables.com for step-by-step directions, including photos: www.instructables.com/id/How-to-make-a-simple-carrying-case-for-the-Asus-Ee.

Wrap it in bubbles

Shortly after buying my first netbook, I remember getting a call about a short-notice opportunity to visit a third-world country and travel around in a Land Rover — both the country and the truck turned out to have seen better days. I wanted to bring the netbook with me but was afraid of it getting trashed by all the bumps and dust. With no time to buy a sleeve, I wondered what Macgyver would do under similar circumstances. *Voilà!* Some old bubble wrap cut to shape, a little duct tape, the netbook stowed safely in a couple of zip freezer bags, and I was ready to go. It didn't look pretty, but the netbook survived the trip.

Pad it with an envelope

Although I wouldn't want to send my netbook through the mail this way, a mailing envelope with the inside padded either foam or bubble wrap makes a cheap, quick-and-dirty sleeve. The folks at Instructables have an even more deluxe version of the same general idea. Check it out at `www.instructables.com/id/Cushioned_Duct_Tape_Laptop_Sleeve`.

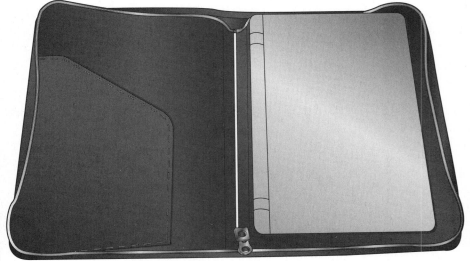

Figure 12-6:
An old planner modified as a netbook carrier.

Chapter 13

Powering Your Netbook

You obviously need electricity to directly run your netbook or charge its battery. Without power, your little laptop is just a high-tech, plastic paperweight — it looks cool, but that's about it.

Most people find that the battery and wall charger included with their netbook meet all of their power needs. But what if there's no electric outlet nearby? What if you're always on the go and a single battery doesn't cut it for your computing needs? What happens when the battery that came with your netbook finally gives up the ghost? What if . . . ?

All good questions that I'm glad you asked. You're in luck, because this chapter is all about ways to power your netbook. I cover batteries (of all different types), charging and running your netbook while on the road (or in the air), some sustainable energy options, and I wrap up with tips for maximizing battery life.

Tackling Battery Basics

Unlike a desktop PC that spends its entire life tethered to a power cord and electrical wall socket, your netbook is designed to go places. Thanks to its small size, you can use it just about anywhere — that is, as long as you have a charged battery.

In the following sections, I give you the juice on batteries. Maybe, after lots of use, your netbook's battery has decided to throw in the towel. Or perhaps you've found that one battery doesn't cut it on transoceanic flights, long commutes, or day outings at the beach. If you need a battery, this is where you can find out about your options.

Current concepts

Before charging up your brain cells with some battery basics, you need to know a few important terms and concepts that relate to your netbook's battery (or any laptop's battery, for that matter):

- ✔ **mAh:** This stands for *milliampere-hour,* a measurement of how much energy is stored in a battery. Generally, the bigger the mAh number, the longer the battery life — and the more expensive the battery.

  Battery life also depends on what you're doing. A netbook with a lower mAh battery rating may run longer than the same netbook with a higher capacity battery — that is, if you were word processing with the wireless card turned off, compared with watching videos and surfing the Net at the same time, which requires more power.

- ✔ **Cells:** Even though laptop batteries look like one big battery, they aren't — see Figure 13-1. They're composed of a series of cells (smaller, individual batteries) that are connected inside the sealed plastic case. More cells typically mean longer battery life — they also make the battery heavier and more expensive than batteries with fewer cells. Manufacturers almost always list how many cells are in a battery. Netbooks are typically powered by three- or six-cell batteries.

  Don't think that having the same number of cells makes batteries the same. For example, a four-cell battery may come in 4,400, 5,200, and 5,800 mAh models.

- ✔ **Battery memory:** You may have heard that batteries have memories and occasionally need to be fully discharged. Not true with lithium ion (li-ion) batteries, which most laptops use these days. They don't have a memory (like older nickel cadmium batteries), and there's no need to fully discharge them. Actually, to maximize battery life, li-ions should be charged when they're down to around 50 percent capacity.

- ✔ **Battery lifespan:** Sooner or later, your battery is going to bite the dust. Batteries have a limited life span that depends on how many times they've been charged and how they've been maintained. As a battery starts to wear out, the amount of charge it holds slowly decreases — meaning you get fewer and fewer minutes of use, even though the battery is fully charged. Eventually, the battery won't power your laptop at all — or it will refuse to completely charge. Depending on use and how you take care of the battery, expect it to last one to three years.

Figure 13-1:
This netbook battery isn't just one battery, but a series of batteries (cells) connected together inside a plastic case.

Brand-name batteries

If you're shopping for a new netbook battery (that is, if your old one didn't seem to last very long and you need a replacement, or if you're considering a second battery so you can use your little laptop longer), you'll probably first turn to a battery that has the same name as your netbook's manufacturer.

This makes sense because you know a battery from the manufacturer is guaranteed to work with your netbook. Manufacturer batteries are also covered by warranties, whereas third-party batteries may not be.

Prices for manufacturer batteries run $65 to $125 depending on capacity — it's worthwhile to shop around on the Internet for the best deal.

If your netbook was available in different colors, there's a chance the batteries are too. Unless you're going for a two-tone look, be sure to order one that matches.

Third-party batteries

An alternative to using a netbook manufacturer name-brand battery is to go with a third-party battery. Many "generic" batteries use the same components as the original batteries that come with the netbooks — they may even come from the same factory as the name-brand battery. Because they don't have the brand name on the label, they're usually priced lower because of reduced business overhead costs.

Third-party batteries generally have the same mAh ratings as manufacturer batteries, but also may be available in even higher-capacity models. For example, some third-party netbook batteries have a rating over 10,000 mAh, and some batteries have nine or more cells.

When buying batteries that have above-normal capacity, always check a photo of the battery and its dimensions. In some cases, the battery may be physically larger than the one that comes with your netbook, — in that event, don't expect a flush fit, because the bigger battery will stick out beyond the back or bottom of the case, increasing the overall size (and weight) of your netbook.

Before you buy a third-party battery (especially from eBay), check what people have to say about the battery and vendor in online reviews — Amazon. com and forums devoted to a particular netbook are a good place to look. For example, Mugen Power Batteries (www.mugenpowerbatteries.info) has received a number of favorable reviews for its extended life batteries.

Burning down the house

No, I'm not talking about those exploding Dell laptop batteries back in 2006 — despite all the hype, only a few actual cases were reported. Instead, I want to mention that sometimes getting netbook batteries can be challenging due to a weak link in the supply chain. Only a few plants make netbook (and laptop) batteries, and they seem to have bad luck when it comes to fires. In March 2008, a fire broke out at LG Chem's Ochang, South Korea battery plant. This severely impacted ASUS, Dell, and HP laptop battery availability. The computer industry was already being impacted by an earlier fire in October 2007 at a battery factory in Japan that caused laptop battery shortages. If you find batteries are backordered, it might be high-demand or another fire.

Power to-go: Universal batteries

If you need extra juice, you don't necessarily need to purchase a battery built expressly for your netbook. There are always universal batteries. These are external lithium-ion batteries that can power all sorts of electronic devices — MP3 players, cell phones, and other types of laptops — as well as your netbook. After the universal battery is fully charged from an included AC or DC adapter, plug the battery into a netbook's power jack (where you normally plug in the wall charger), and your little netbook runs on the external battery until it discharges. When the external battery is depleted, the netbook automatically starts using its internal battery.

One of my favorite universal batteries is the Tekkeon myPower ALL product line (shown in Figure 13-2). Three models are available:

- **MP3700:** Provides up to 20 volts, has a smart sensor that automatically determines the correct amount of voltage to use, a USB charging port, and can be expanded with a spare battery pack. Priced around $170.

- **MP3450:** Provides up to 19 volts, has a USB charging port, and can be expanded with a spare battery pack. Priced around $130.

- **MP3300:** A lower-cost model without all the features of the MP3450, but still provides up to 14 volts of power.

Figure 13-2:
A Tekkeon myPower ALL universal battery.

I've found an MP3450 provides around three-and-a-half to four hours of power before my netbook's internal battery takes over — your mileage may vary.

Universal batteries aren't quite as lightweight and svelte as a netbook's internal battery (they're still very portable though), but they do offer more functionality for around the same price. They're especially a good deal if you have another laptop or need to power other portable electronic devices.

For more information on the myPower ALL batteries, visit `www.tekkeon.com/site/products-mypowerall.php`.

Human-powered netbooks

The One Laptop Per Child XO, which I consider the first netbook, originally was designed to be powered by a built-in hand crank. These computers were destined for off-the-grid developing countries, and the engineers thought it would be smart to make the little laptops human-powered. Unfortunately, the hand crank was dropped from production models due to reliability issues and the fact it took a whole lot of cranking to charge up the battery.

If you want to power your netbook with muscle, you still have a number of options. Here's a quick rundown.

One of my favorite human-powered electrical device manufacturers is Freeplay Energy (`www.freeplayenergy.com`). The company started out producing rugged, hand-crank radios for use in Africa and third-world countries. Since then, they've expanded their products to a number of different human-powered gadgets. Weza (a Swahili word that means *power*) is built around a 12-volt lead-acid battery. You can charge the battery by plugging it into an electrical outlet or solar panel or by stepping on its foot treadle. FreeCharge 12V is a small, lightweight, 12-volt handheld generator.

Attach a cigarette lighter adapter to your netbook, plug it into FreeCharge, and start cranking (at 120 revolutions per minute or more) — be prepared for a couple of hours of cranking and some sore muscles afterward.

Another alternative-energy company called Potenco (`www.potenco.com`), has developed a pull-cord power generator, which should be easier to use than a crank device. At this time, it's not commercially available, but hopefully will be soon.

The least-demanding human-powered way to run and charge your netbook is with a pedal-powered power source. This is a stationary bike hooked up to a generator. As you pedal, the generator creates electricity that you can use to directly power an electronic device or charge a 12-volt battery. For more information on this option, check out Windstream (`www.windstreampower.com`) and the do-it-yourself Pedal Powered Generator (`www.los-gatos.ca.us/davidbu/pedgen.html`).

Have a good workout!

Getting a Charge (Out of Your Car)

A car or truck can power your netbook and charge its battery — although when gas prices are up, it's a pretty expensive generator. If you're going to be on the road with your netbook, you have two options for keeping it charged: a cigarette lighter adapter (CLA) or an inverter. Here's the lowdown on both.

Cigarette lighter adapters

Cigarette lighters first started appearing in cars way back in the 1920s — they were originally designed for lighting cigars; that's why they're the stubby size they are. Thanks to some design changes in the 1950s, it became possible to use the 12-volt, direct current generated by a car to power electrical devices connected to a CLA. By using a CLA like the one in Figure 13-3, you can run and charge your netbook.

CLAs have circuitry that converts the car's 12-volt electricity into power that's usable by a netbook. CLAs also have fuses to protect your little laptop in case a higher-than-normal amount of current comes through the lighter. Fried netbooks don't smell or work all that well.

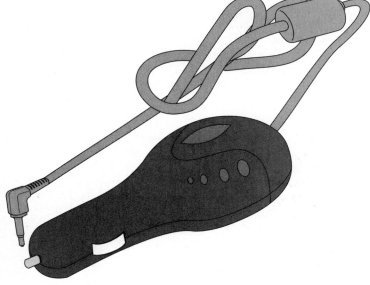

Figure 13-3:
A basic netbook cigarette lighter adapter (CLA).

Sine language

You may read Internet forum discussions about inverters, sine waves, and powering netbooks. Here's what you need to know.

The two types of inverters are

- **True-sine wave inverters** produce power like the kind you get from your electric company. When you look at the power wave through an oscilloscope, it appears as a smooth sine wave.

- **Modified-sine wave (also called square wave) inverters** are the most common type of inverter. They're considerably cheaper than true-sine inverters and produce more of a squared-off looking wave.

Modified-sine wave inverters work fine for powering laptops and most household appliances. True-sine inverters are required for devices that might have problems using an electrical current with a modified sine wave. These include fax machines, laser printers, plasma TVs, and other specialized devices.

Many manufacturers offer CLAs for their netbooks — third-party models are often available cheaper. Another option is to use a universal DC adapter such as those sold by Radio Shack (www.radioshack.com). These units work with a number of different products — plugs are available to fit various electronic devices. A universal adapter and single plug should cost around $45.

If you use a universal, multi-voltage charger, be sure you use the correct voltage for your netbook — check the power rating label, which is usually on the underside of the case. A netbook's power supply can handle a little over and under its rated voltage, but if you use too many volts, you risk damaging the computer. You also need to ensure the power tip is the correct polarity (such as the tip is positive and the outer sleeve is negative or the reverse). Always check a device's user guide or online specifications to find out about its power requirements.

Some airlines offer DC power outlets in their seats (usually business and first class). If you do a lot of flying in addition to driving, CLA chargers are available that work in both car and plane receptacles.

Speaking of charging and flying, when I'm on the road, I always carry a small wall-socket plug with multiple outlets. Public spots in airports for recharging electronic devices are always at a premium, and a multiple-outlet plug lets you get karma points by sharing the juice from a single outlet with other travelers.

Inverters

Another option for powering your netbook while on the road is to use an automotive inverter. This device converts a car's 12-volt DC (direct current) to 120-volt AC (alternating current) — what comes out of standard United States electrical outlets.

Car inverters (two are shown in Figure 13-4) provide one or more electrical outlets that work just like a wall socket. Just plug in any electrical device, and you can run it from your car's electrical system. (When the car is running, its battery is being charged, so you don't need to worry about it discharging.)

Figure 13-4:
Two types of car inverters: They're different in design but identical in function.

Inverters have different wattage ratings. The more watts an inverter can handle, the more it costs. Make sure you have a large enough inverter to accommodate the device(s) you plan on using. Because netbooks draw well under 30 watts, you can use a relatively inexpensive (around $20), 75-watt inverter.

All electrical devices (including netbooks) have a label that lists their wattage. If the device doesn't show watts but lists only volts and amps, use this simple formula: Watts = Volts × Amps

Here comes the sun

How about going green and using the sun to power your netbook? Here are some things to know.

Those little solar panels used for charging cell phones and MP3 players aren't going to charge your netbook — they produce well under 5 watts. At the very minimum, you need a 25-watt solar panel to directly power your netbook while it's running. It's possible to use lower-wattage panels to charge your netbook's battery while the laptop *isn't* running.

A solar panel's rated wattage is the maximum amount of power produced under the most optimal conditions. That means direct, bright sunshine. Add some clouds, and the wattage starts to fall off — the more clouds, the less power. Higher-panel wattage ratings (the more watts, the higher the price and larger the panel) increase the chances you'll get the power you need in less-than-optimal conditions.

In addition to coming in different sizes, solar panels can be rigid or flexible. Figure on spending $200 to $250 for a rigid, 30-watt solar panel and around double that for a flexible panel with the same output. (Solar panels are coming down in price, but aren't cheap yet.)

When you've picked out a panel (or several, because you can combine them) you need to decide whether you'll power your netbook directly from the panel or from an external battery — the solar panel keeps the battery charged, which in turn powers your netbook.

There's much more to solar-powering your netbook than I have the space to discuss. Check out these Web sites for more information: Home Power Magazine (www.homepower.com), SolarPower Forum (www.solarpowerforum.net), and OtherPower.com (www.fieldlines.com/section/solar). Two great retail sites for solar panels and products are Modern Output (www.modernoutpost.com) and Real Goods (www.realgoods.com). Get your green geek on!

The advantage to an inverter is you can use a variety of electrical devices with it and not need special plugs or adapters. Just plug in the wall wart (power adapter) that came with your netbook. Inverters are available in the automotive or electronics sections of most large chain stores.

Many car inverters now come with USB jacks, so you can charge MP3 players and other devices.

Power-Saving Tips

A lot of people instantly think a tiny computer like a netbook means long battery life. It's so small that it can't be using very much power and should run all day. Right?

Not so fast; there's a catch. Smaller computers tend to have smaller batteries that don't have as much capacity as bigger batteries in bigger laptops. So considering this, the typical battery life on netbooks tends to run anywhere from two and a half to around five hours. (Power-stingy processors like Atom increase battery life.)

While bigger batteries and miserly CPUs help extend battery life, laptops are like cars and gas mileage. "Your mileage may vary" — mostly depending on your driving (or computing) habits. Here are some tips to improve your battery life, giving you more smiles per gallon.

Turn off your netbook

Most folks have become accustomed to leaving their PCs turned on when they're not in use — mostly out of convenience due to the painfully long amount of time it takes for a computer to start up and go through the boot process. (Standby and hibernation modes are both attempts to speed up restart time while saving power, and I talk about them next.)

However, a netbook's speedy startup changes these rules. With super-fast boot times, there's no reason to leave your computer turned on when you're temporarily not using it, especially when you're running on batteries and it may be awhile before a recharge.

Use standby mode

Although I recommend turning off your netbook to maximize battery life if you're not going to be using it for awhile, sometimes you may want to use standby mode — this option is available in a dialog box when you use Windows to turn off your netbook.

In standby mode, power is reduced to various netbook hardware components, some of the memory is stored to drive, and the laptop goes to sleep. When you resume (by pressing the power button), the netbook wakes up. After a few seconds, all the windows and programs you had open before you went into standby are restored. This is convenient if you have a lot of browser tabs open or are working with several documents. You don't have to reopen them like you would if you turned off the laptop.

Just keep in mind that power is still being consumed in standby mode, although the amount is smaller compared with when the netbook is turned on and running.

In Windows, in addition to standby mode, you also have an option called *hibernation*. Hibernation mode saves memory to disk like standby, but then turns the computer completely off (instead of reducing power). When the PC is turned back on again, the boot process is skipped, and the stored memory contents are restored. You can enable hibernation and set other power conserving preferences by clicking Power Options in the Windows Control Panel. Refer to Windows online help for more information on hibernation.

Use low power settings

Some netbooks have an option to control the processor speed. The faster a processor runs, the more power it consumes. If the speed is reduced, performance is decreased, but battery life goes up. On models that support changing the clock speed, you can speed up or slow down the chip in the BIOS or a separate utility program. Check your user manual to see whether your netbook supports this feature.

Turn off Wi-Fi

If you don't need a Wi-Fi connection to the Internet (say you're just doing some basic word processing) and your netbook's wireless status light is on, the built-in wireless card is sipping away precious battery power. Even when you're not connected to an access point, the wireless card is still powered up and is sending and receiving data.

If you don't need Wi-Fi, turn it off. (Check your user manual for instructions. This is usually a function key. When you press the function key again, wireless is available — the status light will be illuminated.)

If your netbook supports Bluetooth and you're not using it, turn it off too. Check your user manual for instructions.

Dim the display

In addition to the wireless card, your netbook's monitor is another culprit in eating away at battery life. The brighter the screen display, the more power is required. You guessed it: You can maximize your battery time by reducing the screen's brightness. Dim your screen to a usable level — there's typically a function key that does this; check your user manual.

Treat your battery right

Many people tend to take electronic device batteries for granted. When they get long in the tooth and no longer hold a full charge, the battery (or sometimes the device) gets replaced. I won't get up on a soapbox about our disposable society.

Batteries are pretty complicated chemical power storage devices, and how you treat them directly impacts their longevity. As a battery ages, its storage capacity diminishes, so it makes economic and environmental sense to keep it healthy. Here are a few tips to maximize long-term battery life:

- ✔ **Keep them cool.** Lithium ion batteries exposed to high temperatures have shorter lives. Keep batteries out of the sun and very warm locations. If your netbook feels like it's starting to get overly hot, consider removing the battery. (You need a nearby wall socket to run on AC power.)

- ✔ **Don't run them dry.** Completely discharging a battery decreases its life. Like a car, always leave a little extra in tank before you need a fill-up.

- ✔ **Recharge them often.** Don't be shy about plugging into a wall socket and recharging your battery, even when it's only partially discharged. Laptop batteries like to be treated this way.

- ✔ **Keep the contacts clean.** If you swap your batteries a lot, dirt and grime can build up on the contacts, preventing electrons from flowing freely. Every few months, use a cotton swab and alcohol to clean dirty battery contacts.

- ✔ **Use it or lose it.** Don't leave a charged battery sitting around unused for long periods of time as it will slowly discharge even though it's not being used. Fully discharging batteries shortens their lives. After it's charged, use the battery at least once every two to three weeks.

If you really want to get geeky about the technical aspects of batteries (trust me, it's fascinating), pay a visit to Battery University at `www.battery` `university.com`.

Disconnect USB devices

The USB ports on your netbook (or any computer, for that matter) are powered. Each port makes up to 5 volts available, so anytime you have a USB device connected to your netbook, it's drawing electricity. And when you're not plugged into a wall socket, that power is coming from the battery.

How much depends on the device. A USB flash drive may draw only a small amount of power, whereas an external DVD player without its own power source consumes much more.

As a general guideline, if you have an SD card or a USB thumb drive plugged in the entire time while using a battery, you'll lose from 5 to 15 minutes of power. An external USB hard drive consumes about 20 to 35 minutes of battery time. Your mileage will vary, but the more time a drive is accessed for read and write operations, the more power it needs.

The bottom line is if you're not using the USB device, unplug it. The same holds true for the card reader — remove the SD card if you're not using it. Even with low-consumption devices like memory drives and cards, every electron counts.

Some USB hard drives and DVD players require two USB ports to run. They come with a splitter cable that plugs into two of the computer's USB ports and then into the device. With these devices, this means the power from a single port doesn't provide enough juice to run the device. This isn't a big deal with a desktop PC, but it is with a battery-powered laptop. If you have a choice, external USB devices that require only a single port are much more battery thrifty.

Don't use animated screen savers

Using my trusty Kill A Watt meter (www.p3international.com, a slick device that measures how much power electric appliances use), I discovered something really interesting. Animated screen savers (on all kinds of computers) consume about twice as much power as just a blank screen. It makes sense, because the processor has to work harder drawing all of those intricate geometric shapes and flying icons of various types. A harder-working CPU needs more electricity, so if you use a screen saver, stick to one without animation.

Use a wired Ethernet connection

If you have a choice of connecting to the Internet either wirelessly or wired, pick the cable. The netbook's built-in Ethernet card requires less power than the internal Wi-Fi card. (Also, don't forget to turn off the wireless card to be really battery frugal.)

Know what activities drain batteries

Your netbook doesn't use the same amount of power for everything it does. Some activities require more electricity than others. (This is where a Kill A Watt meter is handy.) For example, these activities require more power than browsing Web pages, reading an e-book, or writing an e-mail:

- Watching videos
- Listening to music (the louder the speaker volume, the larger the battery drain)
- Connecting to external devices (such as hard drives and DVD player/writers)
- Playing games with lots of graphics

If you're trying to be a battery cheapskate because it will be hours before you can get to a wall socket for a recharge, keep the juice-sucking activities to a minimum.

Single task

Whether you like it or not, computers have taught people to become masters of multitasking. But guess what: Multitasking decreases battery life. The more programs and windows you have open at once, the more the processor needs to work. And the harder the processor works, the more power it requires. In addition, when you place a lot of demand on a processor, it generates extra heat. Heat degrades battery life (so does cold, by the way). Heat also causes the fan to come on, which uses even more juice. It's quite the vicious cycle actually.

So if you're away from a wall socket and you're trying to save every possible electron, just do one thing at a time on your netbook. You may find the simplicity is actually refreshing.

Chapter 14

External Storage

*W*hen the first generation of netbooks arrived, storage was extremely limited — solid state drives offered only a puny 4 to 8GB of space. Fortunately, a netbook's SD (Secure Digital) card reader and USB ports provided all sorts of opportunities for adding badly needed storage capacity to the little laptops.

Things have gotten much better since then, and unless you have an older netbook, space shouldn't be as much of an issue — thanks to larger solid state drives and conventional hard drives in the 120-to-160GB range, and even larger.

However, it's worth knowing about all the external storage options that are available for your netbook — whether you're swapping data between computers or accessing a media library filled with music and videos. In this chapter, I give you lowdown on using your netbook with external storage devices.

SD (Secure Digital) Cards

I have yet to see a netbook that doesn't have an SD (Secure Digital) card reader. In fact, built-in SD card readers are one of the features that define netbooks. On netbooks with small solid state drives, an SD card (shown in Figure 14-1) is a cheap, easy, and effective way to add more storage to a little laptop. Just press a card into the slot, and you have more space — the SD card appears in Windows Explorer just like a hard drive, and you can drag and drop files to it.

Digital life

Nothing lasts forever, and the same holds true for memory cards. An SD card's lifecycle is determined by three factors:

- **Insertion/removal cycle:** How many times you push the card into the reader and take it out. Many manufacturers figure 10,000 insertion/removals is a realistic expectation.

- **Read/write cycle:** The number of times the card reader reads and writes data to the card. You're good for about 1,000,000 read/write cycles.

- **Human factor:** I've found this to be the biggest life limiter to memory cards — you lose them, your cat chews on them, they go through the washing machine . . . you get what I'm saying.

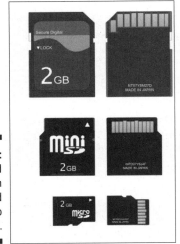

Figure 14-1: An SD card along with mini and micro versions.

Some SD cards have a write protection tab. If you can't save files to a card, check that the write protection tab hasn't accidentally been switched on.

SD cards also offer a way to try out other operating systems on your netbook without overwriting Windows or setting up your system to dual boot. (*Dual boot* means installing a program that allows you to select which operating system to run in case you have several different types installed.) But before I talk about the specifics of using an SD card, it's best that you have a basic understanding of memory cards.

Cavalcade of cards

Netbook SD card readers generally support three types of memory cards:

- ✔ **SD— (Secure Digital):** Flash memory cards that range from 8MB to 4GB.

- ✔ **SDHC (Secure Digital High Capacity):** This is an extension of the SD standard that debuted in 2006. It allows for memory cards with capacities higher than 4GB. The SD and SDHC cards are identical in size and shape; however, older card readers can't read the new format. (High-capacity cards are labeled SDHC so you can tell the two cards apart.)

  Based on the SDHC specification, these cards can theoretically have up to 2,048GB of storage. Wow! However, at the present, card manufacturers have set a maximum of 32GB. Don't be surprised if that goes up in the future.

- ✔ **MMC (MultiMedia Card):** SD and SDHC cards are derived from an older standard known as MultiMedia Cards. MMCs are slower and have less storage capacity. SD and SDHC cards have surpassed MMCs in popularity.

The same SD cards you use in your netbook are also used in digital cameras. For more details on memory cards, check out Steve's Digicams (a digital camera Web site) at `www.steves-digicams.com/flash_memory.html`.

In addition to SD and MMC cards, a few netbook models also support less-popular Memory Stick and XD cards. If you have a camera that uses these types of cards, it's worthwhile to consider getting a netbook that supports them too.

Your digital camera or an older card reader may be able to read only SD cards. If that's the case with your card reader, when you insert an SDHC card, it won't be recognized. Keep this in mind if you're going to be swapping the card between your netbook and another device. Card readers that support SDHC can read SD cards, but not vice versa.

SDXC

SDXC stands for Secure Digital Extended Capacity. This is a new memory card standard announced in 2009 that supports from 32GB to a whopping 2TB (that's *terabytes*) of storage. As I write this, cards and compatible card readers for the new standard aren't available yet. But I certainly expect them to start showing up in netbooks in the near future.

If you have a mini or micro SD card (shown earlier in Figure 14-1), you'll need an adapter to be able to use the card with your netbook's card reader.

Ins and outs

Using an SD card with your netbook is simple. With the label facing up, insert the card into the card reader (with the metal connection points pointing toward the computer) until you hear it click in place. You may need to use your fingernail to press the card all the way in. When fully inserted, the card will be flush with the case.

To remove the card, press on it until you hear it click. The card reader is spring loaded, and the SD card will partially pop up. After the card is released, pull it all the way out of the card reader slot.

When you're done using an SD card, be sure to use the Safely Remove Hardware command before removing the card — on the right side of Windows taskbar, right-click the icon with the small green arrow and then choose Safely Remove Hardware. This ensures all files are properly closed on the card before you eject it. You take the risk of possibly losing data or corrupting files if you remove a card without using this command. If Windows tells you the card can't be removed, a file you've been working on is open or perhaps a Windows Explorer window is displaying the directory contents of the card. Close the file or window and try again.

Formatting SD cards

You can format an SD card in Windows in three ways:

- ✔ **FAT16:** FAT stands for File Allocation Table — in this case, 16-bit. This format dates back to the mid-1970s and was the primary file system for DOS and Windows. The maximum file size is 2GB.

- ✔ **FAT32:** An enhanced, 32-bit version of FAT that debuted in 1996 offering larger volume and maximum file sizes.

- ✔ **NTFS:** NTFS stands for NT File System. (Windows NT was the predecessor of Windows 2000, XP, Vista and 7 with NT standing for New Technology.) It's now the standard file system for Windows, offering many improvements over FAT.

Most SD cards already come preformatted as FAT16 or FAT32, so you shouldn't need to worry about initially formatting them.

If an SD card you purchased needs formatting or if you have a card that doesn't seem to work right, you'll need to format it. Here's how:

1. **Insert the card in the reader.**

2. **Right-click the Start button and choose Explore.**

3. **In Windows Explorer, select the drive letter associated with the card you want to format.**

4. **Right-click the drive letter and choose Format from the shortcut menu.**

   A Format dialog box appears.

5. **Select the format type from the File System drop-down list and give the card a name in the Volume Label text box.**

   Which format type you specify depends on how you use the card:

   - If you're only using the card with Windows computers, format it as NTFS.

   - If you'll be using the card with your netbook and another device (digital camera, cell phone, MP3 player, or a Mac or Linux computer), format the card as FAT32.

6. **Click the Start button.**

   You're asked whether you're sure you want to format the card.

7. **Click OK to continue.**

   A Format Complete dialog box appears after the card is successfully formatted.

If you want to use the SD Card Association's (the SD standards group) official formatting utility, you can download a Windows version here: `www.sdcard.org/about/downloads`.

Booting another operating system

Most netbooks allow you to boot from another operating system that's installed on an SD card. This is handy if you want to see what Linux is all about without installing the free operating system over Windows or going through the hassles of setting up a dual boot system — do a Google search for *dual boot* to find out more.

Hot stuff

Some netbook users have encountered problems with corrupted files on SD cards or a card that won't format properly. If this sounds familiar, the culprit may be excessive heat. On netbook models that run a little hot, it's possible the card reader controller chip overheats and causes write problems — especially when writing large files.

This seems to be an intermittent problem that impacts only some netbook models — and even then, not all of them. If you're having SD card issues similar to the ones I just mentioned, here are some things to try:

✔ Make sure the card isn't defective. It's not unheard of to get a bad SD card. Try using it on another computer.

✔ Make sure the card reader on the netbook isn't to blame. Again, try using the card with another PC.

✔ Reformat the card.

✔ Placing a netbook on a soft surface can block the cooling vents, so keep it on a hard surface.

✔ Use a utility program to set the CPU voltage to a lower level. The lower voltage decreases CPU temperature, which lowers the overall heat. The tradeoff is that system performance is decreased because the processor's speed is lowered to run cooler.

✔ If you need to transfer large files, do so before the netbook starts to warm up.

Booting from another operating system can also be a lifesaver. If Windows gets corrupted or your netbook is infected by a particularly nasty virus, in many cases you can boot from Linux to recover files or repair damage.

Many Linux distributions are available in "live" system versions. That means they boot and run from a CD-ROM, USB flash drive, or SD card, and you don't need to install them on your hard drive.

When it comes to running another operating system on my netbook, I prefer SD cards because they are compact and fit flush in the case — you can easily leave an alternative operating system in the SD card reader, ready to use when needed.

Check some of the user forums that I list in Chapter 22 for Linux distributions that work well with your netbook. Two of my current favorites are

✔ Ubuntu Netbook Remix, www.ubuntu.com

✔ Easy Peasy, www.geteasypeasy.com

Here are the general steps for using an alternative operating system on your netbook:

1. **Install the operating system on an SD card.**

   Follow the instructions on the distribution Web site or from a user forum. You can install the operating system on an SD card using any computer that has a card reader.

2. **Turn off your netbook and insert the SD card into the card reader.**

3. **Press the key sequence to force the netbook to boot from the SD card reader instead of from the hard drive.**

   Check your user manual for details on which key(s) to use.

The operating system should load and run — if you're asked whether you want to install the operating system, say no. You want to use the "live" version, not install the OS to your hard drive. (A *live* version is a copy of an operating system designed to run on an SD card, USB flash drive, or CD-ROM without being installed on a hard drive.)

Have fun exploring Linux!

If you run Linux from an SD card and change any of the default system settings, these settings usually aren't saved when you shut down — a live version is a bit like a demo. If you're going to be frequently using the operating system, you need a way to keep the settings *persistent*. This should be described on the distribution Web site or in a user forum post.

For a complete list, including descriptions, of just about every Linux distribution on the planet, visit `http://distrowatch.com`.

One of the main downsides to running an operating system from an SD card is that operating systems are always reading and writing data. Doing lots of reads and writes wears out an SD card much faster than a conventional hard drive. I can't give you an exact timeframe, but I've heard of users needing to replace an SD card after running Linux daily on the card for six months to a year. If you're going to be running Linux every now and then, using an SD card is fine. If you're a heavy Linux user, look into a distribution that has been optimized to run on a flash memory device with limited reads and writes or bite the bullet and install the operating system on your hard drive — either standalone or dual boot.

USB Flash Drives

I'll bet you remember the good old days when floppy disks were the technology of choice for saving files and moving data between computers. (And you get bonus points if you remember when those nifty 3.5-inch hard-cased floppy disks first appeared and started to replace their flexible 5.25-inch cousins.)

Alas, the poor floppy's fate was sealed in 2000 when IBM and Trek Technology introduced a slick alternative to the ubiquitous floppy disk. The product was a flash memory chip with a USB connector enclosed in a small plastic case and dubbed the ThumbDrive. Plugged into a PC's USB port, the drive offered a whopping 8MB of storage — around five times more than a 3.5-inch floppy disk held at the time.

The rest is history, and USB flash drives (also known as UFDs, pen drives, jump drives, key drives, thumb drives, or in my family, *brain suckers*) have become a part of everyday computing — and have kept the tradeshow trash and trinket industry alive and well.

Flash drives come in all sorts of shapes and sizes (as shown in Figure 14-2) and are available in capacities up to 64GB. (It's difficult to find new drives under 1GB these days.) Storage space seems to always be rising with prices falling, and as I write this, if you shop around, you can get a 16GB thumb drive for around $40 or less.

Figure 14-2:
A collection
of USB flash
drives with
an SD card
on the right.

Flash drive lifecycles

Like any storage media, flash drives aren't immortal. Two primary factors determine how long of a life a flash drive will have.

The first factor is the type of flash memory used. The most common is called MLC (multilevel cell). There's also SLC (single-level cell), which is twice as fast (as well as twice as expensive). SLC also boasts a longer lifecycle of 100,000 write/erase cycles compared to MLC's 10,000 write cycles. (Unfortunately, most manufacturers don't label their products, so you won't know whether a more expensive thumb drive is using SLC.)

Right around the maximum number of write cycles, a flash drive slowly starts to fail — parts of its memory will no longer able to be used. Many flash drives have a five-year warranty, and under normal use should last beyond that.

The other factor that limits a flash drive's life is the USB connector. Manufacturers use a figure known as Mating Durability (I didn't make that up) to predict the maximum number of connections before failure. That number is about 1,500. If you do the math, that's using your flash drive once every day for a little over four years.

You can find lots of USB flash drive reviews on the Web. A relatively comprehensive and recent one (May 2009) appeared in *Ars Technica:* `http://arstechnica.com/hardware/news/2009/05/usb-flash-drive-roundup.ars`. Search for *flash drive reviews* in Google to find more.

Both SD cards and USB flash drives use flash memory. Because more computers have USB ports than built-in card readers, flash memory in the form of USB drives is more popular for data storage — at least on personal computers.

Netbooks have two or three USB 2.0 ports (which are compatible with older and slower 1.1 USB flash drives as well as the more modern, faster 2.0 drives). Just plug a flash drive into your netbook and use Windows Explorer to access the files.

When you're done using a flash drive, be sure to use the Safely Remove Hardware command in Windows taskbar before removing the drive. I discuss this in the SD card "Ins and outs" section earlier in the chapter.

Flash drives are perfect for

- ✔ Adding more storage space to netbooks with low-capacity solid state drives
- ✔ Backing up critical files on your netbook

- ✔ Moving files between your netbook and primary computer
- ✔ Booting alternative operating systems (as I describe in the earlier "Booting another operating system" section)
- ✔ Adding supplemental system memory through ReadyBoost (if your netbook is running Vista or Windows 7)
- ✔ Installing frequently used programs — visit www.portableapps.com to see what I mean

Most USB flash drives are formatted as FAT — see the "Formatting SD cards" section, earlier in this chapter, for more information. If you need to format a flash drive, the same principles and techniques used with SD cards apply.

If you store sensitive documents on a USB flash drive, I highly encourage you to use encryption to keep files safe. I tell you what you need to know in Chapter 9.

Some MP3 players can serve as a USB *mass storage device* (often referred to as MSC or UMS) — that means you can use it with your netbook to transfer and save files. Just connect the player to the little laptop with a USB cable, and the player's memory or drive will appear as a volume in Windows Explorer. Check your MP3 player manual for more information.

U3

A number of USB flash drives come with something called U3 — no, this isn't a band formed by the offspring of Bono and the other founders of rock legend U2.

U3 (www.u3.com) is a technology for automatically launching programs stored on a USB flash drive. It uses a program called LaunchPad that runs whenever the flash drive is inserted into a Windows computer. The idea is for U3 compliant programs to cleanly run on any Windows PC. Normally, program settings are written to the Windows registry, which makes it difficult to install a program on a flash drive and be able to move it from one computer to another with all the settings intact. U3 and compatible programs (a list is here: http://software.u3.com) address this issue.

I'm personally not a big fan of U3 — I've experienced compatibility issues with various hardware and software, I don't like memory and storage space being taken up by something I don't use, plus the original version left a bad taste in my mouth because it was next to impossible to uninstall. For program portability, I'm much more in favor of the Portable Apps (www.portableapps.com) approach. Unless you have a compelling reason to keep it, I recommend removing U3 from your flash drive — either run the uninstaller program or visit the drive's support Web site for instructions.

Microsoft and SanDisk are currently working on a replacement for U3 called StartKey. I've got my fingers crossed it won't have as many issues as U3.

If you're a Windows user who frequently defragments your hard drive to keep it running smoothly, don't bother defragmenting your USB flash drive. Defragmentation works by optimizing access to data on a drive with spinning platters and moving heads. Flash memory has no moving parts and is random-access, so you don't get any performance gains with defragmenting. Additionally, because defragmentation moves data around for optimization, the write/erases decrease the flash memory's life. (See the "Flash drive life-cycles" sidebar.)

USB Hard Drives

USB ports make life easy when it comes to adding external storage to your netbook. A USB hard drive is a traditional hard drive (the same kind you find inside a desktop PC or laptop) with an enclosure and USB cable. Just plug an external hard drive into your netbook (or any other computer) and like magic, more gigabytes appear.

If you're interested in upgrading your netbook's internal hard drive, be sure to check out Chapter 18.

You can get two types of external USB hard drives for your netbook:

- **Mobile:** These drives have a small enclosure (small enough to fit into a pocket) and are designed to be carried around easily. They have limited storage capacity (generally in the 160 to 500GB size range and increasing) but typically don't require a separate power source.

  Choose a mobile USB drive if your netbook has a low-capacity solid state drive and you want to bring more storage with you on the road (or anytime you want to bring a large amount of data with you).

- **Desktop:** These are larger drives, both in terms of capacity (1 terabyte models are common) and enclosure size (bigger cases to handle the bigger capacity drive). Examples of desktop and portable USB drives are shown in Figure 14-3.

  Choose a desktop model for archiving files or if you don't need to bring extra storage capacity with you. For example, instead of keeping your entire music or video collection on your netbook, store it on a larger desktop USB drive and keep only some of the files on your netbook.

Both types of drives are easily moved from one computer to another and make great backup solutions.

Hard drives operate at different speeds — measured in RPMs (revolutions per minute). The faster a hard drive platter spins, the faster the data access. Most PC hard drives run at 5,400 RPM. You generally pay a little extra for a 7,200 RPM drive.

USB external drives are slower than internal hard drives. For day-to-day computing, the speed difference isn't that noticeable. However, if you transfer a large number of files or a single big file, you'll definitely see a lag.

Figure 14-3:
Portable and desktop USB hard drives next to a 10-inch netbook.

Prices for smaller mobile drives range from around $100 to $200. Popular USB drive manufacturers include

- **Iomega,** www.iomega.com
- **Maxtor,** www.maxtor.com
- **Seagate,** www.seagate.com
- **SimpleTech,** www.simpletech.com
- **Western Digital,** www.westerndigital.com

USB power considerations

USB ports not only transfer data back and forth, but can also provide power to a connected device. (That's what an external drive is getting its juice from, unless it uses its own power supply.)

Ideally, you plug a USB hard drive or DVD into your netbook and everything works, with the files and folders all displayed in Windows Explorer. However, to function correctly, some drives need more power than a single USB port can provide.

This is addressed with either an external power source (especially with larger capacity drives)

or a special USB Y-cable. You plug the two ends of the Y-cable into two netbook USB ports and the single end into the drive. This supplies enough power to run the drive from the two netbook ports.

Drives that require power from a single USB port are more energy efficient, which means longer battery life when you're not plugged into a wall socket. They also don't tie up a second USB port. If you have a choice, always go with a drive that needs only a single cable.

When you're done using a USB hard drive, before unplugging it be sure to use the Safely Remove Hardware command in the Windows taskbar. My editor thinks I'm sounding like a broken record with this, but it's a good habit to have. See the SD card "Ins and outs" section earlier in the chapter for more information.

If you have an IDE or SATA internal hard drive from an old PC lying around collecting dust, consider turning it into a cheap desktop storage device for your netbook. Just pick up a USB IDE adapter. Plug one end into the old hard drive (or an old internal CD or DVD drive for that matter), hook up the included power supply if needed, and then plug the USB connector into the netbook. The adapters are reasonably priced under $25 and are available from a number of online retailers. Do a Google search for *usb ide adapter*. If you don't like the unsightly appearance of a naked hard drive, do a Google search for *hard drive enclosure* for places to purchase an inexpensive plastic case.

CD-ROM, DVD, and Blu-ray Drives

The last stop on this tour of netbook external storage devices is in the optical department — not glasses, but optical storage. These devices include the CD-ROM, DVD, and Blu-ray family of drives — all of which use a small beam of laser light precisely focused on a spinning disc that stores the data.

Unlike traditional laptops, netbooks don't come with a built-in optical drive — considering the size, there's no place to put it, plus manufacturers try to keep netbook costs down. Realistically, in its role as an ultra-portable laptop, you can easily get by without ever needing an optical drive for your netbook.

However, there are a couple of reasons that might lead you to purchase an optical drive, such as wanting to

- ✔ Watch movies on commercial DVDs.
- ✔ Restore your system from the recovery DVD that came with your computer.
- ✔ Access files you have stored on DVDs and CD-ROMs.

Before I discuss specifics, it's good to have a basic understanding of the three types of optical storage media that are currently available:

- ✔ **CD-ROM:** Compact discs were the first widely used optical storage media. Depending on the type, a CD-ROM (read-only memory) can store between 650 and 900MB of data.
- ✔ **DVD:** Digital versatile discs (formally DVD-ROM) followed CD-ROMs and can store 4.7GB of data on a single-sided disc.
- ✔ **Blu-ray:** These discs (the name comes from a blue laser the technology uses) are the latest in optical storage and can store a mammoth 25GB of data on a single-sided disc.

Two types of drives are available for these storage mediums:

- ✔ **Read only:** Like the name suggests, a read-only drive can view only data — like a DVD or Blu-ray player you hook up to your television. You can't write data with these types of drives. These days, most optical drives for computers are read/write, which I describe next.
- ✔ **Read/write:** These drives can both read and write data — they're often called *burners*. With each of the optical storage medium types you can buy blank, writable discs — either writable once or many times. Files can be written to but not deleted from a disc labeled with *R* (such as CD-R). Files can be written and deleted from discs labeled with *RW.*

USB versions of optical drives are available, and it's just a matter of plugging them into your netbook to get them running — of course check the user manual for installation instructions.

Drives are generally *backwards compatible.* That means a DVD drive can use both DVDs and CD-ROMs, or a Blu-ray drive can access Blu-ray, DVDs, and CD-ROMs. However, always check the manufacturer's specifications for compatibility information.

Because of backwards compatibility, CD-ROM drives have gone the way of the dodo and have been replaced by DVD drives. For netbooks, I recommend a portable USB DVD drive such as the one shown in Figure 14-4. (This is an LG model GSA-E50N, by the way, which is very popular with netbook users and works quite well with both Windows and Linux models.) Portable DVD drives are priced between $100 and $150 and are available online or from most large electronics retailers.

If you have an old internal DVD drive from a desktop PC or laptop, you may be able to connect it to your netbook with a USB IDE adapter. See the previous section on hard drives to find out more.

Although Blu-ray is the wave of the future, netbooks aren't quite up to speed yet — at least when it comes to viewing Blu-ray videos. At present, most netbooks don't come with high-performance graphics chipsets that allow you to watch high-definition videos. Unless your netbook has a faster processor and compatible graphics chipset, for now I'd stick with a DVD drive and pass on Blu-ray.

Figure 14-4:
LG Slimline USB DVD drive with a 10-inch netbook.

Chapter 15

Netbook Gizmos and Gadgets

· ·

In This Chapter

▶ Personalizing your netbook case

▶ Selecting an external mouse

▶ Connecting an external keyboard

▶ Dialing up with a modem

▶ Adding on Bluetooth

▶ Listening to headphones, headsets, and speakers

▶ Using external monitors and projectors

▶ Tuning in television

▶ Lighting up your netbook

· ·

A netbook is pretty slick all by itself, right out of the box. However, you can find a bunch of tempting and groovy gizmos and gadgets on the market that can make your netbook even more useful — and easier to use.

In this chapter, I round up a collection of nifty add-ons, accessories, and other essential (and nonessential) goodies for your netbook — some battery powered, some not.

Just be forewarned: When you start to equip a netbook with some of the gadgets I mention here (as well as the hardware I mention in other chapters in this part), you can easily equal or surpass the price you paid for your little laptop.

With your credit card safely locked away, feel free to do some window shopping.

Blinging Out Your Netbook

Is your netbook's appearance a little too ho-hum for your personal tastes? Perhaps you're tired of your netbook looking like everyone else's. Then how about adding a little bling to your netbook and turning it into a work of art like the one shown in Figure 15-1? You don't even need to be an artist or have a creative bone in your body.

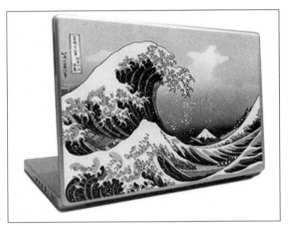

Figure 15-1:
Use a decal to personalize your netbook. (This decal came from Schtickers.)

You too can put a temporary tattoo on your netbook (or any laptop) thanks to a number of companies that offer decals designed to uniquely personalize your PC. Commonly referred to as *skins,* these aren't the cheap bumper stickers you see around town during election time. Instead, they're quality vinyl decals with a reusable adhesive that doesn't leave messy, sticky goo when you pull them off. Priced around $20, they come in solid colors, fine art prints, nature scenes, you name it — you can even submit graphics files to create your own custom decals.

Here are several skin sources to check out:

- ✔ **Schtickers,** www.schtickers.com
- ✔ **DecalGirl,** www.decalgirl.com
- ✔ **GelaSkins,** www.gelaskins.com

Most companies offer skins to fit standard laptop and netbook screen sizes — remember, you can always trim a larger decal. If you have a smaller screen netbook (7 to 9-inch screens) and can't find a skin to fit, order a custom 8.5 x 5.5-inch skin — you shouldn't need to do any extra cutting.

Netbooks with frickin' laser beams

No, I'm not referring to Dr. Evil and his pet sharks. (Refer to the *Austin Powers* movies as needed.) I'm talking about using laser beams to customize your netbook case. The availability of relatively low-cost laser engraving machines has spurred a cottage industry of entrepreneurs who will burn text and images into the top of your favorite laptop's case — without making a melty mess.

You submit the artwork, send in your laptop, and zzzzzzzzzzap, your netbook gets a permanent tattoo. The appearance is stunning and certainly will set your netbook apart from anyone else's. Expect to spend somewhere around one million dollars — not really, more in the $50-to-$150 range, depending on the complexity of the image.

Do a Google search for *laptop laser engraving* to check out photos and find vendors or call a nearby trophy or engraving shop to see whether they can do the job locally for you.

If you're a do-it-yourselfer and want to save some money, invest in a package of inkjet adhesive vinyl sheets. Or take your artwork in PDF format to a commercial print shop (like FedEx/Kinkos) and have someone print the file on an 8.5 x 11-inch clear adhesive label. Carefully cut the label to match your netbook's dimensions, and presto, a custom skin for less than a couple of dollars. (Consider getting two labels: one for the skin and the other to stick over it as a protective layer.) This do-it-yourself approach works great with white netbooks, but it leaves a little to be desired appearance-wise on darker-colored models. If you have a black or dark-color netbook that you want to dress up, I recommend using opaque white labels.

Your netbook manufacturer may offer personalized netbooks off the shelf. For example, Dell's Design Studio (www.dell.com/designstudio) allows you to choose from different designs that can be applied to your netbook's case before it shows up on your doorstep.

Messing Around with Mice

Some people either dislike or can't get used to a netbook touchpad. That's perfectly understandable because a conventional mouse is easier to use and more ergonomic. A touchpad is designed to provide a semi-efficient way to control the cursor in a small package.

If you often use your netbook where you have the room for a mouse on the side, I say go for one. Here are your two choices:

- ✔ **Cable:** This is the tried-and-true mouse that comes with desktop PCs. If you have an unused USB mouse lying around from an old computer (who doesn't?), just plug it in to your netbook — it immediately starts working. In addition to full-size mice, a number of companies make smaller computer rodents designed for laptops and travel use.

- ✔ **Wireless:** With wireless mice, there's no cable — just like the mice in the kid's song, they lost their tails. Instead, these mice work with radio signals that are sent between the mouse and computer. Wireless mice use either a proprietary transmitter/receiver that plugs into a USB port or rely on Bluetooth (either built-in or as an add-on).

When it comes to wireless mice, I've found Bluetooth mice to be a little less reliable than traditional wireless mice.

One of the more popular wireless mice for laptops and netbooks is Logitech's VX Nano — shown in Figure 15-2. This mini-mighty-mouse runs on two AAA batteries and communicates with your netbook through a small dongle that plugs into a USB port. The dongle is teensy weensy and can be stored inside the mouse so you don't lose it. VX Nanos are priced around $55.

Figure 15-2:
A Logitech VX Nano wireless mouse next to a netbook.

Mice come in all sorts of colors, shapes, and sizes. The fancy ones have a range of different features, such as three buttons, scroll wheels, retractable cables, and lasers for more precise tracking. For a new mouse, expect to shell out between $25 and $100 — depending on the features, of course.

A wireless mouse consumes more power than its cousin with a tail, so if you're trying to maximize battery life, go for a traditional cable mouse.

Contemplating Keyboards

During the early days of netbooks, probably the two biggest complaints about the little laptops were the small screens and the tiny keyboards — which caused lots of typos and cramped fingers for more than one user.

Thankfully the screen and keyboard issues are both addressed in today's somewhat larger netbooks. However, the keyboard is still a problem if

- ✔ You have an older netbook and never got the hang of the undersized keyboard.

- ✔ You still can't get used to any kind of a reduced keyboard size — even the 90 percent or larger versions.

- ✔ You like the reduced size and portability of a smaller netbook and can live with the keyboard for casual use, but you prefer a larger keyboard when it's time for serious typing.

If you fall into any of these categories, I have just the solution for you: a USB keyboard. There are four types:

- ✔ **Conventional:** Do you have an ancient and unused desktop PC with a USB keyboard gathering dust in a closet? Just plug the keyboard into your netbook and start typing. It isn't the most portable solution, but if you're going to be on the road a lot, check out the reduced-size travel keyboards available for under $40.

- ✔ **Folding:** Travel-size keyboards are still a little too bulky for some people. If you're one of them, an alternative is a folding keyboard, shown in Figure 15-3. As the name suggests, these keyboards fold in half when not in use. Models range from full to travel size and are priced in the $40-to-$60 range.

- ✔ **Bluetooth:** If your netbook has Bluetooth, wireless keyboards are available for it. These keyboards are slick because you can position them anywhere within 30 feet or so away from your netbook. Prices range from $75 to $150, depending on the model and features.

- ✔ **Roll-up:** The last option is to forget about a rigid plastic keyboard and go with a soft, flexible keyboard that rolls up. These water-resistant keyboards (shown in Figure 15-4) are sold by several companies and are priced between $20 and $40. A downside is the soft silicone keys don't make noise or have the tactile feel of a conventional keyboard.

Figure 15-3:
A USB folding keyboard.

Figure 15-4:
A USB flexible keyboard . . . or a tiny roller coaster. You decide.

Head over to Google and do a search for *travel keyboard, folding keyboard, Bluetooth keyboard,* or *flexible keyboard* for manufacturers and dealers.

Mastering Modems

With Wi-Fi, 3G wireless broadband, and cable/DSL modems, why on earth would you need a dialup modem? (Remember the funny chirping and screeching sounds they made?) Well, depending on where you are in the world, a dialup modem may be the only way to get Internet access. If you and your netbook are in such a situation, read on.

Be aware that getting a USB dialup modem to work under Linux is much more complicated than with Windows. You need to do a lot of configuration and may have to recompile the kernel. In fact, if you plan on getting a netbook and will be exclusively using a dialup modem, for the average user I personally wouldn't consider a Linux model because of the high hassle factor.

Because netbooks don't have a PC Card slot like many other laptops, you need a dialup modem that plugs into one of the USB slots. A popular USB modem that works with many Windows and Linux netbooks is the Zoom 3095 V92 USB Mini modem, shown in Figure 15-5.

USB dialup modems are readily available and cost in the $40-to-$50 range.

A handful of netbooks have ExpressCard slots, a smaller, more up-to-date version of a PC Card slot. If yours does, ExpressCard dialup modems are available.

With Windows netbooks, just plug in the USB modem and configure it in the Control Panel. Depending on the modem, you may also have to install a driver.

You may be able to use your cell phone as a modem with your netbook through a USB or Bluetooth connection. Visit the netbooks forums I list in Chapter 22 and see whether you can find any discussion threads that include your phone model.

Figure 15-5:
The Zoom 3095 USB modem works with many Windows and Linux netbooks.

Beefing Up with Bluetooth

Bluetooth has turned into the *de facto* standard for short-range wireless communications. Compatible cell phones, GPS receivers, mice, keyboards, laptops, PDAs, and other devices all use Bluetooth to exchange data over radio airwaves. (I discuss Bluetooth at length in Chapter 6.)

If your netbook doesn't have built-in Bluetooth, you can buy an add-on adapter. I recommend going with one of the smallest Bluetooth adapters around, made by Mogo. (Figure 15-6 compares the Mogo adapter's size with a Logitech wireless mouse dongle.)

Figure 15-6: The MoGo Bluetooth adapter (round) and the Logitech VX Nano adapter (square) on a netbook.

With any Bluetooth adapter, if you're running Windows, first see whether the device works by plugging it in. If it doesn't, follow the directions that came with the adapter and install the correct driver.

Getting a Bluetooth adapter to work with Linux is a bit more complicated. You'll first need to enter some commands at the console and modify a system configuration file or two. Check one of the netbook user forums I list in Chapter 22 for more information.

Expect to pay between $25 and $50 for a USB Bluetooth adapter.

Headphones, Headsets, and Speakers

If you have an MP3 player, you can use its earbuds or headphones to jack in to your netbook and listen to some tunes — more about music in Chapter 8. If you don't have an MP3 player and listening to music or watching videos on your netbook is starting to annoy your partner (who is trying to quietly read a book), maintain domestic tranquility with a set of headphones. Netbooks have the same size jack as MP3 players, and the marketplace is filled with headphones and earbuds ranging from under $10 to over $100.

All headphones and earbuds are not created equal. One my favorite sources for information on nonprescription hearing aides is a Web site with the in-your-face name of Anything But iPod (http://anythingbutipod.com). This site focuses on MP3 players but also has extensive headphone reviews and a lively and informative forum (http://anythingbutipod.com/forum/forumdisplay.php?f=22). You'll find out you don't have to spend a fortune on earbuds or headphones to get excellent sound quality.

If you use Skype or an instant messaging program that supports voice chat (see Chapter 10), you'll want to invest in a headset for your netbook. This is a pair of headphones that has a microphone grafted on, as shown in Figure 15-7.

Figure 15-7:
A headset is essential for netbook Skyping.

Sure, you can use your netbook's built-in microphone and speakers, but then everyone can hear your conversation if you're in a public place, you have to speak louder or crouch in toward the mic, and the sound quality isn't that great. A lightweight, easy-to-carry headset is a must if you're a Skyping netbook road warrior. And a headset won't cost you an arm and a leg — expect to pay anywhere between $15 and $75; the more you pay, the better the sound and features.

Speaking of speakers, the quality and size of built-in netbook speakers really depends on the netbook — brands and models vary quite a bit. Some speakers are pretty tiny and sound tinny, but others are halfway decent. If the sound from your built-in speakers just doesn't cut it, invest in some external speakers. The popularity of the iPod and other MP3 players prompted an explosion of external speaker options, ranging from cheap products that probably aren't much better than your netbook's to high-end speakers costing hundreds of dollars that integrate with home theater stereo systems.

One product that receives a big thumb's up from serious geeks is the X-mini (www.x-mini.com) series of capsule speakers (shown in Figure 15-8). These lightweight, cool-looking, portable speakers are powered by a rechargeable battery (plug it into a USB port when it gets low) and produce amazing sound for such a small package. Hook two of them together (they're priced around $25 a piece), and you're ready for stereophonic melodies.

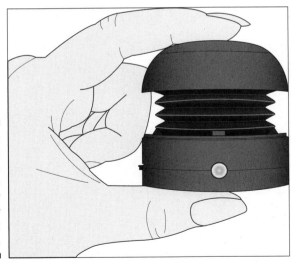

Figure 15-8:
X-mini capsule speakers offer portability and good sound.

Bring On the Big Screen

In my opinion, netbooks make the perfect computer for training and presentations. It's easy to tote a lightweight netbook to a meeting, class, or conference; and with its VGA output, hooking up a netbook to an external monitor or projector is a snap. In the following sections, I share a few thoughts on using external monitors and projectors with your netbook.

Some netbooks come with high-definition HDMI outputs instead of VGA. If you plan to connect your netbook to a monitor or projector, make sure it will be compatible with the external display device you plan to use.

External monitors

Whether you're going to connect your netbook to a 20-inch LCD PC monitor or a big-screen TV, getting the best and most viewable display on an external monitor is often a trial-and-error process. You'll need to try a number of different monitor settings until you find the one that works the best — this is because your netbook supports only a handful of screen resolutions, unlike a desktop PC.

Generally, connecting to a traditional monitor with a 4:3 screen ratio (square in shape) produces the best results. With a more contemporary 16:9 ratio (widescreen) monitor, you may end up with a distorted image — if so, try changing the screen resolution in the display settings in the Windows Control Panel.

With any monitor connected to your netbook, if you get a grainy or distorted picture, keep on trying different settings until you get the best-looking picture.

External monitor resolutions that don't match the resolutions your netbook can display will produce distorted images. This is because the pixels are no longer square, but elongated or compressed.

Projectors

Up until a few years ago, presentation projectors were bulky and expensive devices used only in universities, big corporations, and government agencies. Prices and sizes have both shrunk, and now portable home theater and business projectors are readily available for under $1,000.

When it comes to netbooks, multimedia projectors (often called PowerPoint projectors) are a bit easier to deal with than external monitors. This is because the display devices support only standard resolutions. It's usually just a matter of plugging a projector into the netbook and whatever is displayed on the screen appears on the wall.

Your netbook has a function key that controls the screen output. (Check your user manual for which key to use.) When you press the function key, it toggles through several different modes: netbook screen only, netbook screen and external display device, and external display device only. If you can't get your netbook to work correctly with a projector, try pressing the function key that controls screen output a few times.

Always connect and turn on the external monitor or projector first and *then* turn on your netbook. If the netbook is running when the display device is plugged in, it may not work correctly with the external device.

Creating presentations on a netbook can be a bit challenging because of the small screen and small keyboard (on some models). I typically build a presentation on a desktop PC or a full-size laptop and then copy it to my netbook.

If you're using your netbook only to display presentations, you don't need a full version of Microsoft Office and PowerPoint installed. Microsoft's PowerPoint Viewer is a handy utility that plays presentations on any computer running Windows. PowerPoint Viewer 2007 works with Microsoft Office 2007 and earlier versions of PowerPoint presentations. (You can also download older viewers that work with earlier versions of Office — they tend to be smaller if you're trying to conserve drive space.) The program comes preinstalled on some netbooks or visit the Downloads section at `http://office.microsoft.com`.

Flipping Channels

Just about everyone watches television over cable or on the Internet these days. However, now that the move to digital television has been completed (in the United States and elsewhere), it's possible to use your netbook to watch TV without cable or an Internet connection using something called a *TV tuner*. Here's the lowdown.

First off, you'll be going for something known as OTA (over the air) TV channels — just like in the good old, pre-cable, rabbit ear antenna days. You won't have access to hundreds of channels, only whatever's available in your local area — or wherever you're traveling.

A TV tuner is a hardware device that plugs in to your netbook's (or any computer's) USB port. These are usually priced between $50 and $100. You'll want an ATSC tuner.

ATSC stands for Advanced Television Systems Committee. ATSC digital television (DTV) is the format used for over-the-air digital TV broadcasts in North America, as well as South Korea and Taiwan. (If you're somewhere else in the world, you'll need a tuner that works for your location.)

The tuner receives digital TV broadcasts and decodes the signal so it can be played with Windows software supplied with the tuner. Some tuners give you the ability to record TV shows in MP4 format to watch later on your netbook or another computer.

Although most netbooks don't have the speediest processors or graphics chips, many users report acceptable performance with a TV tuner connected to their Atom processor netbooks.

You'll need an antenna to get the best signal reception out of a TV tuner. If your tuner didn't come with one, they're available online and at electronics stores. Make sure the antenna cable jack will fit the tuner.

Some manufacturers are starting to build tuners directly into their netbooks. For example, Dell offers an ATSC TV tuner as an option on some of its netbook models.

1 Saw the Light

Netbooks that don't have backlit keyboards can be a real pain to use when the lights go out. Small keys and unusual key placement can leave you fumble-fingered, and it doesn't help peeking at a keyboard you can't see.

To quote an old Robert Cray song, "Don't be afraid of the dark." Instead, pick up a USB-powered LED light. These handy little accessories are perfect for when the lights go down or out — LED bulbs also don't need much power, thus prolonging battery life.

Go for a light that sports a flexible gooseneck so you can optimally position it. Depending on the model and features, prices range between $5 and $20. (Don't be penny-wise and pound-foolish and pick up a dollar store variety. They often use low-quality LEDs and have cheap goosenecks that easily break.)

In Case You Gotta Have More USB Toys

I've only scratched the surface when it comes to USB add-ons for your little laptop. You can find many other USB gizmos for your netbook (or any PC). Some are useful (coffee cup heaters, fans, and plug-in rechargeable AA batteries); others are entertaining (dancing robots, toy rocket launchers, and program-mable LED signs). Most online computer accessory retailers have a large selection of USB toys. For excellent coverage of what's available, check out Coolest Gadgets at www.coolest-gadgets.com/category/pc-gadgets/usb-gadgets.

If you can't help yourself and end up with more USB gadgets than will fit in your netbook's two or three USB ports, pick up a *USB hub* — think of it like an electrical extension cord with multiple outlets, but for USB. You simply plug the USB hub into one of your netbook's USB ports. This makes more ports available — four is a common number. Just remember, a single USB port is limited in the amount of power it delivers. If you have several USB devices that need power (external hard drive, DVD player, and so on), you need a self-powered hub that has its own power supply.

Part IV
Checking Underneath the Hood

The 5th Wave
By Rich Tennant

@RICHTENNANT

"I couldn't get this 'job skills' program to work on my PC, so I replaced the motherboard, upgraded the BIOS and wrote a program that links it to my personal database. It told me I wasn't technically inclined and should pursue a career in sales."

In this part . . .

In this part of the book, I present some advanced
netbook topics — don't worry, I don't get too geeky.

First off is some essential information on troubleshooting
your netbook if something goes wrong — although I'm
keeping my fingers crossed that this never happens to
you. I then step you through options for backing up and
restoring your little laptop.

Some netbooks allow you to upgrade storage (as in a solid
state drive or hard drive) or system memory. I tell you
what you need to know to perform these relatively easy
operations.

In the second half of the part, I get a bit more technical
and discuss the various Windows system settings related
to netbooks, the essential drivers a netbook needs to run,
and why knowing what BIOS is may be more important
with netbooks than with other computers.

Chapter 16

Troubleshooting Your Netbook

Sometimes bad things happen to good netbooks — and their owners. Although I have my fingers crossed that you'll be an exception, at some point or another, just about every netbook user will encounter some kind of glitch. It may be a small annoyance that you can easily live with or a colossal problem of epic proportions that you need to fix immediately. Usually it's something in between.

Just knowing about problems and how to fix them is often good juju for keeping gremlins away. That's what this chapter is all about. In it, I give you general guidance on netbook troubleshooting. Then I cover some specific issues you may bump into with your netbook — and how to best remedy them.

How to Troubleshoot

Troubleshooting your netbook is as much of an art as it is a science. Keep in mind that you don't necessarily need to be a computer guru with years of experience to solve a technical problem. What you need is a structured, common-sense, problem-solving approach. Like this one:

1. **Collect the evidence.**

   Treat your netbook problem like a crime scene. To solve the mystery, you need to collect evidence. That means writing down exactly what error messages say, determining what sequence of steps or events caused the problem to occur, and remembering whether you installed a new program, changed a system setting, opened an e-mail attachment, or visited a new Web site before the problems began.

Consider yourself a crime scene technician — just like on *CSI*. As you collect evidence, you might have an "ah-ha" moment that will allow you to solve the case. If not, a more experienced detective (a Web forum member or manufacturer tech support person) should find the evidence valuable when coming up with a solution.

2. **Read the user manual and online help.**

This probably sounds trite, but all too often the solution to a common problem is between the pages of a user manual — or online help. Take a moment to see whether the manual mentions anything that resembles your problem. (If you lost your user manual, visit the manufacturer's Web site and download a PDF copy.) If you solve the problem this way, give yourself a pat on the back. If not, go to Step 3.

Always give yourself a set amount of time to solve a problem by yourself. It's easy to keep beating your head against a wall, trying the same thing over and over again while cursing in frustration. There's a point of diminishing returns, and you need to know when to stop and ask for help.

3. **Visit a Web forum.**

If you can't figure out a problem on your own, pay a visit to a netbook forum. I've found these Web sites invaluable for troubleshooting common and not-so-common netbook problems — especially forums that have a high number of posts and a lot of activity. I list netbook forums, many oriented to a specific manufacturer, in Chapter 22.

These user forums are free — although you need to register to post a message. Use the forum's search feature to see whether any past messages relate to your problem: Enter a few key words that relate to your troubles. If you can't find anything, post a question in an appropriate subforum. (Most forums have subforums devoted to different topics.) Give a clear description of your problem and list the evidence you collected. Over the next few days, check the post to see whether it received any replies. If your problem leaves everyone scratching their heads, go to Step 4.

4. **Contact the manufacturer.**

I consider contacting the manufacturer a last resort step in netbook troubleshooting. I say this not to disparage the manufacturers but because I find that Web forums usually provide quicker and sometimes better-quality information — this doesn't mean you should avoid manufacturer support, though.

Manufacturers usually offer a smorgasbord of support options on their Web sites, including lists of frequently asked questions, searchable knowledge bases, community forums, and e-mail address and phone

number contacts for technical support. I provide a list of netbook manufacturer Web sites in Chapter 22.

If you e-mail or call a manufacturer, have your list of Step 1 evidence in
front of you. The more information a support technician has about a
problem, the better he or she will be able to diagnose what's going on.

Troubleshooting Tools

When it comes to gathering troubleshooting information about your Windows
netbook (as well as diagnosing and sometimes solving problems), I find that
three system tools that come with Windows are indispensable: MSConfig,
MSInfo32, and Windows Task Manager. These tools are available with XP and
Vista and should also come with Windows 7 — Windows 7 has a slightly different appearance but still generally works the same.

Broken Windows

If something goes wrong with your netbook, it's
either a software problem or a hardware problem. If it's a software problem (with a program
or with Windows), that means there's a bug, a
setting was changed, a file got corrupted, or
some malicious software like a virus is running
amuck.

Here are some general suggestions you'll likely
hear from a technical support line for dealing
with a misbehaving netbook:

✔ **Run antivirus software.** A malicious program can cause your netbook to behave
strangely. Check out Chapter 9, where I
discuss virus protection software.

✔ **Make sure you have the latest program or
Windows updates.** Software makers frequently release updates that include bug
fixes — perhaps one that's related to your
problem.

✔ **Exit the program and shut down the netbook.** Sometimes a program has a bug that

isn't easily replicable. Try restarting your
netbook and see whether the problem is
still there.

✔ **If you recently installed a new program
and then started to encounter problems,
uninstall the program.** At times, programs
can install files or change system settings
that accidentally upset the apple cart, so to
speak.

✔ **Use an earlier Windows system restore
point.** Windows allows you to save a snapshot of the system state and then restore
it. This is handy since you can go back to
an earlier version of the system before
you started having troubles. Search the
Windows online help for *restore point* to
find out more.

✔ **Do a complete system reinstall.** This is a
last resort that I discuss in Chapter 17.

For more troubleshooting tips, visit http://
support.microsoft.com.

MSConfig

MSConfig is the Windows System Configuration Utility — shown in Figure 16-1. It provides information about startup programs and processes and allows you to control them. This program is extremely useful for seeing what programs automatically run when your netbook starts up.

To run MSConfig in Windows XP, follow these steps:

1. **Choose Start➪Run.**

2. **Type** msconfig **and click OK.**

To find out how to use MSConfig, visit http://www.microsoft.com/ resources/documentation/windows/xp/all/proddocs/en-us/ msconfig_usage.mspx?mfr=true.

Figure 16-1: With MSConfig, you can see and control what programs are loaded when Windows starts up.

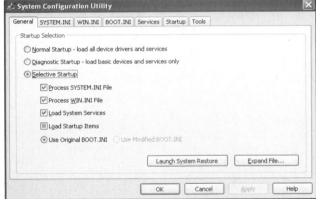

MSInfo32

MSInfo32 (shown in Figure 16-2) provides system information about your netbook. This utility is essential for nosing around the insides of your netbook and finding out about hardware and software. Even if you don't know what it all means, if someone is helping you with a problem and asks for specific information, this program provides it. In addition to system information, MSInfo32 has some diagnostic tools.

To run MSInfo32 in Windows XP, follow these steps:

1. **Choose Start➪Run.**

2. **Type** msinfo32 **and click OK.**

To find out more about MSInfo32, go to `http://support.microsoft.com/kb/308549`.

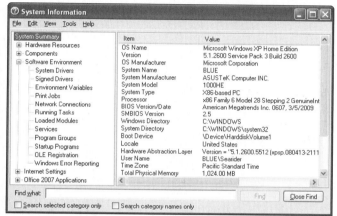

Figure 16-2:
MSInfo32
provides
detailed
information
about your
netbook's
hardware
and
software.

Windows Task Manager

Windows Task Manager (shown in Figure 16-3) provides information about your netbook's performance — including running programs; memory use, processor use, and network activity. The Task Manager can also be used to end programs that are unresponsive.

Be careful about terminating system processes. If you don't know what you're doing, you risk making Windows unstable.

You can start Windows Task Manager in Windows XP three different ways:

✔ Press Ctrl+Alt+Del and click Task Manager.

✔ Press Ctrl+Shift+Esc.

✔ Right-click an empty area of the Windows taskbar and then click Task Manager.

For instructions on using Task Manager, visit `http://support.microsoft.com/kb/323527`.

Figure 16-3:
Windows
Task
Manager
allows
you to get
information
about your
netbook's
performance
plus view
running
programs
and end
them.

Startup Problems

When it comes to solving specific netbook issues, I logically start with startup problems. I assume your netbook shows some form of life like a startup screen, active LED status lights, and so on. If it doesn't, be sure to read the "Dead as a Proverbial Doornail" section at the end of this chapter.

If your netbook seems to be starting up slowly, there's a very good chance you have too many programs running at startup time. You'd be amazed at all the utility programs various applications install — sometimes without your knowledge. On a low-memory computer like a netbook, these little startup programs not only cost start time, but also tax system memory and the processor. See the earlier "MSConfig" section to see what programs are running at startup.

Many programs that appear in the Windows taskbar have a setting for optionally running the program at Windows startup (or not). Click or right-click a program icon in the taskbar and then go to the program options.

If your netbook starts up but never gets to the Windows desktop, there's a problem with Windows. Fortunately, the operating system has a special Safe Boot mode that allows you to boot with minimal drivers and startup programs loaded — press F8 after you turn on your netbook. When you get to the Windows desktop, you can try to diagnose the problem or at least make copies of important files.

To find out more about Safe Boot, go to `http://support.microsoft.com/kb/316434`.

If you can't start up Windows with Safe Boot, you can always bust out an advanced move by booting the netbook with Linux. I discuss operating systems in Chapter 4 and provide information on booting with an alternative operating system.

Forgotten Windows Login Password

Say you set a Windows login password (which I recommend) and then you forgot it (which I don't recommend). Don't despair: There's hope for using your netbook again.

First, make sure Caps Lock isn't on when you log in. (*Psst.* Don't worry: It happens to everyone.)

If Caps Lock isn't on and you're running Windows XP, you have a number of ways to log in to the netbook without a password. Check this handy how-to for one simple method that involves booting into Safe Boot mode as Administrator: `www.wikihow.com/Log-on-to-Windows-XP-if-You-Forget-Your-Password`.

When you're logged in, change your account password to something more memorable and consider writing it down in case there's a future memory failure — yours, not the netbook's.

If you set a BIOS password and forget it, this is going to make life a little more challenging. You need to remove the netbook's BIOS battery — check an online forum for instructions. The BIOS battery is similar to the type used in watches and calculators. When it's removed, it clears all the BIOS settings, resetting them to default values. Wait a few minutes, reinstall the battery, put your netbook back together, and turn it on. I tell you more about BIOS in Chapter 21.

Getting in Touch with the Touchpad

Some netbook touchpads seem to get moody, and for no apparent reason your cursor suddenly starts flying around the screen or maybe gets really, really slow. Another symptom of a touchy touchpad is when multiple copies of a program open when you double-click its icon.

If you're having any unusual cursor and touchpad behavior problems, the touchpad settings need adjusting. Here's how to do it in Windows XP:

1. **Choose Start➪Control Panel.**

2. **Click Printers and Other Hardware.**

   Depending on how your copy of Windows is configured, this step may not be necessary.

3. **Click Mouse.**

   A dialog box is displayed with various setting tabs.

4. **Click a tab labeled touchpad (or similar) to access touchpad settings.**

   Here you control mouse and touchpad options.

5. **Change the touchpad sensitivity so the cursor behaves normally.**

   This typically involves using a slider control to specify a lighter or heavier touch. If the cursor is flying around at the slightest touch, decrease the sensitivity. If you have to press hard to get the cursor to move, increase the sensitivity.

Most netbooks come with touchpad *tapping* enabled. This setting allows you to use the touchpad surface for clicking or double-clicking in addition to the touchpad buttons — for example, moving the cursor over a dialog box button and tapping the touchpad is equivalent to clicking the left touchpad/mouse button. If the tapping sensitivity is set too high, just about every time you brush the touchpad with a finger will be considered a mouse click. The cursor and windows will zoom around, and programs will mysteriously open. If this bugs you (it sure would bug me), change the sensitivity or turn off the tapping feature.

Webcam Issues

Some users have troubles with their built-in webcam not working. They try Skype or some other program that supports the cam but get a blank screen. If this happens to you, try these fixes:

- ✔ **Check whether the webcam is enabled in BIOS.** Don't ask me why, but sometimes a netbook BIOS setting gets changed, and the change disables the camera. Read Chapter 21 for instructions on how to get to the BIOS settings and enable the cam.

- ✔ **Install the latest driver.** Check the manufacturer's support Web site and see whether a new driver is available for the webcam. (I give you the full scoop on drivers in Chapter 20.) Even if you're running the most current version, sometimes a file can get corrupted, so it's worth it trying to reinstall the driver.

Most netbooks feature a LED light next to the camera lens — when the light is on, so is the camera. If the light is on but the camera's not, you might have a hardware problem with the camera. However, my first guess would be that the camera hasn't been configured properly in the program. Check various program options and settings to make sure.

Dealing with Batteries

If you're not getting the amount of runtime out of your battery that you used to, there's a very good chance it reached its prime and is now on the downhill slide. A netbook (or any laptop) battery has a limited lifespan: After a certain point, it begins to hold less and less of a charge, which means you get fewer and fewer minutes of running time when the device isn't plugged in. If you use your netbook a lot, figure a year or two before it's time for a new battery.

If you have a couple of batteries and frequently swap them, visually check that the connection points are clean — grime and grunge on the connectors that may cause problems is clearly apparent. Dirty connectors may prevent a battery from delivering a full charge.

There's more on batteries in Chapter 13.

Repairing Wireless Connections

Unfortunately, wireless problems can be both tricky and mysterious to resolve. Often the culprit is a setting that was inadvertently changed or a temporary glitch in the wireless card, router, or either's interface software. You can try a variety of things in case you run into the following wireless difficulties:

✔ **Is the wireless card enabled on your netbook?** Is the LED status light on, or does the wireless icon in the Windows taskbar indicate wireless is enabled? If it isn't, wireless is disabled. Press the appropriate function key (or click the taskbar icon) to enable wireless and then wait for a connection.

✔ **Do you lose your wireless connection when the microwave oven is on? Or do you perhaps have a baby monitor, cordless phone, garage door opener, or fluorescent light fixture?** You're not hallucinating. These devices all run in the 2.4GHz radio frequency range and can interfere with Wi-Fi connections. Try moving your netbook away from the offending devices (or your wireless router) if possible to eliminate the problem.

✔ **Is your home or office wireless router/access point to blame?** If you have another laptop, can you successfully get a Net connection? If not, reboot or turn the router off and on again. Wait about a minute until the router reconnects to the Internet and then try connecting again with your netbook. (Turn off your netbook and then restart it after the wireless router's status lights indicate there's an Internet connection.)

Check which version of firmware the wireless router is running. If it isn't current, upgrade to the latest. Consult your router user manual or the manufacturer Web site for details.

✔ **Does the router have any security settings (such as MAC address filtering, WEP, or WPA) turned on that may be preventing the netbook from connecting?** If it does, make sure you're using the right settings on your netbook to connect to the router.

✔ **Are you having troubles connecting to just one access point?** Try connecting to a free public Wi-Fi network (at a library, coffee shop, or college). If you're successful, you rule out the possibility that your wireless card is broken. The problem may be with a single connection — usually a security setting or perhaps incompatibility with an older router/access point.

Try right-clicking the wireless icon in the Windows taskbar and selecting Repair. With this command, Windows disconnects from the wireless router, clears cached network settings, and then attempts to reconnect.

If all else fails, check out this detailed wireless troubleshooting guide from Microsoft: http://support.microsoft.com/kb/870702.

Running Slow

If your netbook is running slow, there might not be anything wrong with it. Don't expect as snappy of performance compared with a traditional laptop or desktop PC — a netbook is lacking in both the memory and the processor departments.

I've found common culprits for poor, pokey performance include

✔ Running a processor-intensive program (such as a video player, a game with lots of 3-D animation, or a complex spreadsheet)

✔ Running multiple programs at once

✔ Opening a large number of files or windows

✔ Opening too many Web browser tabs

✔ Having lots of programs running in the background

The solution is to recognize your netbook's limitations and spend more time single-tasking than multitasking. Trust me, it's possible.

Reset

If your netbook stops working (hangs) while a program is running, press Ctrl+Alt+Del to run the Windows Task Manager. You can then shut down the netbook with Task Manager or try closing the offending program — select the program in the Applications tab and click End Task. If you haven't saved what you've been working on in the program, any changes you made are lost.

If it's a serious system crash where Ctrl+Alt+Del doesn't even work (such as an infamous Blue Screen of Death crash), press and hold the power button for 5 to 10 seconds. This forces the netbook to shut down. It's a last-resort option because Windows doesn't do a clean exit. You will definitely lose everything you've been working on, and there's a good chance the netbook will boot up slower when you power it on again as Windows picks itself up, shakes the dust off, and tries to figure out what happened.

Dead as a Proverbial Doornail

I saved the absolute worst case scenario for last. You try to turn on the netbook and nothing happens. Or maybe some LED status lights come on, but the screen is black. Your netbook seems to be a goner.

First, try pressing a key, wiggling your finger on the touchpad, or pressing the power button. Your netbook may just be in standby or hibernation mode (with a blank screen), and you just need to wake it up.

If that doesn't work, there's a chance the netbook's display is set only to appear on an external monitor or projector and not on the netbook's screen. Check your user manual for the appropriate function key to press to toggle screen modes.

Still no luck? Try plugging the netbook into an electrical outlet. It's possible the battery has completely discharged, and there's no power left. By the way, make sure it's a known working electrical outlet — plug a lamp or appliance in if you have any doubts. And make sure all the connections are tight.

Uh-oh, I'm running out of the obvious cures. Next on my list is to read Chapter 17 for instructions on restoring your system — either from a DVD or the recovery hard drive partition.

No luck with that? Not good. I'd be suspicious that it's probably a hardware or BIOS problem. If it's a failed motherboard or power supply, there's not much you can do.

If the BIOS has somehow become corrupted (say you tried to upgrade it, but something happened), you have one last-resort option. Read Chapter 21 where I discuss installing a new copy of the BIOS.

Failing that, here's hoping your netbook is still under warranty. If so, contact the manufacturer, who will likely replace your netbook with a new one rather than repair it.

If your netbook is out of warranty, look on the bright side: All of your data is backed up just as I describe in Chapter 17 (right?), and you were looking for an excuse to get a new model with the latest features. The glass is always either half empty or half full.

Chapter 17

Backing Up and Restoring Your Netbook

*T*ime is precious. If something happens to your netbook (it breaks, is lost, or is stolen), a whole lot of your precious time and effort just disappeared. Think about the amount of time that went into those PowerPoint presentations for your job, or that screenplay you've been writing on the side that you know will be a smash hit, or maybe all of those songs in your music collection you've painstakingly acquired over the years — legally, of course. It may take days, weeks, or months to reconstruct everything — that is, if you're lucky. And that doesn't include the cash you're out from buying all that music again.

Of course that sad scene doesn't need to happen. Backing up your netbook is simple and cheap insurance. If something goes wrong, you won't be crying the blues because a copy of the fruits of your labor exists somewhere else.

In this chapter, I discuss backing up and restoring your netbook (there are several different approaches) and fill you in on the programs that make it easy. I also talk about reinstalling Windows on your netbook — and tell you when you should do it.

I don't want to waste your time, so feel free to get started.

Understanding Simple File Copying

The simplest way to back up your netbook is to copy individual files and directories to another storage medium — USB flash drive, SD memory card, DVD or CD-ROM, an external hard drive, or another networked computer.

Making a duplicate copy of a file or folder and keeping it where the original is stored isn't a smart backup policy. If you make a copy of a folder and keep it on the same hard drive as the original folder, you're probably going to be out of luck if the drive fails.

Some netbooks come with free online storage services that you can use for backing up files. I talk more about some online storage solutions coming up.

In Windows Explorer, select the files and folders you want to back up and drag them to the other storage device. It's as simple as that.

This simple backup strategy works great if you don't have many files (it can take a lot of time copying gigabytes of data) or if you're only interested in archiving documents and other files — simple file copying can't back up the entire Windows operating system or any installed programs.

From an organizational standpoint, it makes sense to keep all your files in the My Documents folder instead of scattered all over your drive. That way you just copy the My Documents folder to back up your files.

Manually copying and dragging files and folders can get a bit tedious — especially when Windows is always asking whether you want to replace a same-named file. If you have a number of files you want to back up to read/ write media (such as a USB flash drive or external hard drive), I suggest picking up a copy of SyncToy, shown in Figure 17-1.

This is a free utility from Microsoft that makes backing up and synchronizing files a breeze. If you don't have very demanding backup needs, I highly recommend this program. To find out more and to download, visit www. microsoft.com/downloads/details.aspx?familyid=c26efa36-98e0-4ee9-a7c5-98d0592d8c52&displaylang=en.

Figure 17-1:
SyncToy
makes
backing up
and syn-
chronizing
files easy.

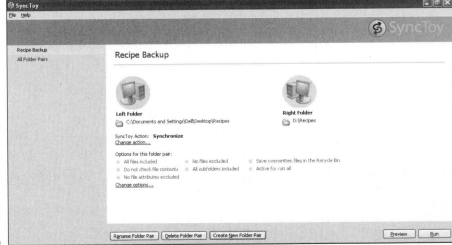

Offsite storage

Backing up important files on your netbook is smart. If you want to be really smart, keep a copy of your backup someplace else. This is a common practice with businesses that have disaster recovery plans. If an office burns down and the backups are kept in the same room as the servers, everyone gets burned.

For personal offsite storage, consider keeping a copy of your backup at a friend's or family member's house, in a safety deposit box, or with an online storage service you can access over the Internet. You don't need to visit the offsite storage site every time you make a backup, just periodically. If something happens to your netbook and your house, apartment, or office, copies of important files will be safe and sound.

This suggestion may seem a little paranoid, but if you live in a natural-disaster–prone area (with floods, wildfires, earthquakes, or hurricanes), it makes sense to have a backup of your backup. Even if natural disasters are rare, it's still not a bad idea to think about safeguarding very important files.

Or if you don't want to type in that long Web address, Google *SyncToy* to go to the appropriate Microsoft Web page.

Backing Up and Restoring Your Drive

Drag-and-drop copying works great if you're backing up only a few files every now and then. But if you have lots of files to archive, want to back up your entire hard drive, and plan to be religious about backup frequency, you need a specialized program. These backup programs (depending on the software) allow you to

- ✔ **Specify which files and folders to back up.** Backup parameters are saved so you don't have to enter them each time. You can back up to different storage media such as DVDs or external hard drives.

- ✔ **Back up the entire drive.** Including hidden system files.

- ✔ **Restore files (or the drive) from a backup copy.** You can restore the backed-up data to your netbook or another computer with a couple of clicks.

- ✔ **Compress backup files.** To save space, archived files are compressed. If you need to restore files, they're decompressed.

- ✔ **Encrypt backup files.** Backup files are scrambled and password-protected to prevent unauthorized access.

- ✔ **Schedule backups.** Automatically run the backup program in the background at scheduled intervals.

✔ **Perform incremental backups.** Automatically compare files being backed up with archived versions. If changes have been made to the original file, a new backup is made. If there haven't been any changes, no backup is made. This saves time.

✔ **Clone a drive.** Some programs support drive cloning; see the "Attack of the clones" sidebar.

In the following sections, I survey different backup programs you can use with your Windows netbook.

Windows backup utilities

I start my discussion of backup programs with Microsoft. Over the years, the company has included different backup utilities with its operating systems. Here's the lowdown on Microsoft backup solutions, depending on which version of Windows you're using with your netbook.

Windows XP

Windows Backup (shown in Figure 17-2) is an easy-to-use backup program for computers running Windows XP. It has basic features and allows you to specify what files and folders you'd like to archive. It can also back up common program and system settings.

For some reason, Microsoft decided to preinstall Windows Backup only on copies of Windows XP Professional — most netbooks run Windows XP Home. If your netbook comes with a CD-ROM that has a "real" copy of Windows XP Home and not just a recovery image, the program is located in the `VALUEADD\MSFT\NTBACKUP` directory. Double-click `Ntbackup.msi` to install the program. If you don't have a CD-ROM, try searching for *ntbackup. msi* in Google to find and download the file — it's available on a number of unofficial Windows XP support sites.

After you install the program, to run it, choose Start➪All Programs➪ Accessories➪System Tools➪Backup.

For more on using Windows Backup with a Windows XP netbook, check out this article: `www.microsoft.com/windowsxp/using/setup/learnmore/ bott_03july14.mspx`.

Vista

With Vista, Microsoft redesigned, simplified, and renamed the Windows Backup program calling it the Backup Status and Configuration tool. Personally, I feel the program was dumbed down a little too much because it prevents you from performing some basic and advanced backup functions that were available in Windows Backup.

Attack of the clones

I briefly want to tell you about cloning hard drives — also known as *disk imaging.* This doesn't require a laboratory or even a working knowledge of DNA. *Cloning a drive* means to make an exact, byte-by-byte duplicate of the drive. Instead of individual files being copied, entire hard drive sectors are faithfully reproduced.

Drive cloning is smart if you're upgrading to a bigger hard drive. You clone the old drive to the new drive, and when you install the new drive, everything is there just like before. No need for reinstalling Windows or other programs.

You can directly clone from one drive to another (you'll need a special adapter and a cable) or save a compressed image of the drive to a DVD or other storage media. You can uncompress

the image later and use to restore the contents of a drive; just remember the storage media needs to be large enough to accommodate all the files on the original drive you're cloning.

Note: If Windows seems to slow down after a couple of years, it's not your imagination. Unused programs, drivers, and registry entries can impact a computer's performance. Keep this in mind when you're thinking about cloning. It may be smarter to perform a fresh operating system install on a new drive than to reinstall programs and copy over backed-up data files.

You can find a number of commercial drive cloning programs on the market, including Norton Ghost and Acronis True Image. Do a Web search for *disk cloning software* to find out more about other programs.

 It's possible to use Windows Backup with Vista if you copy the `Ntbackup.exe`, `Ntmsapi.dll`, and `Vssapi.dll` files from a computer running XP to the Vista Program Files folder. To run Windows Backup (`Ntbackup.exe`), you first need to turn on Removable Storage Management — choose Start➪Control Panel➪Programs➪Turn Windows Features On or Off.

If you're running Vista on your netbook, check the online Help for more information on the Backup Status and Configuration tool.

Windows 7

As I write this, the final version of Windows 7 hasn't hit the streets yet, but if the backup program included in final release candidates is included, netbook users running the new Microsoft operating system should have a smile on their faces.

Vista's Backup Status and Configuration tool is no more and has been replaced by a tool called Backup and Restore — which is much more configurable but still easy to use.

To find out more about the program, use the online Help (which is accessible from the Start menu) to search for *backup.* You can run the program by typing **backup** in the Start menu search box and selecting one of the results.

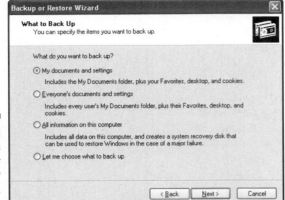

Figure 17-2:
Windows
Backup for
Windows XP
computers.

Commercial backup programs

Although the programs that come with Windows work great for backups, you can also find a number of other freeware and commercial backup programs that have better and more advanced features. Think of it like this: For some people, the basic Windows Paint program meets their needs; for others, it's worthwhile to shell out the extra bucks to get the enhanced features of Photoshop.

Here's a collection of popular, non-Microsoft backup programs for Windows netbooks — or any computer that uses Windows XP (or later). All of these programs are reasonably priced and some have free, limited-feature, or trial versions available. A few even allow you to back up data online, so you don't need to worry about external storage media such as DVDs or spare hard drives. Check out the respective Web sites for more information:

- ✔ **Acronis True Image:** (www.acronis.com) The Home version of Acronis True Image is a traditional backup and disk-cloning program that saves data to CD-ROMs, DVDs, flash memory, and hard drives. It costs $49.99. Acronis also provides a free trial version.

- ✔ **Carbonite:** (http://carbonite.com) This is a popular online backup service. You install a program on your netbook that manages backups over the Internet to a secure server. For $54.95 a year, you can back up as much data as you want. A 15-day free trial is available.

When it comes to online backup services, your biggest limitation is going to be bandwidth. It's not realistic to think you'll be able to back up a full 250GB hard drive online — it would take a very long time. In addition, if your Internet service provider has a metered bandwidth plan, you can use up your allocation pretty quickly if you're performing frequent backups.

- **Cobian Backup:** (www.educ.umu.se/~cobian/cobianbackup.htm) You've got to love developers who release good programs for free. That's what Luis Cobian did with this powerful piece of backup software. If you use it, be sure to send him a donation.

- **Jungle Disk:** (www.jungledisk.com) Jungle Disk is a pay-as-you-go online backup service that uses Amazon's S3 storage service. Rates are currently $2 a month plus 15 cents each month for every gigabyte of storage space, 10 cents per gigabyte uploaded, and 17 cents per gigabyte downloaded.

- **Macrium Reflect:** (www.macrium.com) Reflect is an easy-to-use backup and disk-imaging program that comes with a number of advanced features. It's priced at $39.95 with a free, 30-day trial version available.

- **Mozy:** (http://mozy.com) This online storage service charges $4.95 a month for unlimited backup with its MozyHome product — there's also a professional version with encryption and other features with a higher subscription fee. If you don't have a lot to back up, sign up for a free account and get a complimentary 2GB of storage.

- **SyncBack:** (www.2brightsparks.com/syncback)A feature-rich backup program with easy and power-user modes. Three versions with different features are available, priced at $49.95, $30, and free — you can't beat the price of that last one.

If you're using an online storage service to back up sensitive files, no matter how secure the service advertises itself, I highly recommend encrypting your data. I discuss encryption in Chapter 9.

Reinstalling Windows

Reinstalling Windows means erasing your netbook's hard drive and restoring it to just like it came out of the box. (I'm talking about just the operating system and installed programs — you're on your own for fixing any dings or scratches on the case.)

Reinstalling Windows is a rather extreme measure, and there are four situations that call for it:

- Corrupted system files make Windows unstable.

- Viruses or other malware make your netbook unusable.

    On many occasions, it's faster and easier to reinstall Windows than try to repair a netbook that's been infected by a difficult and stubborn-to-remove virus.

✔ Your netbook doesn't work right and you've tried everything else.

✔ The government (or space aliens) have bugged your netbook to discover Aunt Sally's secret oatmeal cookie recipe.

If you decide you need to reinstall Windows, first back up any files you want to save. (You should have a pretty good idea of how to do this from earlier sections in this chapter.)

Netbook manufacturers provide two different ways to reinstall the operating system. Some manufacturers provide one or the other; some provide both:

✔ **Drive partition:** An image of the operating system is stored on a drive partition.

✔ **Recovery discs:** CD-ROM(s) or a DVD is included that contains a recovery image or a copy of Windows. Some manufacturers don't provide a disc but include a utility program for creating a recovery disc — you supply the CD-ROM or DVD and the drive.

Most manufacturers use recovery images these days in an effort to stem software piracy. Unlike a copy of Windows that can be installed on any computer, a recovery image can be installed only on the computer it came with — also, you can't access any of the individual operating system files on the recovery image.

Any programs you installed or any system updates you applied between the time you got your netbook and when you performed the system reinstall are no longer present. You need to download and install them again.

Using a recovery disc

If a recovery disc (CD-ROM or DVD) came with your netbook, you can use it to restore Windows and other programs. (Obviously you'll need an external drive to access the disc.)

Here are the general steps for reinstalling Windows from a recovery disc (refer to your netbook user manual for specific instructions):

1. **Connect your netbook to an external power source and turn it on.**

   Consider having a fully charged battery, too, just in case the power goes out.

2. **Connect an external DVD drive to your netbook and insert the recovery disc.**

   Some netbooks provide power to USB ports when plugged in to an external power supply. That means if the drive is connected, you can insert and eject DVDs without the netbook being turned on.

Windows System Restore

One of the niftier features that Microsoft included in Windows is something called System Restore. This is a time-machine–like feature that allows you to roll back system files, registry keys, and installed programs to a previous state.

Say you installed some program and suddenly your netbook starts acting strange. Uninstalling the program doesn't help, and you think you may need to reinstall Windows. Before you do, try System Restore. The program will restore your system exactly how it was before you installed the suspect program.

System Restore automatically takes snapshots of the system state . . .

✔ Every 24 hours of computer use.

✔ When software is installed with programs that are designed to work with System Restore.

✔ When Windows Update installs new updates.

✔ Whenever you request it.

These snapshots are called *restore points.* You can display a calendar with various saved restore points and tell Windows to go back in time to a restore point, as shown in the figure. System settings and state are then reverted back to reflect that prior point in time. (System Restore only impacts system files and programs — you won't lose data files such as word processing documents when you go back to an older restore point.)

Windows allocates a certain amount of disk space for storing restore point data. Older restore points are constantly being deleted as newer points are created.

In my book, this is an indispensable tool every netbook owner should know about. There are differences between Windows XP, Vista, and Windows 7 versions of System Restore. For detailed information, your best bet is to consult Windows online Help or visit `www.microsoft.com` and search for System Restore.

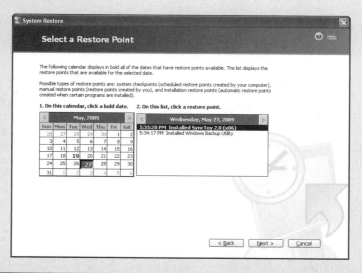

3. **Restart your netbook and press the key sequence to boot from the DVD drive.**

   Your user manual has information on which key(s) to press. If holding down the key doesn't allow you to select which device to boot from, try restarting the netbook and quickly and repeatedly pressing the key(s).

   Some netbooks have a BIOS setting that speeds up the boot process — for example, in ASUS netbooks, it's called Boot Booster. If this setting is enabled, you won't be able to select a boot device with the function key at startup. See Chapter 21 for information on how to change BIOS settings.

4. **Follow the directions that appear on the screen.**

   You'll be prompted if you want to restore the Windows image. If you haven't backed up any important files, now would be a good time to cancel the reinstallation and do a backup.

The process is fully automated and takes between 15 to 20 minutes — your mileage may vary depending on the netbook. You'll see status messages as the system is restored, and you may be prompted to restart your netbook.

When the reinstallation is complete, Windows starts. You'll need to go through the same steps as you did when you first got your netbook, including setting the time zone, agreeing to the licensing terms, specifying computer name and username, and entering other settings.

That's it. When your netbook starts up next, it will be just like it came from the factory. Copy any files you backed up onto the drive, install any programs or updates, and you're back in business.

In addition to the Windows recovery disc, some manufacturers include discs that have other programs that came preinstalled on your netbook. You may need to run the installation programs on these discs to restore other programs that weren't included during the system reinstallation.

Using a drive partition recovery image

If your netbook didn't come with a recovery disc and you need to reinstall Windows, you need to use a recovery image that's installed on a partition of your hard drive or solid state drive. The recovery image includes Windows and all the netbook drivers and utility programs.

Here are the general steps to use a drive partition recovery image (check your user manual for specific instructions that apply to your netbook model):

1. **Connect your netbook to an external power source.**

   You don't want to have your battery die in the middle of a system restore; it's bad luck — especially for your drive as it could get corrupted or possibly damaged.

2. **Turn on your netbook and press the key sequence to begin system reinstallation.**

   This is typically a function key. Check your user manual for the correct one to use. Some netbooks require you to enable a recovery mode BIOS setting before you can reinstall the system. Again, refer to the user manual for details.

3. **Follow the onscreen directions.**

   Your netbook runs a program that erases the main drive partition and copies the image from the recovery partition. You should be able to see this partition with Windows Explorer — for example, there may be a D: drive named Restore with several gigabytes for data. Using a recovery partition should be somewhat faster than using a recovery disc. After the image is copied, Windows starts up and the system is in an identical state to when you first got your netbook.

If you completely reformat your hard drive, you will delete the recovery partition and won't be able to restore Windows — unless you have a recovery disc. I've seen this happen with netbook users who want to try out Linux, format their drives, and end up not being able to restore Windows. If you want to play with Linux, use a *live* version (that is, a customized version) that you can boot from on a CD-ROM, USB flash drive, or SD card without permanently installing on the hard drive. If you format your drive or somehow the recovery partition is damaged, contact the manufacturer and see whether you can get a recovery disc. When you get the disc, if you don't already have a USB DVD drive, you'll need to purchase one.

Chapter 18

Upgrading Storage and Memory

*O*ur society is accustomed to a "more is better" outlook on life. I don't mean to get up on a soapbox, but the computer industry is especially guilty of promoting excess when it comes to processor speed, drive space, and system memory. (In all fairness to the hardware manufacturers, much of this is driven by software companies that continue to produce bigger and more bloated products. Of course, memory, storage, and processing power have all gotten cheaper, so why not take advantage of it? It's a vicious cycle.)

The popularity of the netbook has been a refreshing reversal to the "bigger is better" philosophy. It's amazing how functional a well-designed computer can be when it's based on memory, available storage space, and processing power that was top of the line five or more years back.

Don't worry; this isn't an op-ed piece, and I'm actually going somewhere with all this. Even though a minimalist netbook does a good job of meeting your computing needs, you still may want to amp up the memory or storage in your little laptop. That's what this chapter is about. If you've never upgraded a computer's memory or hard drive before, I tell you everything you need to know — and if you have, I cover a variety of netbook specifics you should know.

Adding More Memory

The first generation of netbooks had a paltry 512K of system memory — system memory is also known as RAM, or random access memory. The majority of netbooks on the market have now mostly standardized on a quite usable 1GB of memory. However, if you're not happy with the amount of memory that came from the factory, many netbook models allow you to upgrade system memory. In this section, I give you advice on whether to upgrade RAM and how to select the right type of memory, and I conclude with a general tutorial on adding more memory to your netbook.

Do you need to upgrade memory?

The first question you should ask yourself is whether more memory will make you a happier and more productive netbook owner.

I believe for most users (with the current netbooks on the market), 1GB of RAM is perfectly acceptable for basic netbook computing needs. You will see only a small performance gain when you upgrade — but it's not like your little laptop will suddenly become twice as fast.

Keep in mind that the reason that most netbooks come with a maximum of 1GB of memory is due to Microsoft licensing requirements. For a netbook to qualify as a ULCPC (that's Ultra Low Cost Personal Computer) under Microsoft's *Designed for Windows XP* logo program, the manufacturer can't ship a netbook with more than 1GB. However, this doesn't prevent a manufacturer from building a netbook that can be user expandable with more memory.

Upgrading memory involves taking your netbook apart — and doing so involves varying degrees of complexity depending on the model, from simple to nearly requiring an engineering degree. I describe the process coming up, but if you're not comfortable installing the memory yourself, that's all right. Your netbook will be fine without more memory.

If you're set on upgrading memory, I certainly won't try to dissuade you. Memory is relatively cheap and depending on the netbook model, is pretty easy to install — even for a novice. So, if you want mo' memory, read on.

Can you upgrade the memory?

If you decide you want (or need) more memory, the next question you must address is whether your netbook's RAM can be upgraded. Turn to your user manual for the answer — or the manufacturer's support Web site. If the user manual doesn't say or is vague, head over to Google and search for the name of your netbook and *memory upgrade*. Other owners no doubt have had the same question, and you'll quickly find out whether you can add more memory to your netbook.

There are several clues that your memory may not be easily upgraded:

- ✔ The manufacturer explicitly says "no dice" on upgrades. (This will be listed in product specifications on the manufacturer Web site and/or in the user manual.)
- ✔ The memory is soldered in place as opposed to removable from a socket.
- ✔ There's no door for accessing the memory module.
- ✔ Opening the case voids the manufacturer's warranty. (If there are tamper-proof, quality-assurance labels sealing the case, that's a hint.)

These factors don't absolutely mean you can't upgrade the memory; they just make it more difficult and mean there are more potential consequences if you mess up. However, if you're technically inclined, and if it's possible (although perhaps a pain) to upgrade the memory, and if you don't care about the warranty, then press on.

If you're stuck with a netbook that you can't upgrade, I recommend making the best of it. Honestly, depending on your use, the netbook may be perfectly fine in the performance department. If it's not, I suggest saving up for a new model that has more RAM or can be easily upgraded.

Memory bytes

When you read about or go shopping for memory, you'll be barraged with a bunch of baffling buzzwords and arcane acronyms. Here's a handy guide to make sense of them:

- ✔ **DDR2:** Double data rate synchronous dynamic random access memory (SDRAM). The second generation, that's what the 2 stands for, of a memory technology.
- ✔ **DIMM:** Dual inline memory module. A card that contains multiple memory chips — used to update a computer's system memory.
- ✔ **MHz:** Just like processors, memory comes in different speeds — measured in megahertz or MHz. Faster memory is better, but keep

in mind that different netbooks support different maximum speeds. If you pay more money for faster memory, you might not get the full benefit of its zippiness — it's like having a Ferrari that can go 140 MPH, but the speed limit is only 60 MPH, and there are police wherever you look.

- ✔ **RAM:** Random access memory or the main, system memory.
- ✔ **SODIMM:** Small outline dual inline memory module. A smaller version of DIMM typically used in laptops and netbooks. SODIMMs have different numbers of pins, so it's important to get the right one that works with your netbook.

Selecting the right memory

After you've confirmed you can upgrade your netbook's RAM, you need to select the right type because there are many types of computer memory on the market. There are two ways to determine which kind of memory is appropriate for your netbook:

- **Read the user manual.** Am I sounding like a broken record throughout this book yet?

- **Check the Net.** First, check the netbook manufacturer's support Web site. You can also do a search for your netbook model and the word *memory.* You'll get lots of retail sites offering their wares and telling you the type of memory you need. Additionally, you can check Web forums devoted to your netbook. There are always discussion threads devoted to memory upgrades.

For system memory, most netbooks use DDR2 SODIMM, shown in Figure 18-1. (Use the acronym guide in the "Memory bytes" sidebar to help figure out what all of those letters mean.)

Figure 18-1:
DDR2
SODIMM for
a netbook.

For example, a manufacturer might suggest you upgrade with this:

2GB DDR2-667 SODIMM

That's a 2GB memory module.

The number that comes after DDR2 is not the memory speed in MHz but the effective number of data transfers per second. Here's how fast the different types of memory are: DDR2-400 — 100 MHz, DDR2-533 — 133 MHz, DDR2-667 — 166 MHz, DDR2-800 — 200 MHz, and DDR2-1066 — 266 MHz.

Don't bother getting memory faster than 166 MHz. The additional cost doesn't justify the benefit.

On most memory upgradeable netbooks, the memory module is installed in a socket. You pull the old memory out and snap a new module (with more memory) in.

Netbook memory is currently offered in nice round numbers, 1GB and 2GB modules. Depending on the brand, where you purchase it, and how much you buy (1 or 2GB) expect to pay between $20 and $50. (Like the stock market, memory prices seem to always be going up or down.)

Netbooks may be limited to a maximum amount of RAM by operating system or hardware constraints. For example, when the Eee PC first came out, Linux models could address only up to 1GB of memory. If you installed 2GB, the netbook would still work but would use only 1GB of the memory. Currently, most netbook system chipsets don't support more than 2GB of RAM — regardless of the operating system.

General guide to upgrading memory

Here I tell you the basic procedure for upgrading your netbook's memory. Remember that each netbook is different, and the following figures and steps might not exactly match your model — but at the very least, they can give you an idea of what's involved.

Before upgrading your netbook's memory, I highly recommend you do some homework. Use Google to search for tutorials dedicated to your specific netbook — you can find many excellent guides with full-color photos and detailed instructions on various Web sites and forums. Also check YouTube, because the site hosts a number of video tutorials that are great for understanding all the steps.

The following steps outline the basic procedure for upgrading your netbook's memory:

1. **Turn off your netbook.**

   Make sure the netbook is powered off and not in sleep mode. Disconnect the power supply from the laptop. It's also a good idea to remove the battery. When the battery is removed, press the power button. This action grounds the system board.

2. **Get to where the memory is.**

   Turn the netbook over so the bottom is facing up. Your netbook will either have a removable panel for accessing the memory (shown in

Figure 18-2; this makes it easy to upgrade memory), or you'll need to take the case apart to get at the memory (which is more of a hassle). With either, you must remove some small screws (usually Phillips head), so have an appropriate size screwdriver handy.

Figure 18-2:
Remove a
netbook's
memory
access
panel.

Put the screws in a small bowl or someplace you won't lose them. It's also a good idea not to work around open heater vents, carpet, or places where small screws accidentally knocked to the floor could disappear forever.

3. **Locate the memory and remove it.**

   With the panel removed or the case opened, find the memory — see Figure 18-3.

   Most netbooks use plastic or metal retaining clips to hold the memory in place (also shown in Figure 18-3). With your fingertips, carefully spread the retaining clips apart.

   The memory module will pop up at an angle. Lift the module up and out to remove it from the socket.

   Be careful when handling the memory module. You should hold it by the edges and not grasp the chips or pins.

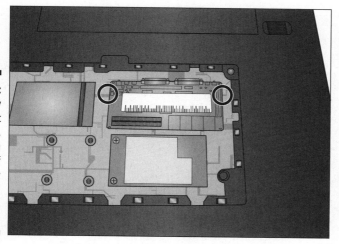

Figure 18-3:
The memory
compartment
is open,
showing the
location of
the memory
module and
retaining
clips.

4. **Place the new memory into the empty socket.**

   This is mostly the same procedure as removing the memory module, but in reverse.

   Aligning the memory module pins with the socket, slide the module into the socket at about a 45-degree angle, as shown in Figure 18-4. Gently press the module down until it clicks into place and is secured by the retaining clips.

   If you don't see and hear it click into place, remove the module and start over again. Something is out of alignment.

Don't give me no static

Anytime you play surgeon and operate on a computer, you need to be careful of static discharge. If you touch something or someone and get a shock from static electricity, it's a harmless surprise. If you touch the wrong component while you're working on your netbook and give it a static shock, the electricity can possibly damage sensitive electronics.

Computer technicians often wear a grounding wrist strap to prevent static discharge. You can also occasionally touch an unpainted, metal surface (such as a connector on the back of your computer) to discharge static from your body.

Static electricity is more prevalent when the humidity is low. I also recommend not vigorously rubbing your feet on carpet prior to swapping out memory or a hard drive — ah, that brings back childhood memories.

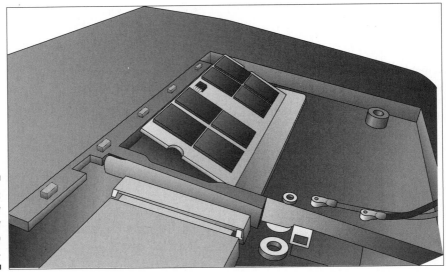

Figure 18-4:
Insert a new
memory
module into
the socket.

5. **Put the case back together.**

   Reattach the panel (or reassemble the case) and put the screws back in. Reinsert the battery into the case.

6. **Turn on your netbook.**

   It's time to check your work. If everything went well, your netbook should now report you have more memory. Some models display the amount of RAM at startup, or you can select My Computer on the Windows desktop and then right-click and choose Properties from the pop-up menu.

   If your netbook doesn't boot, either the memory is defective or more than likely it isn't seated properly in the socket. Go through the preceding steps again and verify that the memory module is in place. If it appears to be, try reinstalling the old memory and see whether the netbook will boot. If it does, there's a good chance the memory is defective, and you'll need to return it.

Swapping Internal Drives

Depending on your netbook model, you may be able to swap its internal drive for a larger drive. In the following sections, I tell you all about swapping drives, including which types of storage drives are available, how to decide whether you need a bigger drive, and the general steps involved in removing and installing a new drive.

As I mention earlier in the "Adding More Memory" section of this chapter, always check your user manual or the manufacturer's support Web site for information on replacing hardware.

Types of netbook drives

Netbooks are sold with two types of drives, solid state drives (SSDs) or hard disk drives (HDDs).

Solid state drives

Solid state drives (one is shown in Figure 18-5), often abbreviated SSD, use memory to store data and don't have any moving mechanical parts — this makes them lighter and less prone to failure. They start up and power down very quickly, are quiet, and have fast read and write times. SSDs were popular in first generation netbooks and still are available in smaller models where maximum low weight and portability are desirable features.

The downside to SSDs is they aren't cheap — at least the high-capacity models. For example a 160GB SSD is currently priced around $900 — ouch, compare that with a hard disk drive the same size, which costs well under $200.

Figure 18-5: Solid state drives use memory to store data.

Hard disk drives

Most computers use a hard disk drive (HDD) as their primary storage media. A hard drive stores digitally encoded data on the magnetic surfaces of rapidly rotating platters.

Traditional laptops use 2.5-inch drives, but in an effort to save space, netbook manufacturers tend to use smaller, 1.8-inch drives — shown in Figure 18-6. Currently, the largest capacity 1.8-inch drive offers 250GB of storage. However, most netbooks are sold with hard drives that range from 60 to 160GB in size.

Figure 18-6: Inside a 1.8-inch hard disk drive (HDD) typically found in a netbook.

Like any hard drive, the more storage available the higher the price tag. Relatively low-capacity 60GB drives cost around $75, whereas a 160GB drive is priced around $175.

Depending on the netbook, it's usually possible to exchange a hard disk drive for an SSD or an SSD for a hard drive. The critical issue is the connector on the motherboard. For example, if the netbook uses a SATA (Serial Advanced Technology Attachment) connector and comes with a SATA hard drive, you should be able to swap the hard drive for an SSD. (See the nearby sidebar, "Drive lingo," for more about SATA.) Things get more complicated when the motherboard connector doesn't match the connector of the drive you want to install. In such cases, adapters may be available. Just remember there's not a lot of space inside a netbook, so the adapter needs to fit.

Do you need a bigger drive?

If you have a netbook with a relatively shrimpy sized drive, should you swap it out for a bigger drive? It depends.

First, can your netbook drive be upgraded? Some manufacturers make it easy to swap out a drive, whereas others make it considerably difficult, and several won't honor the warranty if you open up the case.

Second, is your current drive full or close to full? If it is, are you using the netbook as it was designed — as a portable, travel companion, not as a desktop or full-size laptop replacement (with a big drive cluttered with tons of files and programs)?

Honestly, for the average netbook user, I say don't worry about replacing your drive. It likely has enough capacity to serve your basic computing needs. (If it doesn't, and you're technically inclined, then go for the swap.)

The only netbook owners I would recommend upgrading are those stuck with very small SSDs. Although it's possible to run Linux and Windows on 4 and 8GB netbooks, it doesn't leave you much breathing room for even a minimal collection of programs and files.

Companies such as RunCore (www.runcore.com) and others are starting to offer reasonably priced, upgrade SSDs. For example, RunCore has 16, 32, 64, and 128GB SSDs that are priced between $69 and $389.

Be smart about upgrading an SSD, because at the present you might be able to buy a brand new netbook with lots of enhanced features for the price of a higher-capacity SSD.

If you're considering replacing your SSD, always check the advertised read/write speeds and read reviews. Memory speeds vary, and there are noticeably slower SSDs on the market — the higher the speed, the better.

General guide to replacing a drive

Next, I step you through replacing a netbook's drive. Each netbook is different, so treat the following instructions and figures as a general guide. Although the details may not match your netbook exactly, you'll have a better sense of everything that's involved in a drive swap.

Drive lingo

When you start looking at storage drives, you need to work through some of the jargon. Here's a short glossary to help you out:

- **PATA:** Parallel Advanced Technology Attachment. An older interface standard for connecting storage devices (hard drives) to computer motherboards. Many netbooks come with PATA because it is power efficient — however SATA is now more commonly used on desktop and full-size laptop computers.

- **RPM:** Revolutions per minute. This is the rate a hard drive's platter spins. The higher the number, the faster data on the disk is read. For example a 7,200 RPM is faster (and more expensive) than a 4,200 RPM drive.

- **SATA:** Serial Advanced Technology Attachment. A storage interface for connecting drives to computer motherboards. Has more features and is more compatible with future storage devices than PATA.

- **ZIF:** Zero Insertion Force. A socket-based connector standard. If your netbook uses a ZIF interface to connect its internal drive, a replacement drive needs to be ZIF compatible or you'll need an adapter.

Unless you're a techie, don't be concerned with remembering all of this. If you're shopping for a replacement drive, simply look for a drive that's advertised as compatible with your netbook make and model.

Use Google to search for tutorials on upgrading your netbook's drive — there are many excellent guides with full-color photos and detailed instructions on various Web sites and forums. Also check YouTube for video tutorials.

Here's how to replace a netbook's drive:

1. **Back up the old drive.**

   Unless you want to start completely from scratch, I suggest you first back up the drive you're going to replace. At a minimum, this means copying files you'll want stored on the new drive — use a USB flash drive or external drive. A more advanced technique is to clone the drive. I discuss backup strategies, including cloning, in Chapter 17.

2. **Turn off your netbook.**

   Make sure the netbook is powered off. Disconnect the power supply and remove the battery. After you've done that, press the power button to ground the system board.

3. Get to where the hard drive is located.

Turn the netbook over so the bottom is facing up. Your netbook has a removable panel for accessing the hard drive (shown in Figure 18-7) — some models use the same access panel for memory and drives; others have separate panels. If there's no access panel, you'll need to take the case apart to get to the drive. Remove the screws and try not to lose them.

4. Remove the drive retaining screws.

Whether the drive is an SSD or hard disk, it will be held in place with some type of retaining screws. Depending on the netbook model, the drive may have a bracket that secures it in place (shown in Figure 18-7), or the drive may be screwed directly to the circuit board (shown with a caseless SSD in Figure 18-8). Remove the screws and put them someplace memorable.

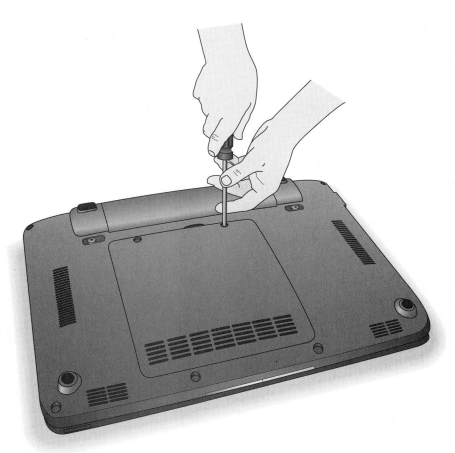

Figure 18-7:
Remove your netbook's drive access panel.

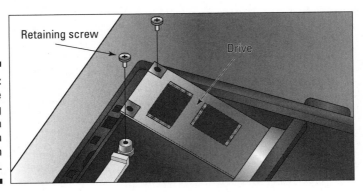

Figure 18-8:
Remove the
retaining
screws on
the drive (in
this case, an
SSD).

Retaining screw

Drive

5. Remove the drive.

With the retaining screws removed, now pull the drive away from the
connector and lift it out of the case. Many hard drives have a pull tab
attached for easier removal as shown in Figure 18-9. For SSDs, handle the
drive by the edges.

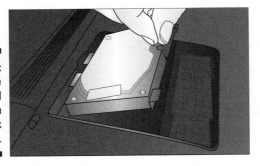

Figure 18-9:
Remove
the hard
drive from
the netbook
case.

6. Install the new drive.

Pretty much the reverse procedure of removing the drive — just slide
the drive into the connector and then screw it into place. Some hard
drives may be enclosed with a bracket; if so, you need to unscrew the
bracket and install it on the new drive.

7. Reassemble the case.

Reattach the panel (or reassemble the case) and put the screws back in.
Reinsert the battery into the case.

8. Turn on your netbook.

Your little laptop should boot up, and the operating system will start to load. If it doesn't, either the new drive is defective or hasn't been installed correctly — the latter being more likely of the two. Go through the steps again and make sure the drive is in place. If you're replacing a drive that works, try reinstalling it and see whether the netbook starts up. If it does, there's a problem with the new drive, and you need to replace it.

Chapter 19

Optimizing Windows

●●●

●●●

*B*ecause of increased gas prices, a new sport called *hypermiling* is becoming popular. You mostly play against yourself with the goal of getting the most possible miles per gallon whenever you drive — you do this by modifying your car and your driving habits. One of the first things *hypermilers* do is ensure their car is tuned up for optimal performance. You should do the same with your netbook.

The simple truth is that a netbook is not a powerful, speed demon of a computer. Its processor, memory, and graphics chipset all limit its performance compared with traditional laptops and PCs. And quite honestly, the way Windows comes configured out-of-the-box can hinder your little laptop's performance even more.

The good news is you can perform a series of Windows tune-up tricks to speed up your netbook, get it running more efficiently, and save drive space. In this chapter, I give you the lowdown on optimizing Windows XP for your netbook — if you're running Windows 7, be sure to read the sidebar "Optimizing Windows 7."

I don't guarantee these tips and tricks will give your netbook the same performance as a traditional PC with a dual core processor and loads of RAM, but hey, every little bit helps, and if you do enough optimization tricks, you can get some noticeable improvements. So pick up that $9/16$-inch crescent wrench over there and get started.

Optimizing Windows 7

As I write this, user tests of beta versions of Windows 7 on various netbooks show the operating system performs just as well if not somewhat faster than Windows XP. That's good news, because by the time you read this, Microsoft's newest operating system will come preinstalled on various netbook models — in a version designed for low-horsepower computers like netbooks.

Of course, that's not to say Windows 7 comes perfectly configured for your netbook. As with XP, you should optionally be able to tune up the operating system to enhance your netbook's performance. (**Remember:** You won't be able to upgrade XP to Windows 7 — you need to perform a fresh install of the new operating system.)

If your netbook is running Windows 7, start by uninstalling any programs you don't need, then move on to turning off unused services as I describe in this chapter. In theory, some of the other tuning tips I offer for Windows XP should also apply — however, how you make the changes will probably be a little different.

Because the final version of Windows 7 hasn't hit the streets yet, there's not as much tune-up information available as there is for prior versions of Windows. However, I expect that to change rapidly. The publishers of one of my favorite sites for tweaking Windows XP (www.tweakxp.com) already have a site devoted to optimizing Windows 7, and it's aptly named www.tweakwin7.com. Check it out for specific performance hints.

Reduce, Simplify

One of my favorite Bruce Lee quotes is "Take what is useful and discard the rest." He was talking about martial arts training and techniques, but his comment is appropriate for lots of other things, too, including netbooks.

Just like any other PC these days, your netbook is going to come with lots of programs installed — many that you'll likely never use. These programs are a drain on your netbook for a couple of reasons:

- ✔ Unused programs take up drive space, which is especially critical on netbooks that have small drives without a lot of storage.
- ✔ There may be programs you don't even know about that are running in the background, taking up precious system memory and processor cycles.

In addition to these programs, your netbook can quickly acquire all sorts of temporary files that rob free disk space.

Your one-stop shop for keeping what's useful and discarding the rest is a Windows program called Disk Cleanup. To run the program, choose Start➪Programs➪Accessories➪System Tools➪Disk Cleanup.

Disk Cleanup displays a list of different types of temporary files and how much space they currently are taking up, as shown in Figure 19-1. Select a check box to indicate the files you want to delete and click OK. The program ferrets out the files and removes them for you.

Figure 19-1:
Use Disk
Cleanup to
free up disk
space.

In addition to getting rid of unwanted temporary files, Disk Cleanup is a convenient jump-off point to three other space-saving programs. When you click the More Options tab, you can

- ✔ **Remove Windows components.** Windows comes with a number of components you may not ever use, such as fax services, MSN, and various system accessories. With this tool, you can add and remove Windows components.

- ✔ **Uninstall programs.** This option runs the Add or Remove Programs utility, which you can also run from the Windows Control Panel. A list of installed programs is displayed. Select a program and click the Remove button to uninstall it.

 If you don't know what a program is, do a little bit of research (with Google) before you uninstall it. It may be more important than you think.

- ✔ **Delete old system restore points.** System Restore is a Windows utility that allows you to roll back the system to a previous point in time. (See the "System Restore" section later in the chapter.) You can get rid of old restore point data to free up more drive space.

Check Windows online Help to find out more about any of these clean-up programs.

RAMeo, RAMeo

"Wherefore art thou RAMeo?" said Juliet to her netbook. Pardon the bad pun. I know this chapter is about optimizing Windows to increase performance, but the single best thing you can possibly do to make your netbook go faster is to add more memory.

Sure Windows XP can run with 512MB of RAM (or even less), but the more memory the better. And if you perform the tweaks in this chapter and add more memory, your netbook will be even zoomier. Take this as a hint to read Chapter 18, where I tell you everything you need to know about upgrading memory on your netbook.

Disable Services

Windows (or any operating system for that matter) is not one single, large program, but a collection of small programs, each of which is responsible for a specific task, such as printing, network communications, and so on. These small programs run in the background and are called *services*. Services consume memory and processor cycles — see where I'm going with this?

Windows runs a number of different services. Some are critical to the operating system working correctly; others are completely optional and may never be of use to you. You should consider turning off the latter.

To find out which services your netbook is running, use MSConfig — the Windows System Configuration Utility. This program provides information about services and allows you to enable and disable them, and it displays other system information.

To run MSConfig in XP, here's what you do:

1. **Choose Start⇨Run.**
2. **Type** msconfig **and click OK.**
3. **Click the Services tab.**

A list of services is displayed, as shown in Figure 19-2. A check mark next to an item means that service is enabled and automatically runs when Windows starts up. If you deselect the item and click the Apply or OK button, the service won't start the next time Windows starts — saving you memory and processor cycles.

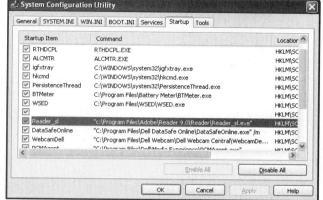

Figure 19-2:
Windows XP
services are
displayed
with
MSConfig.

I could fill this entire book with descriptions of all the Windows XP services. But because I don't have the pages for that, I'll steer you to a very comprehensive Web site that describes all the standard services and even gives suggestions on which ones to disable (and leave alone). And as a bonus, the site provides information on Windows 7 services. Point your browser to www. blackviper.com.

To find out more about MSConfig, visit www.microsoft.com/resources/ documentation/windows/xp/all/proddocs/en-us/msconfig_usage. mspx?mfr=true.

Selective Startups

Look down at the Windows taskbar. See all those little icons down there to the right? Do you even know what half of them are or what they do? I'll tell you what they're doing: Those potentially unused programs are consuming system memory and possibly processor cycles. On a traditional laptop or PC with lots of memory and a fast processor, it's not a big deal. But on a netbook, the more of the little goblins that inhabit the taskbar, the less snappy your little laptop will perform.

First things first. Click each of the icons to see what it is. All the programs in the taskbar are being automatically loaded when Windows starts up. If you don't use the program, it's silly to have it wasting resources.

Many programs that end up in the taskbar have an option that says Run at Startup or something similar. Try right- or left-clicking the icon to display a pop-up menu. You may need to do some sleuthing to find the location of the right setting, but just make sure the program doesn't run when Windows starts.

Another way to find out which programs are run when Windows loads is to use MSConfig, which I introduce in the "Disable Services" section, earlier in this chapter. To run MSConfig, you need to

1. **Choose Start⇨Run.**

2. **Type** msconfig **and click OK.**

3. **Click the Startup tab.**

A list of startup programs is displayed, as shown in Figure 19-3. A check mark next to an item means the program runs when Windows starts up. If you deselect the item and click the Apply or OK button, the program won't run the next time Windows starts.

You'll need to play detective with some of these programs to see what they are — many are part of the operating system and are required for your net-book to work correctly, so don't blindly turn off programs.

Use Google to search for a program's name that appears in the list. For example, if you searched for *Reader_sl.exe,* you'd find out it was Adobe Reader Speed Launch, a program that doesn't really need to run at startup.

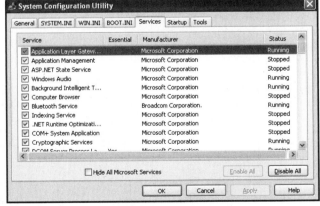

Figure 19-3:
Startup
programs
displayed
with
MSConfig.

Ditch the Glitz

I remember when Windows 3.0 came out. Wow, did it ever have a cutting-edge, fancy user interface. Today, it looks quaint and antiquated in comparison with the animated, eye-popping operating system interfaces you find in the current versions of Windows, Linux, and Mac OS X.

There was a reason earlier generations of Windows didn't have all those glitzy interface features you see on present day operating systems. That reason was performance — computers of the time just didn't have the power to do all the fancy graphics stuff you see today.

By default, Windows XP has a number of graphics features turned on that enhance the user interface. If you turn them off, you free up processor cycles and memory. Here's how:

1. **Right-click the Start button and choose Explore from the pop-up menu.**

   Windows Explorer appears.

2. **Right-click My Computer and choose Properties.**

   The System Properties dialog box appears

3. **Click the Advanced tab.**

4. **Click the Settings button under Performance.**

   The Performance Options dialog box appears, as shown in Figure 19-4. Here you find a variety of user interface visual effects. You have two options to increase system performance:

   • *Select the Adjust for Best Performance radio button.* This turns off all the different graphics interface options shown in the list.

   • *Select the Custom radio button.* With this choice, only the visual effects options that are selected are used. Turn off any effects you don't want to run.

5. **Click OK to save your changes and you're done.**

I have to warn you, though: Turning off all the graphics effects is probably going to seem odd at first. Your eyes tell you something seems just a little off, and you can't quite put your finger on what it is. If you don't like the results, try turning selected effects on and off. Or, go back and enable all the effects again.

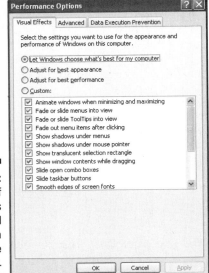

Figure 19-4:
Turn off
Windows
visual
effects for a
performance
boost.

Pictures of puppies, landscapes, children (or whatever) for your desktop background add a nice personal touch to your netbook. However, a custom background also consumes system memory. Consider using a simple, solid color instead. It's boring but efficient.

Industrial Space Saving

Aside from uninstalling programs and temporary files you don't use (as I mention earlier), if you have an extremely space-constrained netbook, you need to perform some industrial-strength space saving. You can tweak several Windows features to maximize your storage space, as I describe in the following sections.

These space-saving tips are primarily for netbooks with small solid state drives. Don't feel compelled to use them if you have a netbook with a hard disk drive — unless you're really trying to scrimp on space.

Compression

You may not know it, but Windows has a feature that allows you to save drive space by compressing individual folders or the entire drive. Here's how to do it.

To compress a folder, take these steps:

1. **Right-click the folder and choose Properties.**

   The folder Properties dialog box appears.

2. **Click the Advanced button.**

   The Advanced Attributes dialog box appears.

3. **Select the Compress Contents to Save Disk Space check box, as shown in Figure 19-5.**

4. **Click OK.**

Figure 19-5:
Compress
a folder to
save space.

Any files in the folder (or that are moved to the folder in the future) are automatically compressed. When you open a file in the folder, Windows transparently uncompresses it to allow program access. When the file is closed, it's compressed again.

You can also compress individual files using the same technique.

To compress the entire drive, here's what you do:

1. **Right-click the Start button and choose Explore from the pop-up menu.**

   Windows Explorer appears.

2. **Right-click on the C: drive and choose Properties.**

   The (C:) Properties dialog box appears.

3. **Select the Compress Drive to Save Disk Space check box, as shown in Figure 19-6.**

4. **Click OK.**

Windows begins compressing the drive. The length of time it takes depends on the size of the drive and how full it is.

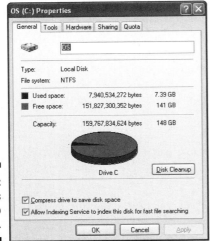

Figure 19-6: Compress the drive to save space.

Compressing the entire drive might seem like a good idea, but keep in mind that although available space increases, your performance may decrease. When programs and certain system files are compressed, they must be uncompressed before they can be run or used. This can really slow down your system.

Page file

In addition to system memory (commonly known as RAM), modern operating systems also rely on something called *virtual memory*. Virtual memory is drive space that's treated as memory. Windows allocates a certain amount of drive space and reads and writes data to it, thus extending the physical memory.

By default, Windows XP allocates 1.5 times the amount of physical memory for virtual memory — so with a netbook that has 1GB of RAM, 1.5GB of drive space is used for virtual memory. Virtual memory is kept in a *page file,* also known as a *swap file,* as data is being swapped in and out of it.

Needless to say, on a netbook with a small solid state drive, virtual memory can consume a big chunk of space. Here's how to turn it off:

1. **Right-click the Start button and choose Explore from the pop-up menu.**

   Windows Explorer appears.

2. **Right-click My Computer and choose Properties.**

   The System Properties dialog box appears.

3. **Click the Advanced tab.**

4. **Click the Settings button under Performance.**

   The Performance Options dialog box appears.

5. **Click the Advanced tab.**

6. **Under Virtual Memory, click the Change button.**

   The Virtual Memory settings dialog box is displayed, as shown in Figure 19-7.

7. **Change the size of the page file (or elect not to use it). When you're done, click OK.**

   Windows restarts and resizes (or removes) the existing page file.

If you decide to ditch the page file, you'll have to make do with whatever physical memory you have installed in your netbook. Try to single-task and not open lots of browser tabs to avoid Windows complaining about running out of memory. If your netbook's performance really suffers after disabling swapping, turn it back on.

Hibernation

Windows XP has two ways of putting your netbook to sleep when you won't be using it for awhile.

- ✔ **Standby:** This is an energy-saving mode where the monitor and drive are turned off and your netbook uses less power.

- ✔ **Hibernate:** In this mode, Windows writes an image of the system state and everything in memory to the drive and then shuts down your netbook. When you come out of hibernation, your netbook is exactly the same as you left it, with the same programs running and files open — no booting required.

Figure 19-7:
Change
the page
file size
or disable
swapping to
save space.

Hibernation is great for shutting down your netbook for the night or the weekend, but Windows needs to store that sleepy bear data someplace. Figure the amount of system memory you have plus a little more will be written to disk — for example, a 1GB netbook needs a bit more than 1GB of disk space to support hibernation.

If you're tight on drive space, turn off hibernation. In the Windows Control Panel, go to Power Options, and on the Hibernate tab, deselect the Enable Hibernation check box.

System Restore

Windows has a slick feature called System Restore that allows you to roll back system settings and installed programs to a previous point in time. It's very useful if your netbook starts misbehaving after you install a new program or update. (I talk more about this feature in Chapter 17.)

The downside to System Restore is its associated data takes up space. A certain amount of drive space is allocated to save all the data included with a restore point. However, you can turn off System Restore or change how much space is allocated by doing the following:

1. **Right-click the Start button and choose Explore from the pop-up menu.**

   Windows Explorer appears.

2. **Right-click My Computer and select Properties.**

   The System Properties dialog box appears.

3. **Click the System Restore tab.**

   System Restore options are displayed, as shown in Figure 19-8.

4. **Either turn off System Restore or use the slider bar to change the amount of space the service uses. Then click OK.**

   Reducing the space does reduce the number of restore points that can be saved.

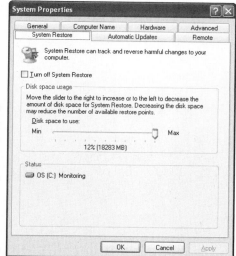

Figure 19-8: Save space by turning System Restore off or changing the amount of space it uses.

There's a case for weighing the usefulness of System Restore with the amount of space it takes up. My recommendation is if you've been running Windows on other computers for awhile and have never used System Restore, consider disabling it on your netbook if you need the extra space.

Chapter 20

Discovering Drivers

This chapter isn't about using a netbook to keep track of your golf clubs or how to discover whether hackers known as *war drivers* are eavesdropping on your netbook's Wi-Fi connection.

The drivers that I'm talking about are *device drivers* — software that allows Windows and other programs to interface with your netbook's hardware, such as its wireless LAN card, webcam, and SD memory card reader.

Device drivers come preinstalled on your netbook and work quietly behind the scenes — you don't need to run the programs or usually even worry about them. However, there may come a time that you need to install a driver, download a new version of one, or are just curious about what drivers are all about. You've come to the right place, because that's what I cover in this chapter.

The Dope on Drivers

For the most part, you can go through life being blissfully unaware of device drivers. They sit unnoticed in the background, chugging away, doing the important job of interfacing with various hardware components. Both Windows and other programs rely on drivers to use hardware such as wireless cards, webcams, sound cards, and more. If a correct driver isn't installed or a driver file becomes corrupted, the hardware device won't work. Bummer. Then you're forced to come up to speed on drivers.

Generally, there are three types of device drivers:

- ✔ **System drivers:** These drivers come with Windows and are part of the operating system. Microsoft includes drivers for many different kinds of popular hardware products.

- ✔ **Computer manufacturer drivers:** These drivers are provided by the PC manufacturer based on a specific computer's hardware components. These drivers, as well as the system drivers, are preinstalled on your netbook.

Drivers tend to be netbook model specific. That means although the same hardware component may be used in a number of different netbooks, you should use only a driver the manufacturer says is for your little laptop.

- ✔ **Third-party hardware drivers:** Certain types of add-on hardware may require a driver to be installed for the product to work correctly — printers are a good example. These drivers are provided on CD-ROMs or DVDs that come with the hardware (or from support Web sites). You need to install the driver if it doesn't come with Windows.

Essential netbook drivers

Lots of drivers are preinstalled on your netbook (many are part of the Windows operating system). Here's a list of common drivers that manufacturers put on your netbook to ensure all those nifty hardware features work as advertised:

- ✔ **Audio:** Interfaces with the sound card for playing and recording audio.

- ✔ **Bluetooth:** Controls the Bluetooth card (if present).

- ✔ **Camera:** Communicates with the webcam.

- ✔ **Card reader:** Interfaces with the memory card reader.

- ✔ **Chipset:** Interfaces with the processor and other integrated chips.

- ✔ **Graphics:** Communicates with the graphics processor.

- ✔ **LAN:** Controls the network card.

- ✔ **Power:** Controls power consumption options.

- ✔ **VGA:** Interfaces with an external display device such as a monitor or projector.

- ✔ **Wireless LAN:** Provides Wi-Fi functionality with the wireless card.

Some manufacturers may provide additional drivers depending on the netbook features, such as for a 3G (as in Third Generation) modem, TV tuner, or GPS receiver. All these drivers (the type will vary depending on the netbook make and model) should be available on the manufacturer's support Web site.

A device driver is a program — just like a word processor, a spreadsheet, or an operating system. That means it can have bugs (that need to be fixed), or whoever wrote the program may have released updated versions with new features or functionality.

What I'm getting at is it's not uncommon for Microsoft and netbook and hardware device manufacturers to release updated versions of their drivers — which I talk about next.

Updating Drivers

Perhaps you were reading on a netbook Web forum that a new version of a wireless driver is available. Or maybe you're having problems with your netbook and someone suggests you get an updated release of the webcam driver. Where do you get updated drivers from and how do you install them?

First off, updating a device driver is usually a three-step process:

1. **Find out what version of the driver you have.**
2. **Check what the latest version of the driver is, and if there's a newer version, download it.**
3. **Install the driver.**

Some netbook manufacturers automate the entire process by providing a utility program that connects to a support Web site, compares driver versions, and downloads and installs the correct drivers (if you don't have the latest version). Check your user manual or online Help to see whether you have this option.

In the coming sections, I give you the details on each of these three steps.

Determining the installed version

You need to know what version of an installed device driver you have before you can find out whether a newer version is available. To determine the version, run the Windows Device Manager. Here's how:

In Windows XP (Classic File Manager view)

1. **Choose Start⇨Settings⇨Control Panel⇨System.**
2. **On the Hardware tab, click Device Manager.**

In Windows XP (Category File Manager view)

> **1. Choose Start⇨Control Panel⇨Performance and Maintenance⇨System.**
>
> **2. On the Hardware tab, click Device Manager.**

In Windows 7

> **1. Choose Start⇨Control Panel⇨System and Security⇨Device Manager.**

Next, with the Device Manager running (as shown in Figure 20-1), select a driver you want to get information about.

Figure 20-1: Windows Device Manager displays hardware devices.

Hardware devices are organized by type — for example, the Disk Drives item contains information about internal drives. Click the plus sign (+) to the left of a hardware device type icon to expand the list. (The Network Adapters item is shown expanded in Figure 20-1.)

When a list is expanded, the plus sign turns into a minus sign (–). Click the minus sign to condense the list.

With the selected hardware device, right-click and choose Properties from the pop-up menu. A Properties dialog box is displayed. Click the Driver tab to get details about the driver, as shown in Figure 20-2. The release date and version number are shown.

Make a note of the version number and release date. You need this to find out whether the driver is current.

Figure 20-2:
The device
Properties
dialog box
shows the
driver
version
number
and release
date.

Getting the latest version

When you know which version of a driver your netbook is running, it's time to see whether a newer release is available.

Device driver updates are free. You may have to register to download a driver, but you won't have to pay for it.

Go to the manufacturer's support Web site for your netbook. There will be a download section where you can get the latest versions of drivers and utility programs. (You may need to do a little bit of hunting because sometimes manufacturers bury downloadable files in the oddest places or make you jump through all sorts of hoops to get to them.)

After you specify your netbook model, a list of available files is displayed. Read through the list until you find the driver you're interested in and then take a look at the information provided about it. An example is shown in Figure 20-3.

Compare the driver version number and release date on the support site with the driver version that's currently on your netbook — remember, you wrote it down:

✔ **If the versions are the same,** there's no sense in downloading the driver — unless you suspect the driver on your netbook may have become corrupted and you're planning to reinstall it.

✔ **If the support site has a newer version of the driver,** follow the instructions to download it; however, first read the "To update or not" sidebar.

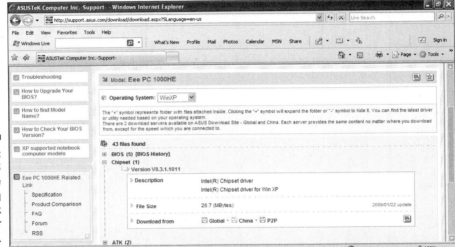

Figure 20-3:
The ASUS support site showing netbook driver information.

 Some manufacturers provide a CD-ROM or DVD that contains all the required drivers for your netbook. If a device isn't working properly and you suspect a corrupted driver file may be the culprit, you can use a driver from the disc instead of downloading one from the manufacturer support site. Additionally, if you have to reinstall Windows, you may need to install these drivers so your netbook works correctly. You need an external drive to access these files. If you don't have one, download the drivers from the support Web site with another computer and then transfer them to your netbook with a USB flash drive.

Installing the update

After you've obtained a device driver (either downloaded or from a CD-ROM that came with your netbook), the installation process is straightforward. Here's what you do:

1. **Follow the steps listed in the section, "Determining the installed version," earlier in this chapter, to run the Device Manager.**

2. **In the Device Manager, select the device driver you want to update.**

3. **Right-click the selected driver and choose Update Driver from the pop-up menu.**

4. **Follow the Hardware Update Wizard prompts and instructions.**

Specify the location of the updated driver — either downloaded to your hard drive, on a USB flash drive, or on the manufacturer CD-ROM. There is an option that queries a Microsoft Internet site for updated drivers, but because you already have the driver you need, asking Windows to search for a newer version isn't necessary.

If you decide to use the search feature instead of manually downloading a driver from a manufacturer site, keep in mind that searching works great for system drivers but may not always find the latest manufacturer drivers.

Windows then replaces the current device driver with the one you specify. You may need to restart your netbook for the new driver to start working — Windows lets you know if that's the case.

To update or not

If you discover that a new version of a driver is available, should you automatically download and install it? Newer is better, right? The computer industry has done a very good job of training all of us to believe that's the case. But hold on a minute.

Personally, I believe in the old adage of "if it's not broken, don't fix it." Unless I have a very compelling reason to use a new release of a driver, I generally won't update an older version. Unless you have a bit of a technical bent, the update process can be a bit confusing as well as time consuming — especially if your netbook doesn't work correctly after a new driver version is installed.

At the very least, I'll get as much information as I possibly can to help me decide whether to update. That includes

✔ Checking out the read-me file that comes with the driver. This file usually contains some notes on what's new and has been changed.

✔ Reviewing netbook forums to see whether I can find any user comments about a newly released driver.

Even if I do decide to update, I won't do it immediately unless the driver is supposed to fix a bug that I've been cursing about for awhile. I like to wait at least a few weeks after a release to make sure it's stable — and let other users play test pilot ahead of me.

As always, check your user manual, the manufacturer's support site, or a netbook forum for specific information about upgrading drivers on your particular model.

Windows is only halfway intelligent when it comes to upgrading drivers. It's possible to replace a driver with one that's not compatible with a hardware component. When that happens, at the very least the hardware won't work — at the worst, the hardware won't work and Windows will become unstable. Always make sure you have the right driver. If you get yourself in trouble, try using the Roll Back Driver command in the device Properties dialog box, shown earlier in Figure 20-2.

Chapter 21

BIOS Basics

*B*IOS stands for *basic input/output system*. This is firmware (a program in hardware) that runs when a computer starts up. The BIOS recognizes and initializes various system hardware components, such as storage drives, the keyboard, video card, and other devices. This startup process gets the computer ready for Windows (or some other operating system) to load and take charge.

You may have been using computers for years and never had to deal with BIOS before, so why am I devoting a chapter to it in this book? The answer is that netbooks may require you to work with the BIOS more than your average laptop or desktop PC does — at least that's what some evidence suggests.

I don't want to say it's certain you'll have to muck around with your netbook's BIOS, but just in case you do, this chapter prepares you. I describe what the BIOS is and how it works, how to access and change netbook BIOS settings, and the pros and cons of updating the BIOS, and even how to do the updating.

Boiling Down BIOS

As I mention in the introduction, BIOS (basic input/output system) is program code that runs when your netbook is powered on. The purpose of BIOS is to make sure essential hardware components are working correctly before Windows loads and runs. In addition, the BIOS also contains a library of code used to control the keyboard and display and to store different system settings.

The BIOS is incorporated into a chip — a *CMOS* (complementary metal oxide semiconductor) chip, to be precise. This chip contains rewritable memory, and it's possible to update the BIOS code with new versions — a process commonly known as *flashing,* which I talk about later in this chapter, in the section "Updating the BIOS."

A handful of companies manufacture BIOS for computers — a few of the more popular brands are AMI, Award, and Phoenix. Netbook manufacturers install BIOS chips with code customized to work with their little laptops on system *motherboards,* the board that contains the *brains* of the computer, including the processor, memory, and graphics processor.

That's BIOS boiled down without getting into the real geeky stuff. The reason I'm bringing you up to speed on BIOS has to do with an observation: I've been hanging around personal computers for a long time now, and for some reason, I see netbook users mentioning more BIOS-related issues than traditional PC users. For example, here's a sampling of topics frequently discussed in netbook user Web forums:

✔ My webcams aren't working because of a BIOS setting.

✔ My wireless isn't working after a BIOS update.

✔ What's involved in changing the BIOS boot order sequence to use an operating system on an SD card?

✔ My netbook died after a failed BIOS upgrade.

✔ Should I change the processor speed in BIOS?

I don't exactly know what the BIOS fixation is (and personally, I've never had any BIOS-related problems with any of the netbooks I've used), but I decided it was best to devote some time to the subject — just in case.

The best place on the Web to get detailed information on all sorts of aspects of BIOS is Wim's BIOS site at www.wimsbios.com.

Getting to the BIOS Settings

All BIOSes have a setup program for changing settings. To run the program, you need to press a certain key (or keys) right after you turn on the netbook.

Some netbook user manuals refer to the time that immediately follows pressing the power button as POST (power-on self test). POST checks your hardware to ensure that necessary components are present and working.

On some netbooks, a startup screen briefly appears. Somewhere on the screen, a message, such as `Press F2 to run setup`, tells you which key(s) you need to press to edit BIOS settings. When you see the screen, press the key.

Other netbooks don't include a helpful reminder screen before Windows starts to load — the screen is disabled in a BIOS setting that speeds up boot time. If this is the case, you'll need to press the BIOS setup key(s) immediately after you press the netbook power button.

Unfortunately, the computer industry has never standardized on a common key sequence to get to the BIOS settings — the key(s) will vary depending on your netbook manufacturer and the BIOS used.

Some common key sequences for running the BIOS setup program include:

- ✔ Del
- ✔ Esc
- ✔ F1
- ✔ F2
- ✔ Ctrl+Alt+Esc

Your user manual (or the manufacturer support Web site) will tell you which key(s) works for your netbook.

Some netbooks are very picky about exactly when you need to press the key. If pressing and holding the correct key doesn't bring up the setup program, restart your netbook and then try rapidly and repeatedly pressing the key.

Changing BIOS Settings

When you press the appropriate key(s), a very old-school text screen appears, and it looks similar to what's shown in Figure 21-1. Information about your netbook (including the memory, processor type and speed, and BIOS version) is displayed.

Congratulations! You're now running the BIOS setup program, where you can make various system changes.

This isn't the place to be changing settings for things you don't understand. If you don't know what you're doing (and why you're doing it), you can mess your netbook up pretty good — as in bad. Don't play around with BIOS settings unless you have to, and even then, be careful.

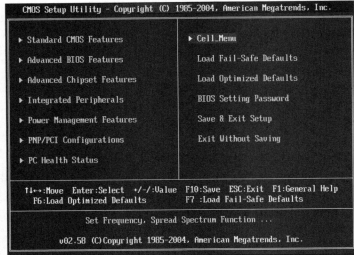

CMOS Setup Utility - Copyright (C) 1985-2004, American Megatrends, Inc.

```
▶ Standard CMOS Features          ▶ Cell_Menu

▶ Advanced BIOS Features            Load Fail-Safe Defaults

▶ Advanced Chipset Features         Load Optimized Defaults

▶ Integrated Peripherals            BIOS Setting Password

▶ Power Management Features         Save & Exit Setup

▶ PNP/PCI Configurations            Exit Without Saving

▶ PC Health Status


↑↓←→:Move  Enter:Select  +/-/:Value  F10:Save  ESC:Exit  F1:General Help
    F6:Load Optimized Defaults        F7 :Load Fail-Safe Defaults

            Set Frequency, Spread Spectrum Function ...

        v02.58 (C)Copyright 1985-2004, American Megatrends, Inc.
```

Figure 21-1:
Expect the
BIOS setup
program to
look and run
like an
old DOS
program.

Navigating the screens

If you're used to Windows, don't expect fancy fonts, graphics, or icons in the BIOS setup program. Heck, you can't even use your mouse to select menu items. Instead, expect a text-based interface that looks like it escaped from the 1980s. You even have to use your keyboard to navigate the screen.

The BIOS setup program has different screens that are organized around types of settings. The screen names appear at the top of the screens — they're like tabs. For example, all the security-related settings may appear on a screen named Security.

A list showing available keyboard commands always appears on the screen, so you'll know how to navigate the screens. As an example, here's a quick rundown of various AMI BIOS commands:

- ✔ **Right- and left-arrow keys:** Selects a screen — click one of the arrow keys to move to the next or previous screen. The currently selected screen name is highlighted at the top of the window.

- ✔ **Up- and down-arrow keys:** Selects a setting in the current screen. Brief information about the setting and commands appears to the right.

- ✔ **Plus (+) and minus (–) keys:** Changes an option — the currently selected option is highlighted in white.

- ✔ **Enter:** Selects a setting and displays another screen with additional related settings.

- **Tab:** On settings that have multiple fields, moves to a field. For example, if you were changing the system time setting, pressing Tab would move between the hours, minutes, and seconds fields.

- **Esc:** Exits the current screen. If you press Esc in any of the main screens, you're asked whether you want to save your changes before you quit setup.

- **F1:** Displays a Help dialog box with commands. Press Esc to close the dialog box.

- **F10:** Saves any changes you've made and exits the setup program.

If a dialog box with buttons is displayed, use Tab to move between the buttons and press Enter to click a button.

After you exit, the setup program closes, your netbook continues booting, and Windows starts.

The preceding commands are found in the AMI (American Megatrends, Inc.) BIOS setup utility. Depending on which BIOS your netbook comes with, the commands may be different.

Setting options

The BIOS setup program allows you to change a number of system settings — think of it as a low-level Windows Control Panel for netbook hardware. You can change many settings, but in the following sections, I focus on those most important to netbook users.

Hardware

The BIOS contains settings for a number of hardware devices, including

- **LAN:** Wired network card
- **Audio:** Sound card
- **Card reader:** SD memory card reader
- **Camera:** Webcam (if built-in)
- **WLAN:** Wireless network card
- **Bluetooth:** Bluetooth wireless (if built-in)

In the popular AMI BIOS, these settings are found in the Onboard Devices Configuration item in the Advanced screen.

These hardware devices can all be enabled or disabled. Use the + (plus) key to enable a selected item or the – (minus) key to disable an item.

If one or more of these hardware components aren't working on your netbook, check whether it's enabled. If a setting is disabled, that particular device won't function. If you enable the device, save the change, and then exit the setup program, there's a good chance you will just have solved your problem.

Some of these hardware components can be turned on and off with function keys. Try enabling a device that doesn't work with a function key first before running the BIOS setup program and changing settings — it's much easier. Check your user manual for details.

Boot

These settings control your netbook's boot (startup) options, including

- ✔ **Boot Device Priority:** Sets the booting order of storage devices. For example, you could specify that your netbook boots from an operating system installed on an SD card (if present) before Windows on the hard drive loads and runs.

  Most netbooks have a key command for selecting which device to boot from. When you press a certain key after you power on the netbook, a dialog box appears and allows you to choose the boot device (SD card reader, internal hard drive, or external drive). Check your user manual for more information.

- ✔ **Boot Settings:** Many netbooks have a BIOS option that speeds up booting by skipping some startup tests — as well as the startup screen. You can enable or disable this setting here. In most cases, it doesn't hurt to disable startup tests. If you do, and at some point your netbook doesn't seem to be working correctly, enable the tests. If there's some type of hardware problem, information about it will appear after you turn on the netbook.

Security

Several different security settings in BIOS are available to protect your netbook. If you're storing sensitive information on your little laptop, consider using one or more of the following options:

- ✔ **User Password:** This setting requires a password when the netbook starts up. If you don't get it right, you're out of luck.

- ✔ **Supervisor Password:** With this setting, you need a password to access the BIOS setup program. If the supervisor password isn't set, anyone who knows the user password can change it in the BIOS setup program. If the supervisor password is set, it's impossible to reset the user password without knowing the supervisor password.

- **HDD User Password:** If this option is enabled, the netbook's hard drive won't be accessible until a correct password is entered. Some BIOS versions use encryption to secure the drive. (See Chapter 9, where I discuss software encryption options.)

- **HDD Master Password:** Similar to the supervisor password, if a master hard drive password is set, you need to correctly enter it in order to change the HDD User Password. Yes, it's a password you need to enter to change another password. For years, BIOS users have been scratching their heads over these rather confusing collections of password setting.

If you use BIOS passwords, be sure to write them down and keep them in a safe place. If you forget them, it can be difficult (or sometimes impossible) to access a protected netbook.

There are ways of defeating BIOS security, depending on the computer. This means two things:

- BIOS security measures won't stop a determined and skilled adversary from getting into your netbook — they can stop most people, but not everyone.

- If you forget your password, there's some possible hope. Do some Google searching on *BIOS password* for more.

CPU

Some netbook models contain a BIOS setting for controlling the speed of the processor. The faster a processor runs, the more power it draws. By reducing the speed of the processor, you increase battery life. To better handle high-definition video, some manufacturers offer an option of running the processor faster than its advertised speed (known as *overclocking*). The downsides to overclocking are battery life is decreased and the computer runs hotter.

Updating the BIOS

Manufacturers often release updates to a netbook's BIOS for fixing bugs and adding new features — remember that the BIOS code is stored in a chip with rewritable memory. Many netbooks include programs for updating to the latest version of the BIOS — this is commonly known as *flashing,* but it has nothing to do with a seedy-looking character in a trench coat. In general, none of this sounds out of the ordinary. In fact it probably sounds like a common software update, the kind where you check whether there's a new release, download and install it, and everyone's happy.

Not so fast. Despite appearances, it's really not that simple, and many netbook manufacturers are a little guilty of glossing over some important details that could bite you in the behind.

What the friendly user manuals often neglect to mention is if something goes wrong during a BIOS update, there's a chance you'll turn your netbook into a brick — or, to quote an old *Monty Python* skit, "it will be pushing up the daisies."

If corrupt code or data gets written to the BIOS while flashing, the odds are good that your netbook's motherboard won't be able to communicate with hardware components. Trying to flash the BIOS a second time may not help either.

If this happens while your netbook is under warranty, off it goes to the manufacturer, and you patiently wait for a replacement laptop to arrive — you did back up your files, I hope.

If the BIOS gets messed up after your warranty expires, it probably means buying a new netbook. (It's possible to install a new BIOS chip or motherboard, but considering the servicing costs, it usually makes more economic sense to opt for a whole new computer.)

Computer and BIOS manufacturers are aware of the risks that BIOS updates pose and typically include some safeguard measures during the update process. However, these safety procedures aren't infallible. If you suspect you've messed up the BIOS, consult the netbook manufacturer's support site to see whether you can find utilities or procedures that might help you get your netbook working again.

When it comes to BIOS upgrades, I'm an advocate of "if it ain't broke, don't fix it." Unless you have a compelling reason to update the BIOS (such as a known hardware bug that's been troubling you gets fixed in a new BIOS version), don't.

Just because a new version of the BIOS is available, don't rush out and update — avoid the Pavlovian response of automatically updating whenever a manufacturer rings the "new version" bell.

Usually a manufacturer supplies a list of what's been fixed or added in new BIOS releases — although the information can be pretty terse and sometimes difficult to understand. If you're having an issue that seems related to one of the described fixes, consider updating — but recognize the risks, especially if the warranty on your netbook has expired.

When a new version of a BIOS is released, there's often lots of discussion about it in netbook Web forums. You may glean some insights from other users who've already installed an update as to whether a specific problem has been fixed. Be suspicious about reports of faster boot times. It seems like any time a new BIOS is released, someone is always claiming his computer (whether it's a netbook, laptop or desktop PC) starts up faster — even if there were no changes to boot-specific code. Oh well.

Check your user manual or the manufacturer's Web support site for details on updating your netbook's BIOS. Updating is usually done with a supplied utility program or by downloading a BIOS file to an SD card and pressing a key sequence after the netbook is powered on — the BIOS file on the SD card replaces the current BIOS.

BIOS update hints

If you decide to flash your BIOS, here are a few hints to ensure a successful experience:

✔ Always update the BIOS with the netbook plugged into an electrical outlet. Losing power midway through a BIOS flash is a recipe for disaster.

✔ Make sure your battery is fully charged just in case the main power goes out.

✔ Never turn off or reset your netbook during a BIOS flash.

✔ Follow the manufacturer's update instructions to the letter. Read through the directions several times so you understand them. If something doesn't make sense, try searching on Google for your netbook model and the keywords *BIOS update* — you'll find tutorials and user commentary that helps explain unclear steps.

✔ Make sure you get the right BIOS for your netbook. Flashing a BIOS update for another model can cause big trouble.

✔ Use the most recent version of the BIOS update utility — check the manufacturer's Web site.

✔ If you've overclocked your netbook (performed a tweak to speed up the processor to get it to run faster), be aware that flashing a new BIOS can possibly lock up your little laptop.

✔ If there's a way to flash the BIOS without running a utility program from within Windows, do it. I've heard of instances where Windows processes and antivirus software have messed up a BIOS update. Play it safe if you can.

Good luck!

Part V
The Part of Tens

The 5th Wave   By Rich Tennant

"I'll be right there. Let me just take care of this user. He's about halfway through a three hour download."

In this part . . .

Welcome to The Part of Tens. If you're a connoisseur of other fine *For Dummies* books, you've undoubtedly noticed that all *For Dummies* titles have this part — and who am I to break with tradition?

For your reading pleasure, in this part you find a chapter that lists essential Internet information resources for netbooks and another that describes ten netbook hardware hacks.

Chapter 22

Top Ten Internet Netbook Resources

You can find a tremendous amount of technical support information about netbooks available on the Internet. Some of it comes from official sources (like manufacturer Web sites), but an increasing amount is provided by individual netbook users who are passionate about their little laptops and want to spread the word as well as help other users. In this chapter, I list the top places to get free technical support for your netbook.

In addition to these sites, I point you toward some of the best Net sources for netbook news and reviews. The netbook world is always changing — new products are released, old products are dropped, hot technologies emerge, and so on. If you want to stay up on the latest happenings, these news and review Web sites are indispensable.

Also, I guess I lied when I said I'd cover only the top ten Net resources — it's more like the top 40. But you don't mind that, do you? I didn't think so. Here they are.

Official Support

When you need netbook technical support, the place to go is the World Wide Web. The first stop should be your netbook manufacturer's Web site. Here you find how to get technical support, software updates you can download, user manuals, and additional information about your netbook.

When I'm checking out support sites, I always use my primary computer for the browsing, with my netbook running at its side. That makes it easy to read directions on the main PC and then do whatever you need to do on your netbook.

Because netbook manufacturers are international companies, they often have a different Web site for each country or region. Considering that, I list the primary Web addresses for the major netbook manufacturers. From here you can click until you find a support site for where you live — often localized in your language.

- **Acer,** www.acer.com
- **ASUS,** www.asus.com
- **Dell,** www.dell.com
- **Everex,** www.everexstore.com/everex
- **Fujitsu,** www.fujitsu.com/global/services/computing
- **HP,** www.hp.com
- **LG,** www.lg.com
- **Lenovo,** www.lenovo.com
- **MSI,** www.msimobile.com
- **One Laptop per Child (OLPC),** www.laptop.org
- **Samsung,** www.samsung.com
- **Toshiba,** www.toshiba.com

If you don't see your netbook manufacturer in this list, enter the company's name in Google and jump to the manufacturer's Web site.

I've found netbook manufacturer information (especially downloads) can vary among different country Web sites. If you feel like doing a little globe-trotting and exploring, try checking out various international sites.

Functional Forums

If you're having problems with your netbook and can't get a good answer from an official support site, visit a Web forum. A number of user communities have popped up around popular brands and models of netbooks. I've found at times I can get faster and more accurate information from these unofficial sources than I can from an official manufacturer's technical support site.

All access to these forums is free so that anyone can read them, but if you want to post a message, you'll need to register for a free account. If you're new to netbook forums, I have several pieces of advice:

- ✔ **Read through the forum posts first to get a general idea of how the group works.** Also, if you have a question, there's a pretty good chance it may have already been answered in the past. It's also not a bad idea to read any FAQs (Frequently Asked Question lists) or wikis that are associated with the forum.

- ✔ **Use the forum's search function before you post a question.** You should do this just in case the question has already been answered. Search for some pertinent keywords that relate to your question.

- ✔ **When you post a question, provide as much detail as you can.** Avoid "My netbook doesn't work. What should I do?" A better approach is "My Eee PC 900A won't boot after I accidentally left it on a picnic table overnight and it rained."

 Although most forum "elders" are kind and provide sage wisdom, some can get a little grumpy, especially when they think someone isn't asking a worthwhile question. Don't sweat it if someone gets a little testy. It's the Internet after all.

Here's a collection of independent netbook forums to consult, organized alphabetically by brand:

- ✔ **Acer,** www.aspireoneuser.com/forum
- ✔ **ASUS,** http://forum.eeeuser.com
- ✔ **Dell,** www.mydellmini.com/forum
- ✔ **Everex,** http://forums.cloudbooklounge.com
- ✔ **HP,** www.hp2133guide.com/forums
- ✔ **MSI, Wind** http://forums.msiwind.net
- ✔ **OLPC,** www.olpcnews.com/forum
- ✔ **Samsung,** www.sammynetbook.com/plugins/forum/forum.php

In addition to these brand-specific forums, here are some general netbook forums that cover many different makes and models:

- ✔ **Netbook User,** http://forum.netbookuser.com
- ✔ **Netbook Forums,** http://netbook-forums.com
- ✔ **Netbook Boards,** http://netbookboards.com/forums

News and Reviews

If you want to stay up-to-date with the latest on netbooks, you can turn to a number of Web sites and blogs. Here I tell you about the ones considered some of the best — presented in alphabetical order.

ASUS's Eee PC was the first netbook to hit the market, and a lot of Web sites appeared with some variation of Eee in their names. However, the name doesn't necessarily mean the site is only about Eee PCs. As netbook popularity increased, many sites started covering all makes and models of netbooks but never changed their site names.

If you're shopping for a new netbook, several of these sites not only provide news and reviews, but also have a deals section devoted to bargain-priced netbooks from various sources.

- **ASUS EEE Hacks:** (`http://asuseeehacks.blogspot.com`) This blog is one of my favorite daily reads, with fresh news and useful information on many types of netbooks — plus, as the name suggests, some cool hardware hacks.

- **Blogeee:** (`www.blogeee.net`) This is a netbook blog from France that always seems to get the scoop on upcoming netbook releases. The problem for English-only speakers is the site is in French — so if you don't *parle vous,* use Google's translation service at `www.google.com/translate_t` to see what the Web site has to say.

- **Eee PC Blog:** (`http://eeepc.net`) Despite its name, this blog covers news on all types of netbooks.

- **EeeUser:** (`www.eeeuser.com`) By far the most definitive Eee PC site on the planet with news, reviews, forums and a wiki. If you own an ASUS, bookmark this site.

- **GottaBeMobile:** (`www.gottabemobile.com`) Covers tablet PCs, mobile PCs, and netbooks.

- **JKKMobile:** (`http://jkkmobile.com`) A great site devoted to ultra-mobile computers. In addition to run-of-the-mill blog entries, the hosts post a number of review and technical information videos.

- **LAPTOP Magazine:** (`http://blog.laptopmag.com`) This is the *LAPTOP Magazine* blog on all things laptop — with a heavy emphasis on netbooks these days, due to their popularity.

- **Liliputing:** (`www.liliputing.com`) This is my favorite news site devoted to small laptops. Lilliputian computing, get it? It's an excellent resource for all the latest netbook news.

- **My Dell Mini:** (http://mydellmini.com) The source of all things related to Dell's Mini line of netbooks.

- **MSI Wind:** (http://msiwind.net) News and information on MSI netbooks.

- **NetbookTech:** (www.netbooktech.com) More netbook news and commentary.

- **Netbook User:** (http://netbookuser.com) Netbook User is a news aggregator that pulls headlines from many popular netbook sites. No photos or frills; just the facts, ma'am.

- **Portable Monkey:** (http://portablemonkey.com) This blog's author lives in Tokyo, Japan, so you find out what's happening in Asia. Most netbooks debut in Taiwan and Japan before appearing in the United States and Europe, so you get a sneak peek.

- **Sammy Netbook:** (www.sammynetbook.com) If you're into Samsung netbooks, this site has everything you need.

- **Trusted Reviews:** (www.trustedreviews.com/laptops) This is a British computer review site that provides some of the best, no-holds barred reviews of netbooks on the Web.

As you can see, there are a whole lot of Web sites devoted to netbook news and reviews — and I haven't even come close to listing them all.

For any netbook blog, check whether the author offers an RSS (Really Simple Syndication) feed or Twitter tweet. That way you can easily check whether new content has been added without visiting the full Web site.

Chapter 23

Ten Cool Hardware Hacks

*G*ood, Igor. You're just in time. (Cue high voltage electricity arcing through the air in a dark, dank, evil scientist's dungeon lair.) The subject is on the table, and I'm about ready to begin. Yes, I'm going to turn this mild mannered netbook into a . . . Bwah, ha, ha, ha!

If you're one of those mad scientist types who's never happy with things as they originally came from the manufacturer, because you just know you can make them better, this chapter is for you. Here I supply the inveterate tinkerer with ten (actually a few more than that, but who's counting) hardware projects for modifying various models of netbooks.

I absolutely have to throw one of those little bomb icons in here. Be forewarned: Many of these projects require a steady soldering hand and a rudimentary knowledge of electronics. There's a good chance you can turn your netbook into a brick if you mess up — and forget about a manufacturer honoring your warranty.

With the disclaimers out of the way, please follow me down to the laboratory. Walk this way. (Even if you're not planning on modding your netbook, it's still fun to see what other people have done.)

Add a Keyboard Backlight

If you're a touch typist who's used to normal-size keys, using a netbook with a small keyboard can be a bit challenging — enough to make you look down at the keys every now and then. When the lights go out, it's even worse — especially for hunt-and-peck typists. If you can't see what you're pressing, the typo count will be sky high.

The first hardware hack in this chapter is installing a keyboard backlight inside the case. This provides a soothing glow between the key spaces, softly illuminating the keyboard (as shown in Figure 23-1) — kind of like having a nightlight inside your netbook.

Popular Science has step-by-step instructions, using an Eee PC. The cost is under $15, and the work takes just a couple hours of your time. Check it out at

```
www.popsci.com/diy/article/2008-05/eee-pc-school-add-
             keyboard-backlight-under-15
```

Figure 23-1:
Light shines up through the spaces between keys, back-lighting the keyboard.

Add Internal GPS

In Chapter 11, I tell you about using an external GPS receiver to turn your netbook into a nifty, nimble navigator. But wouldn't it be nice if you could dispense with the cables or Bluetooth connections and forget about yet another accessory to carry around?

Although a few netbooks are available with built-in GPS chips, most aren't. However, with a little bit of hardware hacking, you can add GPS functionality to just about any netbook.

Thanks to folks like Tom Beauchamp, adding GPS isn't as hard as you might think. Tom bought a USB GPS receiver (shown in Figure 23-2) and engineered a way to fit it into his Dell Mini's case. Tom shares instructions and photos with you in this informative forum post:

```
http://mydellmini.com/forum/integrated-gps-on-my-mini-
            9-t167.html
```

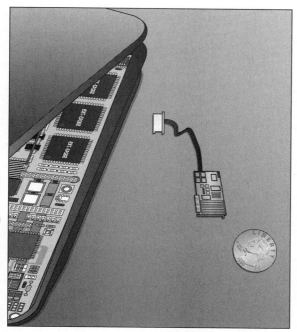

Figure 23-2: This GPS receiver is ready to be installed in a Dell Mini.

Swap in a Touch Screen

When netbooks first came out, a lot of users were clamoring for touch screen models. About two years later, manufacturers are finally starting to release little laptops that give you a tablet computing experience. But in the meantime, hardware hackers have been modifying existing netbooks right and left with touch panels — and if you're a bit of a geek, you can too.

A good place to start is with netbook guru and blogger JKKMobile. He's been building touch screen Eee PCs since a few months after they first hit the streets. Check out this URL for video instructions:

```
http://jkkmobile.blogspot.com/2007/12/asus-eee-pc-with-
          touch-screen.html
```

From an engineering standpoint, it's not that difficult to swap a default net-book screen with a touch panel. With a little searching through Google or through Web forums devoted to your netbook make and model, you should be able to find hacking instructions — or people offering customized models. Or you could just wait and buy a new touch screen netbook.

Make Your Own Extended Battery

Do you want to power your netbook with an extended-life battery but don't want to shell out the bucks to purchase a new one? No worries, because those crazy French hackers over at `www.blogeee.net` show you how — using an MSI Wind netbook as shown in Figure 23-3. Here's the URL:

```
www.blogeee.net/2008/07/31/une-batterie-9-cellules-pour-
          msi-wind-u100-faite-maison
```

Oops, I forgot to mention the tutorial is in French. There are enough photos to give you a pretty good idea of what the process is, but understanding the words that go with the pictures is always nice.

If your French is as bad as mine (or even worse), head over to Google's free translation service at `http://translate.google.com`. Type in the Web address and specify to translate from French to English. *Mon dieu!* The transla-tion is a bit fractured, but quite usable.

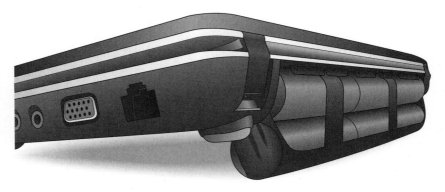

Figure 23-3:
A do-it-
yourself
extended
battery.

Hack your Dell Mini

I have to hand it to Dell. Whereas other manufacturers treat the internals of their netbooks like state secrets, Dell happily provides the service manual online for free.

If you're a hardware hacker, you know how much easier it is to have the service manual available to find out about all the components and how they're connected. For example, say you have a Mini 910 and want to swap out the

built-in digital camera for something a bit better. No problem; just point your browser at

```
http://support.dell.com/
support/edocs/systems/ins910/
en/sm/index.htm
```

You get step-by-step instructions, including color photos. That's what I call hardware hacker friendly — yet another reason why the Dell Minis are turning into a favorite of geeks.

The original article on this how-to came from an MSI Web forum and is in English (but is missing the photos). Check it out at

```
http://forums.msiwind.net/viewtopic.php?f=17&t=1245
```

Mod the Case

An interesting subculture of hardware hackers known as *case modders* has cropped up. These artistic hackers hack the outside of a computer — and sometimes the insides, too. In a nutshell, they swap the original computer case for something infinitely cooler. Modders have put computers in mannequins, old radios, movie props, and just about anything you can possibly think of — do a Google search for *case mods* to see what I mean.

The popularity of netbooks is focusing modders' attention on the little laptops. For example, Figure 23-4 shows a sleek Eee PC crafted by a Japanese modder who ditched the original case and keyboard and turned it into a tablet PC. You can check out more photos at

```
http://dvice.com/archives/2009/02/gutted_eee_pc_d.php
```

Figure 23-4:
An Eee PC
modded and
transformed
into a
tablet PC.

No-Soldering Hardware Mods

I've always thought that if you're going to hack hardware, you need a cool hand with a hot soldering iron. Touching the wrong component with the soldering iron tip or blobbing solder in the wrong place is a recipe for disaster.

I was pretty amazed when I saw the following tutorial on installing a touch screen in an Eee PC with no soldering involved — and for under $50, mind you.

```
www.instructables.com/id/how_to_touchscreen_EEE_without_
            soldering_/
```

The secret to holding everything together without the silver melty stuff is simply pieces of high-temperature tape. Wow, that opens up all sorts of possibilities for soldering-phobics.

Add a Second Memory Card Reader

One of the defining features of a netbook is a built-in SD memory card reader. The reader allows you to boot different operating systems and transfer photos from digital cameras — on first-generation netbooks, it was essential for expanding storage on models that came with low-capacity solid state drives.

But more is always better, so why not add another memory card reader? After all, you do have two or more USB slots.

Your friends at *Popular Science* were so enamored with modding the Eee PC they ran a series of hardware hacking how-to articles. This article shows you how to install a microSD card reader (shown in Figure 23-5):

```
www.popsci.com/diy/article/2008-05/eee-pc-school-2-add-
                second-microsd-card-reader
```

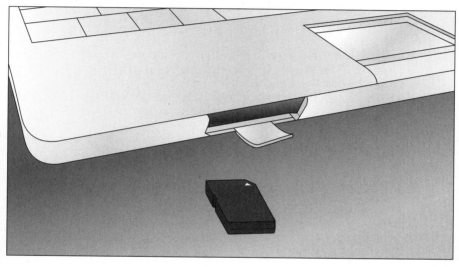

Figure 23-5:
A netbook with a second memory card reader installed.

There's also another set of instructions for adding an old-school, Compact Flash (CF) card reader to another netbook brand at

```
www.popsci.com/diy/article/2008-05/add-versatile-compact-
                flash-boot-drive-inexpensive-laptop
```

Turn a Netbook into a Picture Frame

Digital picture frames were a big hit a few Christmases ago. The novelty has since worn off, and the prices have dropped, but that hasn't stopped the hardware-hacking community from continuing to play around with the idea.

There's an old saying that if you give a bored hacker some old hardware, you'll probably be surprised at what that hacker comes up with. A case in point is a hacker who goes by the name of Q, who took a cheap, first-generation Eee PC and turned it into a digital picture. His meticulously documented how-to is here:

```
http://awooga.nl/the-eee-pc-digital-picture-frame
```

Q also has some detailed information on hacking Dell Minis elsewhere on his site.

Add an External Wi-Fi Antenna Jack

For a tiny PC, most netbooks get surprisingly good Wi-Fi reception — especially considering the space available for an internal antenna is much less compared to a full-size laptop.

However, there may be times when you want to boost reception with an external antenna — for example when war-driving, er, I mean, performing wireless security audits. Unfortunately, netbooks don't come with PC card slots where the simple solution would be to purchase a Wi-Fi card that supported plugging in an external antenna.

But a hardware limitation can't stop a determined hacker. In an excellent tutorial, Terry Porter shows you how to install an SMA jack into the back of an Eee PC (shown in Figure 23-6). When attached to an external antenna, signal strength for the built-in Wi-Fi card is considerably increased.

Here's the Web address for more information:

```
http://wiki.portertech.org/doku.php?id=eeepc900-ext-
          antenna
```

Swiss Army Knife Mod an Eee PC

I love Swiss Army Knives — they feature tools of every manner and are ready for any job. And I have to give a tip of the hat to Torsten Lyngaas, who performed one big Swiss Army Knife of a modification to an Eee PC. He stuffed over $400 of additional hardware into the little laptop, including a USB hub, GPS with antenna, Bluetooth, card reader, flash drive, new power switch, FM transmitter, modem, touch screen, temperature sensor, and heat sink.

The cool thing is that he provides detailed information about the parts he used and how he added them — complete with close-up photos. Check out his wiki at

```
http://beta.ivancover.com/wiki/index.php/Eee_PC_Internal_
          Upgrades
```

Figure 23-6:
An Eee
PC with
an added
external
Wi-Fi
antenna
jack.

Find out about even more hacks

I close by pointing you toward even more net-book hardware hacks — I just scratch the surface in this chapter, and new hacks seem to appear every week.

Two of my favorite Web sites for keeping up with little laptop hardware hacks are

✔ **JKKMobile:** `http://jkkmobile.blogspot.com/search/label/hack`

✔ **Hack a Day:** `http://hackaday.com/tag/netbook`

In addition to these sources, check out Web forums that are devoted to the make and model of your netbook — there's almost always a section devoted to hardware hacking.

Get your soldering iron warmed up and have some fun!

Index

• *D* •

Notes

Notes

Business/Accounting & Bookkeeping

Bookkeeping For Dummies
978-0-7645-9848-7

eBay Business
All-in-One For Dummies,
2nd Edition
978-0-470-38536-4

Job Interviews
For Dummies,
3rd Edition
978-0-470-17748-8

Resumes For Dummies,
5th Edition
978-0-470-08037-5

Stock Investing
For Dummies,
3rd Edition
978-0-470-40114-9

Successful Time
Management
For Dummies
978-0-470-29034-7

Computer Hardware

BlackBerry For Dummies,
3rd Edition
978-0-470-45762-7

Computers For Seniors
For Dummies
978-0-470-24055-7

iPhone For Dummies,
2nd Edition
978-0-470-42342-4

Laptops For Dummies,
3rd Edition
978-0-470-27759-1

Macs For Dummies,
10th Edition
978-0-470-27817-8

Cooking & Entertaining

Cooking Basics
For Dummies,
3rd Edition
978-0-7645-7206-7

Wine For Dummies,
4th Edition
978-0-470-04579-4

Diet & Nutrition

Dieting For Dummies,
2nd Edition
978-0-7645-4149-0

Nutrition For Dummies,
4th Edition
978-0-471-79868-2

Weight Training
For Dummies,
3rd Edition
978-0-471-76845-6

Digital Photography

Digital Photography
For Dummies,
6th Edition
978-0-470-25074-7

Photoshop Elements 7
For Dummies
978-0-470-39700-8

Gardening

Gardening Basics
For Dummies
978-0-470-03749-2

Organic Gardening
For Dummies,
2nd Edition
978-0-470-43067-5

Green/Sustainable

Green Building
& Remodeling
For Dummies
978-0-4710-17559-0

Green Cleaning
For Dummies
978-0-470-39106-8

Green IT For Dummies
978-0-470-38688-0

Health

Diabetes For Dummies,
3rd Edition
978-0-470-27086-8

Food Allergies
For Dummies
978-0-470-09584-3

Living Gluten-Free
For Dummies
978-0-471-77383-2

Hobbies/General

Chess For Dummies,
2nd Edition
978-0-7645-8404-6

Drawing For Dummies
978-0-7645-5476-6

Knitting For Dummies,
2nd Edition
978-0-470-28747-7

Organizing For Dummies
978-0-7645-5300-4

SuDoku For Dummies
978-0-470-01892-7

Home Improvement

Energy Efficient Homes
For Dummies
978-0-470-37602-7

Home Theater
For Dummies,
3rd Edition
978-0-470-41189-6

Living the Country Lifestyle
All-in-One For Dummies
978-0-470-43061-3

Solar Power Your Home
For Dummies
978-0-470-17569-9

Internet
Blogging For Dummies,
2nd Edition
978-0-470-23017-6

eBay For Dummies,
6th Edition
978-0-470-49741-8

Facebook For Dummies
978-0-470-26273-3

Google Blogger
For Dummies
978-0-470-40742-4

Web Marketing
For Dummies,
2nd Edition
978-0-470-37181-7

WordPress For Dummies,
2nd Edition
978-0-470-40296-2

Language & Foreign Language
French For Dummies
978-0-7645-5193-2

Italian Phrases
For Dummies
978-0-7645-7203-6

Spanish For Dummies
978-0-7645-5194-9

Spanish For Dummies,
Audio Set
978-0-470-09585-0

Macintosh
Mac OS X Snow Leopard
For Dummies
978-0-470-43543-4

Math & Science
Algebra I For Dummies
978-0-7645-5325-7

Biology For Dummies
978-0-7645-5326-4

Calculus For Dummies
978-0-7645-2498-1

Chemistry For Dummies
978-0-7645-5430-8

Microsoft Office
Excel 2007 For Dummies
978-0-470-03737-9

Office 2007 All-in-One
Desk Reference
For Dummies
978-0-471-78279-7

Music
Guitar For Dummies,
2nd Edition
978-0-7645-9904-0

iPod & iTunes
For Dummies,
6th Edition
978-0-470-39062-7

Piano Exercises
For Dummies
978-0-470-38765-8

Parenting & Education
Parenting For Dummies,
2nd Edition
978-0-7645-5418-6

Type 1 Diabetes
For Dummies
978-0-470-17811-9

Pets
Cats For Dummies,
2nd Edition
978-0-7645-5275-5

Dog Training For Dummies,
2nd Edition
978-0-7645-8418-3

Puppies For Dummies,
2nd Edition
978-0-470-03717-1

Religion & Inspiration
The Bible For Dummies
978-0-7645-5296-0

Catholicism For Dummies
978-0-7645-5391-2

Women in the Bible
For Dummies
978-0-7645-8475-6

Self-Help & Relationship
Anger Management
For Dummies
978-0-470-03715-7

Overcoming Anxiety
For Dummies
978-0-7645-5447-6

Sports
Baseball For Dummies,
3rd Edition
978-0-7645-7537-2

Basketball For Dummies,
2nd Edition
978-0-7645-5248-9

Golf For Dummies,
3rd Edition
978-0-471-76871-5

Web Development
Web Design All-in-One
For Dummies
978-0-470-41796-6

Windows Vista
Windows Vista
For Dummies
978-0-471-75421-3

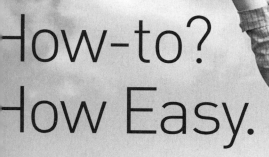

How-to?
How Easy.

Go to www.Dummies.com

From hooking up a modem to cooking up a casserole, knitting a scarf to navigating an iPod, you can trust Dummies.com to show you how to get things done the easy way.

Visit us at Dummies.com